# JESSE JAMES IN IOWA

# Jesse James in Iowa

John Koblas

North Star Press of St. Cloud, Inc.
St. Cloud, Minnesota

Cover photo: The Adair Train Robbery
(Courtesy of the Library of Congress)


Copyright © 2006 John Koblas

ISBN: 0-87839-232-7

First Edition
First Printing: June 2006

Printed in the United States of America by
Versa Press, Inc., East Peoria, Illinois

Published by
North Star Press of St. Cloud, Inc.
P.O. Box 451
St. Cloud, Minnesota 56302
northstarpress.com
nspress@cloudnet.com

For Virgil C. Julian, Gentleman of the Old West

# Acknowledgments

T HE AUTHOR OF THIS VOLUME wishes to express his gratitude to the following persons and their organizations for valuable assistance with this book: Beth Beckett, James Farm, Kearney, Missouri; Brenda DeVore, manager Prairie Trails Museum of Wayne County, Corydon, Iowa; Jan Donaldson, Wayne County Historical Society, Corydon, Iowa; Hugh Doty, *The Times-Republican*, Corydon, Iowa; Jim Driscoll, Plymouth County Historical Society, LeMars, Iowa; Mark Fagerwick and Hayes Scriven, Northfield Historical Society, Northfield, Minnesota; Scott and Julie Fisher, Inn of the Six-Toed Cat, Allerton, Iowa; Kelly Green, *The Messenger*, Fort Dodge, Iowa; Louise W. Hampton, Scholl Family Research Association of America, Winchester, Kentucky; Karen Laughlin, Iowa State Historical Society, Iowa City; Iowa; Librarians, Fort Dodge Public Library, Fort Dodge, Iowa; Library of Congress, Washington, D.C.; Arnie Lillo, Jesse James Theme Park, Good Thunder, Minnesota; W.E. Littler, Jr., *The Adair News*, Adair, Iowa; Minnesota Historical Society; St. Paul, Minnesota; David Parker, Fort Dodge Historical Foundation, Fort Dodge, Iowa; Scott Sorensen, Sioux City Public Museum, Sioux City, Iowa; Lowell R. Wilbur, Iowa Historical Library,

Des Moines, Iowa; Mrs. Jackie Wilson, Jesse James Museum, Adair, Iowa.

A special thanks as well to the following individuals for their contributions in various ways: Ron Affolter, Roger Brezina, John Caldwell, Marilynn Cierzan, Chip DeMann, Jan Goodman, Emmett C. Hoctor, Eric James, Virgil C. Julian, Rex Macbeth, Rick Mattix, Paul Meredith, Mabel Guth Ohde, Chuck Parsons, Diana Pierce, Claire Ryan, Tom Ryther, Nancy Samuelson, Robert L. Shelburne, Shirley Wells, Mrs. Fred Wingert, and Jan Winslow.

# Contents

# A TYPICAL STRANGER

A horseman rode up to the farmhouse in style—
A slow, easy gait on a fine, gallant steed.
He asked for some food, as politely he smiled,
Some fresh bandages for he started to bleed,
And he needed to rest. Could he sleep in the loft?
His mannerisms seemed like some minister;
His voice was commanding yet gentle and soft
So why did the stranger appear sinister?
He'd given no reason for them to be scared
And seemed in much pain but alighted with grace.
He helped with their chores chopping wood though he fared
So weak that they feared he might fall on his face.
Then later at supper this true gentleman
Left silver dollars to pay for the meal.
At dawn he was gone, never heard from again
But why did the stranger so sinister feel?

Roger Brezina

# Chapter One

# The Iowa Frontier

*"Through it runs a coulee from the Little Maquoketa all the way to the Great River. The coulee is a fine level prairie surrounded by bluffs and forests, and interrupted here and there by hollows with more bluffs, and more forests, and springs. Where the hollows merge with the coulee, the bluffs descend to ledges just above the bottoms that are always safe from flooding and sheltered from the coldest of winds, perfect for a house. It is said that in the bottoms of the coulee and smaller hollows grew the best corn planted by the Indian women. The bluffs and hollows give way to high rolling prairies a short distance to the east. On ridges above the coulee and hollows the Indians find 'float lead' in the shallow little pits they are capable of digging. We noticed a few of them near our diggings."*
—Dr. Stephen Langworthy[1]

IOWA, ONE OF THE NORTH CENTRAL STATES of the United States, is bounded on the north by Minnesota, on the east by Wisconsin and Illinois, on the south by Missouri, and on the west by Nebraska and South Dakota. The Mississippi River forms much of the state's eastern border.

Iowa entered the Union on December 28, 1846, as the twenty-ninth state, only one year before the birth of Jesse Woodson James to the Reverend Robert Sallee James and Zerelda Elizabeth Cole on September 5, 1847, in what is now Kearney, Missouri. Jesse's older brother,

Jesse James. (Courtesy of the Library of Congress)

Alexander Franklin James, or Frank as he came to be known, had preceded him in birth on January 10, 1843. Another son, Robert, was born July 19, 1845, but he lived only thirty-three days. A sister, Susan Lavenia James, was born November 25, 1849.[2]

When gold was discovered in California in 1849, thousands rushed to the West Coast to seek their fortune. Reverend James was among them. Whatever dreams he may have entertained were never realized, as shortly after his arrival in California, he died of a stomach ailment on August 18, 1850, at a Placerville gold camp.

On September 30, 1852, Zerelda married a neighboring farmer named Benjamin Simms. The James children, however, would not accept his authority, and, despite protests from Zerelda, he often beat them. Simms was killed in a horse accident before the Simms could obtain a divorce.

Zerelda fell in love with and married Dr. Reuben Samuel on September 25, 1855. Dr. Samuel was highly respected and loved by the James children, and he became the only father they really ever knew. The children attended school, regular church services, and worked on the 275-acre farm. With the slaves Reverend James had brought with him from Kentucky to work the land, and his fine Kentucky breeding horses, the farm prospered.

Although the James Farm was situated on good Missouri soil, the best land lay just over the border to the north. Iowa had some of the richest farmland in the United States, and its economy had always been dominated by farming. Iowa is known for its production of corn, hogs, and cattle and took its name from the Iowa River, which is named for the Iowa Indians. Iowa was part of the Louisiana Purchase, a transaction arranged between President Thomas Jefferson and Napoleon Bonaparte of France that brought a vast tract of the continent under the control of the United States. The area, however, was closed to white settlement until the early 1830s.

Following the Black Hawk War—a conflict that ended in 1832 near present-day New Albin—the Sauk and Fox Indian tribes were forced to make their first land concessions west of the Mississippi River. The United States government gave the Sauk and Fox a small amount of cash, forty barrels of salt, forty barrels of tobacco, and some blacksmithing services in exchange for the fertile Mississippi Valley lands of eastern Iowa. The tribes were ordered out of the area a year later.

That same year, a "Journal of Occurrences," as required by government regulation, was maintained by Daniel R. Dunihue during the period he was engaged to help conduct the removal of a group of Seneca and Shawnee Indians near New Lebanon, Ohio, to Missouri. The removals resulted from treaties negotiated at Lewistown and Wapaghkonnetta by Dunihue's cousin James B. Gardiner, a specially appointed commissioner, and Indian agent John McElvain. According to Dunihue's journal, the Indians were not happy about the land in Missouri where they were forced to live:

> Monday, December 3, 1832: We started about 10:00—the Indians going one road and the waggons [sic] the other. The cause of this separation of the Indians from the teams was that the ridge road, as it is called, for about

Daniel Dunihue. (Author's collection)

3

[forty] miles, is very good for wagons [sic]—and the lower road much better for the Indians in consequence of there being an abundance of good grass—while on the other road there is none at all.[3]

Dunihue's entry for Friday, December 14, 1832, is even more negative regarding the Missouri land:

> In the evening a general council was held by all the chiefs and head men of this tribe and of those of the Senecas who are settled here. Afterwards a general dance was held. The cause of their remaining here is this: They are told by their brethren, the resident Senecas, that their land is nearly all prairie and entirely unfit for them to settle on; and further, that the privilege of refusing it and having a new selection made for them. They, therefore, after learning that Lieutenant Lane, the District Agent had sent an express to F.J. Gibson for information upon this subject determined to remain with their friends until the express should come back, and until a delegation from their own people should go and examine the land now laid off for them and make their report.

Eager to open the West to settlement, President Thomas Jefferson commissioned Captains Meriwether Lewis and William Clark to explore the newly acquired Louisiana Territory. Lewis and Clark led forty soldiers and boatmen on an epic trek from the Mississippi River to the Pacific Ocean during 1804 and 1806. Lewis and Clark mapped their journey, created a record of the natural resources they encountered and made contacts with Native Americans.

It was in Iowa that the explorers held council with chiefs of the Missouri and Oto tribes at a place they named "council bluffs." Sergeant Charles Floyd, the only member of the Lewis and Clark party who died during the expedition is buried at Sioux City.

Steamboat paddle-wheelers reigned supreme on the Mississippi and Missouri rivers in the nineteenth century. The steamboat *Bertrand* sank in the Missouri River near what is today the town of Missouri Valley.

At this same time, Lieutenant Zebulon Pike was sent up the Mississippi River. Pike was instructed to gather information about the river and note sites that would be favorable strategic locations for the construction of forts. In June 1809, Congress reserved Rock Island, or "big island," as Pike called it, for federal military use. Fort Armstrong was built in 1816 following two battles against the British near Rock Island in 1814.[4]

After white settlement began with the Black Hawk Purchase, Iowa became part of Michigan Territory. When Michigan achieved statehood in 1836, Iowa then became a part of Wisconsin Territory. Finally, two years later, Iowa Territory was carved out of the area of Wisconsin Territory west of the Mississippi River. The first Iowa Territory legislature met in Burlington before a territorial capital city was finally selected in Johnson County. In Iowa City, the government seat was established in a grand structure known as Old Capitol. Built in the early 1840s, Old Capitol served as the last capitol of Iowa Territory and the first capitol of the state. Under the 1857 Iowa constitution, the seat of state government was moved to Des Moines, a more central location.

Unlike Missouri, which nurtured an eruption of violence with Mormons that had settled within the state's borders in 1831, Iowa had no quarrel with the Saints. Joseph Smith and his followers were convinced that God had selected Jackson County, Missouri, as the place where the Saints should gather to await the holy summons. Independence was chosen as the Saints' Zion, which angered many Missourians, who feared the Mormons would drive all other settlers away.[5]

By 1833, a third of Jackson County's population was Mormon. The area's first settlers, mostly Southerners who had come to Missouri with slaves, kept a spiteful eye on both the Mormons and the Indians, who had settled just across the border. The Southerners were uncomfortable and angry over the religious sect, composed mostly of wealthy Yankees because they not only welcomed the Indians into their fold, but the free blacks as well.

Church members were also heavily persecuted, largely because the non-Mormons believed that the church was promoting the establishment of a religious dictatorship (a theocracy). They were also distressed by the Mormon's belief that the Book of Mormon was the revealed work of God, with the same status as the Hebrew Scriptures

(Old Testament) and Christian Scriptures (New Testament). In spite of the opposition, much of it state-sponsored or condoned, the church increased greatly in numbers.

The persecution of the Mormons commenced in November 1833 with a frightening meteor shower. Citizens of Jackson, Clay, Ray, Caldwell, and Daviess counties concluded that the meteors were a sign that the end predicted by the Mormons was near, and they gathered a force to drive the Saints from their area. From 1833 to 1839, the Mormons endured six years of brutality. Their homes were destroyed; many Mormons died while trying to survive winter without adequate shelter. The church was expelled from Jackson County and re-settled in Far West, Missouri, in Caldwell County, which had been reserved for them.

A public Danite organization was formed in the Mormon community to organize defense, construct homes and obtain provisions. The original settlers were concerned that the Latter Day Saints might become a political majority in their locality and planned an attack as a method of preventing Mormons from voting. The state militia became involved. Sampson Avard, who is believed to have been both a captain within the Danites and an officer in the militia, persuaded his men to become a "covert renegade band" and to avenge outrages against the Mormons. When Joseph Smith heard of this group's illegal activity, he removed Avard from command and disbanded his criminal group.

On October 27, 1838, Governor Lilburn Boggs of Missouri had issued an "Extermination Order" to treat all Mormons as enemies and exterminate them or force them out of Missouri. Ignorance, fear, and rumors fueled the fire of hatred against the Mormons, which finally led to the extermination order by Governor Boggs.

Governor Boggs' Extermination Order read "The Mormons must be treated as enemies and must be exterminated or driven from the state if necessary for the public peace."

With this order the Missouri Militia dispatched a party of men on October 30, 1838, to a small Mormon settlement at Jacob Haun's Mill in Caldwell County, Missouri, where they massacred seventeen persons. The militia consisted of 200 men while only thirty families resided at Haun's Mill. The residents were unaware of the extermination order and believed they were living under a truce that had been reached several days earlier between the Missouri government and the Mormons. They were totally shocked and unprepared for the brutal attack.

When the militia invaded the settlement on horses and began firing rifles, the women and children ran across a stream and into the woods to hide. The men ran indoors to find defensive positions, but were massacred by bullets from the militia, which were fired through the wood slats of the cabins. Any Mormons that were found alive were later shot.

When the massacre ended, seventeen Mormons had been killed, including a ten-year-old boy. The boy had been huddling behind a stove, unable to escape with his mother into the forest. When the militia found him, they raised their rifles and blew his head off. Another victim was a seventy-eight-year-old, feeble grandfather. He was shot by one of the militia and then was mutilated with a knife. Thirteen Mormons had been injured, including women and children. Three militia men were injured, which indicates that the Mormans had put up a fight.

After the militia left, the frightened settlers remained in hiding until after dark, afraid the militia would return to finish them off. When it was clear they were safe, they hid the bodies of their dead in a well, and ran into neighboring settlements for help. The Mormons surrendered after being faced with diminishing supplies, the approach of winter, an aggressive militia, and the anti-Latter Day Saints extermination order from the governor.

> The people of western Missouri are, in some respects, very peculiar, [related James-Younger Gang Outlaw Cole Younger years later]. We will take Jackson County (where I was born) for instance. In that section the people seemed to be born fighters, the instinct being inherited from a long line of ancestors.
> Joe Smith and Brigham Young laid out Independence, but very soon thereafter enough citizens of the county collected to drive them off, after several stubborn fights. The Mormons withdrew from the state and settled their community at Nauvoo, Illinois, but

in a few years afterward about fifty of them again came into Missouri and settled in Platte County.

They had scarcely established themselves, however, before another company of Jackson County citizens, chiefly from around Independence, organized to drive them off. Among these determined citizens were Richard Fristoe, my grandfather, Wood Nolen, Smallwood Nolen, and Sam Owens. While crossing the river in a hand-ferry-boat, the ferryman, who had been bribed by the Mormons, succeeded in turning the boat over midway in the Missouri River. A large number were drowned, but the four I have mentioned succeeded in swimming ashore.[6]

Following their rude reception in Missouri, the vanguard of the Church of Jesus Christ of Latter Day Saints (Mormons) trekked across southern Iowa on their way to establish their "New Zion" in the Rocky Mountains. The journey from Nauvoo, Illinois, to Council Bluffs, Iowa, tested the endurance of the Mormons, their animals, and equipment. Crossing the Mississippi River into Iowa at Montrose, the Mormons regrouped in the area of Sugar Creek where about 2,000 persons organized their first winter camp.[7]

In March, the Mormons made their first trek across Iowa. Because they were free of the hostilities they had endured in neighboring Missouri, 70,000 Mormons walked hundreds of miles in suffocating dust, violent thunderstorms, mud, and temperature extremes, experiencing bad water, poor forage, and sickness and death.

Those hardy pioneers who followed the southern trail across Iowa entered Wayne County, where Corydon was later located, on April 3, 1846. Prior to this, they had followed existing roads and trails, but the Wayne County line was the "jumping off place." The Mormons faced an unexplored, trackless prairie with no settlements. The first camp in the county was in the southeast corner at Hickory Ridge. Traveling in a northwesterly direction through axle-deep mud, it took them three full weeks just to cross the county.

Those Mormons following the upper trail across Iowa entered Adair County on June 4, 1846. Along the way, they encountered the

Pottawattamie Indians, who had been transplanted from their lands in Indiana and were living peaceably in the Iowa Territory.

But like all the territories of the frontier, Iowa had its share of marauding outlaws and hostile Indians. One of the most shocking incidents connected with the early history of Davenport and Scott counties was the murder of Colonel George Davenport at Rock Island on July 4, 1845. The country on both sides of the river had been infested by a lawless band of freebooters, with their supposed headquarters at Nauvoo. They had organized themselves into bands and engaged in horse-stealing, counterfeiting, burglary, robbery, and murder. Rumors circulated that men in official positions and of good standing were associated with them.[8]

On the fatal Fourth of July, Colonel Davenport's family was away at Stephenson attending a celebration when three men attacked him in his own house, one of whom shot him with a pistol through the thigh. The colonel was bound with strips of bark and blindfolded. The intruders searched for the key to his safe but were unable to find it.

Returning to the wounded man, they carried him upstairs where the safe was located and ordered him to unlock it. The marauders obtained about $600 from the safe, as well as a gold watch-chain and seals, a double-barreled gun, and a few articles of minor value. Colonel Davenport lived long enough to relate the incidents of the robbery.

For several weeks, no trace could be found of the murderers. Edward Bonney, of Lee County, Iowa, took it upon himself to ferret them out. About the middle of August, he rode to Nauvoo were he obtained information by representing himself as one of the gang.

On the eighth of September he arrested a man named Fox at Centerville, Indiana, and committed him to jail there. On the nineteenth, he arrested two others—John Long and a man named Birch, at Sandusky, Ohio, and brought them to Rock Island. Three others were also arrested as accessories—Richard Baxter and Aaron Long, near Galena, Illinois, and Granville Young, at Nauvoo. Aaron was a brother of the already captured John Long.

On the sixth of October, they were all indicted by the grand jury of Rock Island County, with the exception of the prisoner named Fox, who had escaped from the jail in Indiana on the seventeenth of September. On the fourteenth of October, the two Longs went to trial, were found guilty, and sentenced to be hanged on the twenty-seventh. Birch, one of the ringleaders, turned state's evidence. Baxter was tried separately, convicted and sentenced to be hanged on the eighteenth of November. Granted a second trial, he was again found guilty and sentenced to the penitentiary for life, where he died two years later. Birch took a change of venue to Knox County, and while awaiting trial escaped from jail. Upon the gallows, John Long confessed all, but died a hardened wretch without sign of repentance or fear of death.

During the same decade, the Cedar River Gang of outlaws terrorized the Cedar Rapids area of Iowa. "All winter, it had been evident that we had in our midst some persons who were giving aid and comfort to the outlaws; but we were not able to identify them or put a stop to their work," John Weare later wrote.

In the spring, one of the "Regulators" joined the outlaws, and so learned that a party on a certain night would pass Cedar Rapids, conveying a large amount of stolen goods to their cave on the bank of the Cedar River, at the point known as "The Palisades." Plans were made by the Regulators to intercept this company, on their way through Cedar Rapids, capture the goods and the thieves and bring them to justice. We greatly desired to secure their leader, a desperate Missourian.

The Regulators were stationed along the road where the outlaws were expected to pass. When the band stole into the guarded road, at a given signal they were surrounded, and nearly captured, but they fought like tigers. In the contest the leader escaped, although he was known to be wounded. All the plunder was seized and most of the outlaws were captured. After seeing the gang lodged in our block house—built for defense from the Indians—I returned home, not more than half satisfied with our night's work. My wife met me at the door with the information that one of the Regulators from Marion, who had been wounded in the attack, had started home and found himself too weak from lose of blood to go on. Knowing mine was the house of a friend he sought its shelter, and had gone to bed in our room. I made haste to go to the man, wondering who he could be. By the "Law Harry!" there lay, in my own bed the leader of the outlaws! It swept over me in a moment, his whole audacious plan. When he knew how badly he was wounded, he made straight for my house, knowing I was not at home, and that any sufferer had but to let his sufferings be known to my wife and he would have a friend. I was greatly enraged with him, but my wife pleaded for him. She knew he would be hung by the Regulators. With all this in mind I spoke to him. He answered and, looking me straight in the eye, said, "John, you're not the man to strike even a dog when he's down." I went right out and called a physician, and my wife, the doctor, and I took the best care we could of him. He died the next night.[9]

The fears of western Iowans regarding the Sioux tribes can be traced back to the 1850s. In the late 1840s and the early 1850s, settlers in northwest Iowa moved beyond Fort Dodge and into areas unprotected by military garrisons. Considered intruders by the Indians (in this case, the Wapekutah Sioux), the settlers were bound to face difficulties. In 1848, a band of Wapekutahs, led by Sidominadotah (Two Fingers), traced some stolen horses to the cabin of Henry Lott, who was living at the confluence of the Des Moines and Boone rivers. Lott and his fourteen-year-old son, Milton, fled but became separated during their escape. The boy froze to death before his father could return with help.

Lott struck back at the Sioux in January of 1854. Finding Sidominadotah and his band camped on the Des Moines River about thirty miles north of Fort Dodge, Lott and his stepson attacked the camp, killing the chief and six of his relatives. Inkpadutah, Sidominadotah's younger brother, became the new leader of the band and vowed revenge. Lott and his stepson left Iowa for California.

On March 8, 1857, Inkpadutah and his band attacked the scattered cabins of settlers in the vicinity of Spirit Lake and Lake Okoboji. The bloodshed also spread to the nearby town of Springfield, Minnesota. Thirty-eight settlers were slain, including James and Mary Mattock and their five children. A relief expedition from Fort Dodge, led by Major

William Williams, buried the victims and made a futile attempt to track down the perpetrators of the massacre. Four women had been carried off from their cabins at Spirit Lake. Lydia Noble was beaten to death and Elizabeth Thatcher was drowned. Margaret Noble was bought from Inkpadutah's band for $1,000, and Abbie Gardner was purchased by a $1,200 ransom appropriated by the Minnesota legislature.[10]

Soon after the beginning of the Civil War, the Sioux Indians, on the Minnesota reservations, began to make hostile demonstrations in the northwestern counties of Iowa. Horses and cattle were stolen, and, on the ninth of July, two members of the Frontier Guards, Hobert Thomas and Henry Cordna, were killed within three miles of Sioux City. Several parties of Sioux Indians were seen in the Little Sioux Valley. The settlers became alarmed, and companies of "Home Guards" were organized in several of the northwestern counties. Under the authority of Judge A.W. Hubbard, a military company of the Sioux City Cavalry, under command of Captain A.J. Millard, was ordered into state service for protection of the frontier.[11]

There were at this time about 8,000 Sioux Indians on the reservations along the Minnesota River, at a distance of from sixty to one hundred miles from the north line of the state. Aware that thousands of the natural defenders of the frontier were away fighting the Confederate army, the Sioux entered into a conspiracy to march upon the settlers and exterminate them before aid could reach them. So well had the plans of the Indians been concealed that no intimation of the impending doom had reached frontier settlements.

On the seventeenth of August 1862, the massacre began near the Upper Agency. On August 21st, while the men were gathered at a public meeting, on the upper Des Moines River, near Jackson, to devise means for common defense, the Indians suddenly fell upon the settlement, murdering the defenseless families, plundering their homes and killing the livestock. When the news of the massacre reached the settlements at Spirit Lake and Estherville, parties of armed men were hastily organized, and the men marched to the aid of their neighbors. At

Jackson they received reinforcements. They headed up the river to the scene of the massacre. Finding that the Indians had disappeared, they buried the bodies of the fifteen victims and returned to their homes.

Throughout northern Iowa, the sturdy pioneers erected strong stockades into which their families were gathered, preparations being made for a vigorous defense. Scouts were sent out and every precaution taken to guard against surprise. Efforts were at once made to secure state protection. A detachment of Sioux City cavalry was immediately sent to the lakes and the Dickinson County courthouse was fortified. Here the families were gathered under the protection of the soldiers, while men worked on the defenses. A sawmill was kept running, cutting logs into plank four inches in thickness. A trench, three feet deep, was dug around the court-house, about thirty feet from its walls and into this the palisades were firmly planted, making a defense against any weapons in possession of the Indians. Here the settlers remained in security while the terrible massacre was desolating western Minnesota. Thousands of the Sioux were on the war path, and troops were hurried to the frontier.

The chiefs had planned to sweep swiftly down the Des Moines Valley and the Little Sioux by way of the lakes of Dickinson County, thus exterminating all of the settlements in northwestern Iowa above Fort Dodge and Sioux City. They soon met with vigorous resistance, however, in Kossuth and Palo Alto counties, as preparations were at once made by the settlers to defend their homes.

The Minnesota authorities were soon thoroughly aroused, as they came to realize that they were assailed by the greatest Indian uprising of the century. The settlers seized such arms as they could find and hurried to the aid of their frontier neighbors. Such troops as were within reach were hastily called to their assistance, but, before the savages could be checked, more than 1,000 men, women, and children had been slaughtered and 5,000 driven from their homes.

Houses were pillaged and burned, stock killed or driven off, fields devastated and more than two hundred and fifty women and children taken into captivity. In magnitude the Indian uprising exceeded any massacre ever perpetrated in North America, and in atrocities it has never been surpassed in any country.

Attacks such as these, however, were few and far between. Iowans frequently had to defend their homes from a bigger threat during this period—Missourians, loyal to the South, who crossed the border and wreaked havoc across the state. The last raid into Iowa by Missouri guerrillas was in October 1864. On the morning of the twelfth, twelve young men, dressed in federal uniforms and mounted on good horses, entered Davis County from the southeast corner and, riding along the road at a rapid gait, began to plunder the farm houses and people they met on the road. They seized such arms as they found, and destroying them, took some of the citizens prisoner. Their leader was Lieutenant James Jackson, who sent out small detachments on intersecting roads to bring in plunder. The point at which they entered the county was about sixteen miles from Bloomfield, and, as they advanced with a large number of prisoners, they presented a formidable appearance that so terrified the inhabitants that it was several hours before the news of the raid reached the county seat.

The first man killed was Thomas Hurdy, a farmer, who refused to give up his team. The leader shot him in his wagon and robbed his body of about four hundred dollars. The next man killed was a returned soldier from the Third Iowa Cavalry, Eleazer Small, who was shot by the leader, who dismounted and coolly rifled the pockets of the dying man. At Springville, the marauders went to the residence of Captain Philip Bunce, an officer of the Thirtieth Iowa Infantry, who happened to be at home on a visit. They robbed him of his uniform and were about to shoot him when he walked up to the leader and in a low voice, that he might not be heard by his terrified family, requested that he might not be killed in the presence of his wife. He was accordingly taken several miles from home and brutally murdered.

When the news of the bloody raid reached Bloomfield, the county fair was in session. The men rushed to the arsenal, where arms and ammunition were hastily distributed, horses were taken from the wagons and mounted, and Colonel J.B. Weaver was called to the command. A company of mounted men was soon organized, and, led by Weaver, started in pursuit of the guerrillas, while Lieutenant-Colonel S.A. Moore took command of the militia to protect the town. The party under Weaver struck the trail of the outlaws at Hurdy's and followed it with great rapidity until the place was reached where Captain Bunce had been murdered. It was now midnight, they were in Missouri and five hours behind the raiders, as they learned from the citizens. It was impossible to track them in the darkness and in a region where the raiders knew every bridle path and were among their friends, who would give no information to the pursuers. It was useless to proceed further, and Weaver's party reluctantly turned back, taking the body of Captain Bunce.

On the seventh of November, while three men in Davis County were attempting to arrest suspicious characters, one of them, William Wallace, was shot by the raiders and killed. During these troubles in Teat County, thirteen of the guerrillas were captured by the militia, and delivered to the proper authorities.

Several northerners in Iowa denounced the war as an "Abolition Crusade" and missed no occasion to endeavor to create sympathy for the leaders of the Southern Confederacy. These people were called "Copperheads" and were, for the most part, of that class in the North who were not opposed to slavery. Orator Henry Clay Dean, whom the James-Younger Gang would later confront in Corydon, was the most prominent leader of this faction in Iowa. Like other copperheads, he opposed the emancipation of the slaves and considered the war to be an illegal aggression. In his article "The Bloodmarket of the Rich," he argued that the entire war was conceived by an international conspiracy of bankers and "stock-gamblers."

> The war between the States of the Union was not a riot, [proclaimed Dean in one of his speeches]. It was deliberate, systematic and orderly, upon the part of the Southern States. It was not an insurrection or rebellion; everything was done in subordination to

the law and sovereign power of the states in which it transpired, with no more violence than is common to warfare. It was not a revolution. It changed none of the organic laws of the states; the people armed themselves according to law to repel a threatened invasion of their country, overthrow of their government and violation of their political, legal and social rights.

The pretext for war was the preservation of the Union—an organized Union fighting against organized States. It was a war of states, with all of its attendant evils, in which the government was guilty of usurpation. Lincoln tore up the Constitution and set up his arbitrary will instead. Lincoln selected the weakest, worst and most corrupt men in the country, who served him cheerfully as instruments of usurpation. Lincoln dissolved the government and left the country in anarchy. Lincoln corrupted one part of the church to engage in warfare with the other part, and burned 1,200 houses of worship; he mutilated graveyards, and left whole cities and churches in ashes; dragged ministers from their knees in the very act of worship; tied them up by their thumbs; had their daughters stripped naked by negro soldiers under command of white officers.

Again, in speaking of the bonds issued by the government to meet the expenses of the war, Dean said:

> This debt was incurred to carry on a war conceived in the foulest passions of depraved human nature, carried on for the mercenary purposes of personal gain by systematized corruption, cruelty and crime. In all this wicked, cruel war, there has been but these unchangeable objects in view: to glut the avarice of the rich, to satiate the vengeance of the spiteful, minister to the most groveling appetites of the vicious; to make the people the slaves of money, and their armies the tools of tyrants. The people are not bound in justice to pay this debt. Every consistent friend of peace must oppose the payment of this debt.
>
> The popular mind was wrought up to an artificial frenzy. At a given signal the mercenary ecclesiastical politicians broke loose in their Sabbath day harangues to inflame the passions and prepare the public mind for war. They made their absurd charges against the Southern people. They appealed to the people to fly to arms in defense of their homes—to fight for liberty. The manufacturers closed up their mills and sold their operatives to the recruiting sergeant; merchants refused credit to the poor to drive them into

the army; every manner of argument was used, and every kind of bait held out as an inducement to the poor to rush to the army to fight the battles of plunder for the rich.

Early in the second year of the war, it assumed a purely mercenary character, stimulated by the hope of plunder. The public was undermined; licentiousness reigned to an extent without parallel or precedent among us. Thousands of enlisted soldiers, having first entered the army without bounty, became excited over the bounty mania, and engaged in bounty-jumping. They would leave the ranks at every available opportunity, re-enlist several times, take bounties and share the spoils liberally with their delinquent commanders. This mercenary spirit spread throughout every part of the army like a contagion. The soldiers caught the infection until the army became a reckless, mercenary mob of unfortunate conscripts driven to the slaughter. The degradation of society was consummate. Parents might be seen selling their children in the conscript market and walking complacently away with the price of their own blood in their pocket.[12]

But the Civil War and its Unionist-Copperhead dissentions had fostered instability and motivated settlers to bury bullion.[13] Mud and plank roads, winter blizzards, prairie fires, and especially, robberies constituted misery for rural Iowans. In the early 1800s, horse thieves operated in the area of Sabula, Iowa. Outlaw Henry Plummer was seen in the state and is said to have buried loot from several stagecoach robberies. Following a robbery of 700 pounds of gold, currency, diamonds, and finished jewelry at Canyon Springs, a Black Hills relay station, Atlantic City, Iowa, William Ward, the stage line's superintendent and a Deputy United States Marshal arrested "Duck" Goodale in Atlantic City, Iowa.[14]

After the Civil War, Iowa's agriculture underwent considerable change. By the 1870s, farms and small towns blanketed the entire state. Also in that decade, Iowa farmers established definite production patterns, which led to considerable prosperity. During the Civil War, Iowa farmers had raised considerable wheat. After the war, however, prominent Iowa farmers like "Tama Jim" Wilson, later to be national secretary of agriculture for sixteen years, urged farmers to diversify their production, raise corn rather than wheat, and convert that corn into pork, beef, and wool whenever possible. For many generations, Iowa farmers have followed Wilson's advice.

Once the land had been cleared, the farmers' concerns were about weather, infestation of pests, plant disease, fencing, transportation of crops to market, and market prices. With thousands of acres under cultivation, the fungi of rust, scab, and orchard blight, followed by the grasshoppers, spelled disaster for many tillers of the soil.[15]

Early settlers recognized other disadvantages of prairie living. Many people complained that the prairie looked bleak and desolate. One woman, newly arrived from New York State, told her husband that she thought she would die without any trees. Emigrants from Europe, particularly the Scandinavian countries, reacted in similar fashion. These newcomers also discovered that the prairies held another disadvantage—one that could be deadly. Prairie fires were common in the tall-grass country, often occurring yearly. Diaries of pioneer families provide dramatic accounts of the reactions of early Iowans to prairie fires, often a mixture of fear and awe. When a prairie fire approached, all family members were called out to help keep the flames away. One nineteenth-century Iowan wrote that in the fall, people slept "with one eye open" until the first snow fell, indicating that the threat of fire had passed.[16]

Pioneer families faced additional hardships in their early years in Iowa. Constructing a farmstead was hard work in itself. Families not only had to build their homes, but often they had to construct the furniture used. Newcomers were often lonely for friends and relatives. Pioneers frequently contracted communicable diseases such as scarlet fever. Fever and ague, which consisted of alternating fevers and chills, was a constant complaint. Later generations would learn that fever and ague was a form of malaria, but pioneers thought that it was caused by gas emitted from the newly turned sod. Moreover, pioneers had few ways to relieve even common colds or toothaches.

In the early 1870s, Bill Lyons, a resident of Wayne County, was believed to have been a member of a band of outlaws organized in the area. Considered a dangerous character, Lyons was charged with being one of the gang members who pursued a local citizen with every intention to rob and murder him. The evidence was not sufficient to identify Lyons or to show that he was guilty of other crimes charged against him. While Lyons was in jail awaiting his fate, however, a mob collected one night, took him from the jail, and hanged him. None of the other members of the mob were ever identified, and no one was prosecuted for the crime.[17]

"Horse thieves got rough treatment in those days," recalled an early Corydon resident while referring to the Lyons case. "I remember that one night a mob broke into the jail, where a man was being held for trial, and taking him several miles out of town, they hanged him to a pile driver that was being used in the building of a new railroad. The man's name was Bill Lyons."[18]

Another criminal, a young man named Loux, professing to be a traveling salesman for an Omaha firm, insisted he had an account at a bank in Creston, Iowa, and at one time he evidently did make a deposit there. He wrote a small check to a party in Corydon, but upon presentation of the check, the bank refused to pay because he had no funds in the bank. Loux was duly indicted for obtaining money by false pretenses and was locked away in jail to await his trial.

Loux conveyed to the party he had swindled that, if he was released, he could make the necessary money and pay them back. Arrangements were made for his release upon this promise to pay back the money. Loux, however, made arrangements of his own and was not seen again.

Feared throughout the state was a notorious gang of outlaws and cattle rustlers known as the Banditti of the Plains, headquartered near the mouth of the Boone River in the 1800s. Although working far to the east of their area of operations, these men were "executioners, cold, determined, and implacable."[19]

Outlaws such as Frank and Jesse James and Cole Younger made forays into Iowa, but other men of legend actually lived there. Wyatt Berry Stapp Earp, named for his father's neighbor and commanding

Earp home, Pella, Iowa. (Courtesy of the Library of Congress)

officer in the Mexican War, was born in Monmouth, Illinois, on March 19, 1848. When Wyatt was but a year old, his father, Nicholas, moved

Wyatt Earp. (Courtesy of the Library of Congress)

the family to a little farm in Lake Prairie Township, near Pella, Iowa. While living in Pella, Nicholas held the office of United States Provost Marshal of Marion County.[20]

Wyatt's father wanted to farm more land in addition to his farm, to put his roots firmly into the Iowa soil. According to the Federal Census of 1850, Nicholas was listed as a "cooper and farmer." Wyatt's brother, Morgan, later to die by violence in Tombstone, Arizona, was born April 24, 1851 near Pella.[21]

In February 1860, the citizens of Pella were excited to learn that Virgil Earp, Nicholas's third born and first to marry, had run away to the adjoining county and married Ellen Rysdem, a neighbor girl. Virgil was only seventeen years old and Ellen even younger. They had borrowed a wagon and made the thirty-mile trip from their homes near Pella.[22] At the time of their marriage, Wyatt was only twelve years old, and along with his brothers, spent most of his spare time working on his father's farm.[23]

Nicholas Earp's experience as a captain in the Mexican War earned him the responsibility of training troops for the Union Army. Wyatt's three older brothers enlisted in the Union Army, while Wyatt stayed home and tended the farm. Finally, at the tender age of fifteen, the lure of the Civil War overwhelmed Wyatt. He ran away from home and enlisted in the army. As luck would have it, the first person Wyatt encountered among the army ranks was his father, who promptly sent him home, back to the cornfields.

In 1864 Nicholas's hitch in the army ran out. Although Nicholas was against secession, he disagreed with freeing the slaves. In May, the elder Earp organized a wagon train of forty families with similar ideas against emancipation, and, by way of Omaha and across the Great Plains past Salt Lake City, they headed to California. Sixteen-year-old Wyatt joined his father's wagon train. Before the Earps started westward, Nicholas gave Wyatt his first firearm. It was a clumsy weapon, but it proved to be a valuable tool for a wagon train on the move. Wyatt kept the party well supplied with fresh game. Dangers encountered on this trip changed Wyatt from a boy to a man, and they arrived in California's San Bernardino Valley seven months later.[24]

Just southeast of Pella at the time Wyatt Earp was growing up lived Katherine Elder, or "Big Nose Kate," as she was later known in the Southwest. Kate had been born Mary Catherine Elder Haroney in Hungary on November 7, 1850, and was reported to have been the wife of Doc Holliday, although there are no records of such a marriage. She was from an Aristocratic family; Kate's father, Michael, made a living as a doctor.

In 1862 Mexico's Emperor Maximillian appointed Kate's father to the position of personal surgeon. With the appointment, the Haroney family packed up and left for Mexico. In 1865 Maximillian's rule crumbled, and the Haroney family fled Mexico and moved to Davenport, Iowa. On March 26, 1865, Kate's mother died, and the following May her father passed away. Kate and the rest of the children were placed in foster homes. But in 1867, Kate was put in the care of Otto Smith. The stay with Smith was short. Kate ran away and, by her own account, stowed away aboard a steam ship headed for St. Louis. Kate was caught by the captain of the ship, but he befriended her and saw her safely placed in a convent in St. Louis.[25]

Ironically, others who would later show up for a confrontation at the O.K. Corral in Tombstone—Will, Robert, and Tom McLaury—lived with their father, Robert, in Hazelton, Iowa. The McLaury boys' sister lived in Toledo, Iowa, not far north of Pella.

Also growing up on the Iowa frontier were Dan and John Harlan. Later both would be reckoned with on the Western frontier for years. Sixty miles south of Pella lived Ed T. Beard, later to become notorious in the West as well. All these persons would later share each other's lives out West. As was frequently the case, many of the "sporting" young men, left the Midwest for the Kansas cow towns.

It seems that every small, southern and central Iowa town, however, claims a connection to the infamous James Gang, perhaps the deadliest, and undoubtedly the most well known of all the desperado bands throughout 1865 to 1882. Whether it was a sighting, a direct contact, or the smoldering embers from an overnight campfire, some reality or myth fueled this legend.

Frank and Jesse James had early become experts in the use of firearms and were noted pistol shots "almost before they owned their first pair of boots or could properly appreciate the beauties and comforts of a pair of suspenders. In handling an "Arkansaw toothpick, they rivaled the famed [Jim] Bowie himself. Among their commoner feats, while out for practice, was what was known as 'girdling a tree'—walking around a tree at a distance of forty-five feet and firing alternately, each shot chipping the bark until the circle was complete. At fifteen feet they could send a Bowie knife quivering into a two-inch sapling with unerring precision."[26]

The *Columbia* (Missouri) *Herald*, however, felt differently, and despite the robberies and murders committed by the gang, considered them victims of geography:

> This much can be said of the Youngers and Jameses: They were not original crooks or outlaws. They were the product of the most vicious and terrible warfare of which history tells. For four years they were in a constant carnival of blood and devastation. It was enough to turn men into demons. At the close of the war they found themselves outlawed. They kept on in the life they had led, justifying themselves on the ground that they were still in the enemies' country. Their crimes cannot be excused, but they can be forgotten and forgiven now that they have been pardoned under the law and can and should be covered with that Christian charity which hides a multitude of sins.[27]

At the south edge of Franklin, Nebraska, between the railroad tracks and the Republican River, was a piece of farmland immersed in the lore of Jesse James. The legendary outlaw talked of buying 160 acres in Franklin as a home for his family after robbing just one more bank. In late 1881, weary from hiding, Jesse, living under the name Thomas Howard, talked of ending his outlaw ways and settling down to farm in Nebraska.

He answered a *Lincoln Journal* advertisement for 160 acres, with a creek running through it, for sale at Franklin, saying: "I want to purchase a farm of that size—I will not buy a farm unless the soil is No. 1." He apparently visited the land in 1882, but was killed before moving ahead with the purchase. The 160 acres is still farmland. The creek no longer runs through the site. It was rerouted after the 1935 Republican River Flood.[28]

The Franklin land is one of many connections Jesse James and his brother Frank had with Nebraska and Iowa. Reported Nebraska locales include Omaha, Rulo, Nebraska City, the Devil's Nest area near Niobrara, Obert, Sumner, Washington, and Lowell. Jesse James frequently visited a friend in Nebraska City. A resident recalled that Jesse, "with a price on his head, used to ride boldly down Central Avenue in Nebraska City." One of the best photographs of Jesse was made in a studio in Nebraska City.

Otoe County also is the supposed setting for a popular tale about the James Gang. The gang reportedly rode to a widow's farm home one evening and asked for a meal. As she fed them, she began crying. The gang leader asked why. She said a banker was coming the next day to foreclose on the mortgage, and she didn't have money to pay him. The gang leader assured her things might work out. As she cleaned up after the men left, she found under the table a leather bag that contained enough gold to pay off the banker. The next day, as he rode in his carriage back to town after collecting the money, the banker was robbed by a gang of masked men. He said they looked like the James Gang.

There are many other tales of Jesse and Frank hiding out in Nebraska and sleeping in barns en route to and from robberies. One newspaper reporter said of Jesse James: "The legends that have sprung up concerning the bandit were as thick as dandelions, and he must have had the ability to be in a hundred different places simultaneously if all the several million people who 'saw' him are to be believed."[29]

Iowa was chiefly virgin prairie. Prairie schooners flocked into the region to take advantage of the free land for homesteading following the Civil War. Buffalo still roamed the prairie, cowpunchers and miners were everywhere, the occasional Indian uprisings broke the stillness of dawn, and pioneer railroading stretched from Council Bluffs to Denver and Ogden. The National Census of 1870 showed the population of Iowa to be 1,191,720. Davenport was the largest city with a population of 20,141.[30]

Iowa stories of Jesse and Frank James allege sightings in Adair, Corydon, Council Bluffs, Hamburg, Bartlett, Hinkletown, Greene Valley, North English, Millersburg, Wellman, Fairview, and the Honey Creek area in Harrison and Pottawattamie counties. Many of these communities formed groups of men known as "vigilantes," who upheld the law and tracked down criminals, the James-Younger Gang included.

In the 1870s, Johnny Corridan, who owned land a quarter-mile directly south of Hinkletown, claimed that Jesse James had camped on his land to the north of Kinross. According to Old Johnny, Jesses James and his notorious bunch of outlaws were passing through the area when they reportedly stopped over for the night. He remembered them making camp a short distance east of the Corridan home. One of the gang slipped into Wellman for a haircut and a shave.[31]

Johnny Corridan was a member of the "Union Horse Company," a well-organized early law enforcement group also known as the "vigilantes," which tracked down many horse thieves and criminals in the vicinity. The unit was composed of thirty men, many from

The Corridan house in the 1850s. (Author's collection)

John Corridan. (Author's collection)

An advertizement for the Union Horse Company in the Friday, February 14, 1893 edition of the *Wellman Advance*. (Author's collection)

Hinkletown and a several-mile perimeter, who had mustered together to fight the outlaws. These thirty men set forth their constitution, by laws and articles, which appointed officers and their duties, and addressed membership criteria, meeting times, dues and duties of the members, and behavior.[32]

Talk of recent crimes, criminals, and strategies comprised the meetings. Each member kept a full description of his horses and mules in the event of theft of his own or being ordered to look for and identify the property of others. Hand signals and passwords were used to identify each other in the dark, and to test dubious members.

There was a jail at Hinkletown on the Keokuk County side of "Main Street," as well as a large oak tree where hangings were said to occur at the top of a hill on the Keokuk County side of Hinkletown, which caused many outlaws to avoid the area. Apparently, Jesse James paid them little heed, however, if the stories of his being there are true.

Greene Valley, only one-mile east of Hinkletown, also had its share of thieves. One Sunday the F.M. Berry family returned home from church only to notice some strange men by one of their log cabins. Being very hospitable, they invited these men in for dinner. Just as they were preparing to sit down to eat, the sheriff from Marengo arrived and arrested the guests; the men were a group of horse thieves.[33]

Numerous other bands of horse thieves roamed the area, and as in Hinkletown, a Vigilante party was organized to protect the civilians and their property. The captain of these vigilantes was William Popham of Yankee Lane. It was reported to Mr. Popham that the thieves were operating around Greene Valley but had their headquarters in North English or Millersburg. A Mr. Johnson and a Mr. Grimm both reported seeing suspicious looking men near Yankee Lane. Upon investigation they discovered these men had their camp near Greene Valley. Soon Mr. Johnson and Mr. Grimm missed some good horses. Popham and Grimm went in pursuit of the thieves, but lost their trail in some heavy timber near Millersburg. They questioned a Mr. McCarthy, who said they had gone to St. Joseph, Missouri. Grimm and Popham split up, Grimm following them, and Popham moving ahead on a train to head them off. A little after sun-up the next day, Mr. Grimm captured the thieves as they were attempting to trade off the stolen horses. He turned them over to officers who returned them to Iowa County for trial. While waiting to be tried, the thieves broke out of jail and were not captured again. Local citizens believed the horse thieves in this area were part of the infamous, "law-breaking Jesse James Gang."

The Billy Hull farm near Fairview was a busy place with several workers coming and going. One evening, an able-looking young man allegedly rode in on a lame horse. He asked if he could stay until his horse's leg healed. He insisted he would do anything about the place in return. The stranger was polite when spoken to, but he volunteered no information. They liked him since he appeared to be a good man and apparently clean spoken. Any man who used foul language was immediately asked to leave. This man kept to himself, devoting his attention to caring for his horse. When there was no task he could perform, he rested. Some of the young boys were curious and began watching him. They found that he was not only tending a sore leg on his horse, but one of his own as well. The boys reported what they saw to their father, but he told them to mind their own business, believing the man had suffered an accident as riders often did.

The horse healed and so did the stranger. One morning he was gone, leaving a note of thanks and wishing them well. About two weeks later, Mr. Hull came home from town carrying a newspaper he had picked up. The newspaper featured a photograph of their late guest— Jesse James—and an account of a train robbery in which he had taken part. According to a family member, "No matter what others might have said or thought, the Hull boys always had a good word for Jesse."[34]

Another account alleges that Frank and Jesse James stopped at the George and Nora McNamara farm near Rhodes, Iowa, after attempting to rob the First National Bank of Northfield, Minnesota, in 1876. The boys took two of the McNamara horses, leaving one of their own as partial payment.[35]

In 1881, notorious outlaw Pat Crowe, alleged by some as being an acquaintance of Jesse James, had moved with his family to Crawford County, Iowa, and purchased a farm nine miles north of Aspinwall. The farm had been sold by the railroad to Samuel Miller in 1871, then to the Crowes in 1881, and, afterwards, to Peter J. Martens of Westside in 1884. Martens, upon moving in, found that the front enclosure of the house still had a piece of tin nailed over a hole where Pat Crowe had used a gun, shooting through the floor.[36]

In later years, the Martens often talked about Pat Crowe and the James Brothers. Although it is doubtful that Crowe had any communication with the James-Younger Gang, he had already commenced his outlaw career at the same time that the James Brothers were said to be hanging out in Cherokee, Sac, and even Crawford County, Iowa.

According to another account, the James Gang had a hide-out on the John Wieble place, eight miles south of Manning, Iowa, a convenient location for planned robberies north of Missouri about 1880. One summer day before noon a band of about twelve horsemen rode up to the farm home of the White family, who lived on the old Bill Wegner place north of Aspinwall.[37]

Mrs. White and her daughter were terrified when the men alighted. The leader walked up to them and politely asked if they could be served a dinner. The young girl was sent out to the field to get her father to help prepare the meal, for the men said they were in a hurry. Mr. White was ordered to kill and dress the chickens and to peel potatoes. The daughter ran to get fresh vegetables from the garden and prepare them for the table. Two of the strangers chopped wood. Mrs. White fried the chicken. One of the gang brought in a bag of lemons and asked that she make lemon pies with meringue.

Dinner was served in grand style on a linen tablecloth with cloth napkins. The gang feasted and all of the men were orderly. As each one rose from the table, he left a silver dollar at his plate.

The White family was amazed, but was grateful that the outlaws left without harmful incident. They heeded the strict warnings given not to divulge the whereabouts of the James Gang. It was some time before the affair was thus told to the neighbors of the Aspinwall community.

In the spring of 1881, Jacob Wiecks rented a farm west of Aspinwall. When it came time to pay taxes and rent at Denison, the county seat, he loaded a flock of turkeys on his spring-board wagon pulled by his two fastest horses. It was about a twenty-mile trip along the Ridge Road to Denison, so Wiecks departed early in the morning. After transacting his business, he began the long trip back to Aspinwall. As his team and wagon passed under the Northwestern Railroad Bridge, east of Denison, a man leaped from the bridge onto his wagon seat, landing at Wieck's side. The man pulled out a revolver, pointed it at the frightened driver, and ordered him to move at a fast clip up the hill and along the Ridgeway toward Aspinwall and Botna.[38]

Jacob Wiecks was a powerful man, having been a soldier and fencer in the Danish Army. With a sure quick motion, he grabbed the wrist of the stranger's revolver-holding hand. He held that position and the men sat side-by-side for the rest of the trip to Aspinwall.

Wiecks's horses were fatigued and slowed down. Finally, when Wiecks released the stranger's wrist without further harassment, the man asked about the Chicago Great Western Railroad connections at Botna.

Upon reaching the crossroads of the old Milwaukee right-of-way just west of the Marvin Lamp place, the stranger spied a beautiful black riding stallion tethered near a barn belonging to a Jones family. Suddenly and without warning, the stranger leaped from the wagon and ran up to the gentle black stallion, mounted him, and galloped away south down to Botna. While the curious Wieck looked on, the stranger watched and waited for the advancing train. He slid from the gentle stallion's back, pulled out a sharp knife and cut the tendons at the horse's hocks. The poor animal fell no longer able to walk. The stranger had guaranteed that no one would use that fleet horse to follow him as he jumped on the passing train. The poor animal later had to be shot.

About a week later, Wieck went to Aspinwall to buy groceries and pipe tobacco. Here he saw "WANTED POSTERS" of the Jesse James gang and allegedly recognized Cole Younger as the man who had leaped into his wagon.

## Notes

[1]Michael J. Perry, "A Territorial Period Site in Dubuque," Office of the Iowa State Archaeologist Archives.

[2]Phillip W. Steele with George Warfel, *The Many Faces of Jesse James*, Gretna, Pelican Publishing Company, 1995, pp. 17-20.

[3]Daniel Dunihue, "Journal of Occurrences, August 1832," Indiana Humanities Council, Indianapolis, Indiana.

[4]Ron Diess, " Fort Armstrong at the Rock Island Rapids," Unpublished manuscript; E.S. "A Visit to Fort Armstrong." *Rock Island Banner and Stephenson Gazette*, Rock Island, 1840, p. 2.

[5]Paul C. Nagel, *Missouri: A History*, Lawrence, University of Kansas Press, 1977, pp. 120-121.

[6]J.W. Buel, *The Border Outlaws: An Authentic and Thrilling History of the Most Noted Bandits of Ancient or Modern Times, the Younger Brothers, Jesse and Frank James, and Their Comrades in Crime.*

[7]L. Matthew Chatterley, "Explore Iowa's Historic Mormon Trails," Iowa Mormon Trail Association.

[8]Benjamin F. Gue, *History of Iowa from the Earliest Times to the Beginning of the Twentieth Century*, Four Volumes, New York, Century History Company, 1903.

[9]*Annals of Iowa*, Volume VI, Number 7, October 1904, 3D Series, "Pioneer Perils."

[10]*Annals of Iowa*, Vol. XVIII, No. 5, Des Moines, Iowa, July 1932, Third Series, F.L. Herriott, "The Origins of the Indian Massacre Between the Okobojis, March 8, 1857," p. 323.

[11]Abigail Gardiner, *History of the Spirit Lake Massacre! 8th March 1857, and of Miss Abigail Gardiner's Three Months Captivity Among the Indians*, New Britain, CT., L.P. Lee, Publisher, 1857, p. 5; Benjamin F. Gue, *History of Iowa from the Earliest Times to the Beginning of the Twentieth Century*, Four Volumes, New York, Century History Company, 1903.

[12]Ibid.

[13]J. Frank Dobie, *Legends of Texas*, Austin, Texas Folk-Lore Society Number 3, 1924, p. 10; Charlton Grant Laird, Iowa Legends of Buried Treasure, Lincoln, Foundation Books, 1990, p. 4.

[14]*Treasure Cache Magazine*, January 2002, p. 81; Donald E. Bower, *Ghost Towns & Back Roads*, Stackpole Books, Harrisburg, Pennsylvania, 1971; George A. Thompson, *Throw Down the Box!* Dream Garden Press, Salt Lake City, Utah 1989.

[15]Joseph Frazier Wall, *Iowa: A History*, New York, W.W. Norton & Company, Inc., 1978, p. 124.

[16]Dorothy Schwieder, *Iowa State Register, History of Iowa*; Glenda Riley, *Frontier Woman: The Iowa Experience*, Ames, Iowa State University Press, 1981, p. 81.

[17]Wayne and Appanoose counties, Iowa, Biographical and Historical Record, 1886, in collection at Prairie Trails Museum, Corydon, Iowa.

[18]William Lee Burton, "Adam Ripper, Corydon Resident for 62 Years, Tells of Town's Thrilling History," 1932, in collection at Prairie Trails Museum, Corydon, Iowa.

[19]A.S. Mercer, *The Banditti of the Plains*, Norman, University of Oklahoma Press, 1954, pp. xxv.

[20]Ed Bartholomew, *Wyatt Earp: The Untold Story*, Toyahvale, Texas, Frontier Book Company, 1963, pp. 10-11.

[21]1850 Federal Census for Marion County, Iowa.

[22]Ed Bartholomew, *Wyatt Earp: The Untold Story*, p. 14.

[23]Richard E. Erwin, *The Truth About Wyatt Earp*, Carpinteria, California, The O.K. Press, 1993, pp. 12-13.

[24]Casey Tefertiller, *Wyatt Earp: The Life Behind the Legend*, New York, Wiley & Sons, Inc., 1997, p. 3; Frank Waters, *The Earp Brothers of Tombstone*,

Lincoln & London, University of Nebraska Press, 1960, pp. 28-29; Johnny D. Boggs, "Following Wyatt Earp," *True West*, November/December 2005, p. 87; Ed Bartholomew, *Wyatt Earp: The Untold Story*, pp. 14-15.

[25]Glenn G. Boyer, "On the Trail of Big Nosed Kate," *Real West*, March 1951, pp. 14-15.

[26]*Kansas City Journal*, April 4, 1882.

[27]*Columbia, Missouri, Herald*, August 28, 1903.

[28]*Omaha World-Herald*, June 1, 1998, Fred Thomas, "James Had Nebraska Connections."

[29]Ibid.

[30]Benjamin F. Gue, *History of Iowa from the Earliest Times to the Beginning of the Twentieth Century*, Four Volumes, New York, The Century History Company, Volume 3, 1903.

[31]Scott Romine and Steve Miller, *History of Kinross , Iowa*, 1979.

[32]*Wellman Advance*, February 14, 1893.

[33]Donna Miller, *A Glimpse of Greene Valley*, 1964.

[34]William Hull Family Papers and biography.

[35]Claire Ryan letter to author dated September 20, 2002. Author's collection.

[36]*A Little Bit of Paradise*, Aspinwall, Iowa, centennial book, 1992

[37]Mabel Guth Ohde letter to author dated September 22, 2002. Author's Collection.

[38]Mabel Guth Ohde letter to author dated September 24, 2002. Author's Collection.

*Chapter Two*

# The Puke War

"Ye freemen of this happy land,
Which flows with milk and honey,
Arise!  To arms!  Your ponies mount!
Regard not blood or money.
Old Governor Lucas, tiger-like,
Is prowling round our borders,
But Governor Boggs is wide awake-
Just to listen to his orders:
Three bee trees stand about the line
Between our state and Lucas.
Be ready all these trees to fall
And bring things to a focus.
We'll show old Lucas how to brag,
And seize our precious honey!
He also claims, I understand,
Of us three bits in money."
—A Missouri Wag[1]

A S EARLY AS 1854 MISSOURI BUSHWHACKERS were engaged in a border war with Kansas Jayhawkers (named for a mythical Irish bird) and the Redlegs (named for their maroon leggings). The founder of the Jayhawkers, Charles R. "Doc" Jennison, once declared an outlaw by the federal government, was commissioned to command the Seventh Kansas Volunteer Cavalry Regiment. The Redlegs, under command of General James C. Blunt and Kansas Senator Jim Lane, became the Ninth Kansas Volunteer Cavalry Regiment. Jesse James' family, living in pro-Confederate Clay County, witnessed and endured many of the atrocities committed by Jim Lane and his Union loyalist Redlegs or Jayhawkers.

Missouri's friction with its neighbors, however, was not limited to Kansas. Although pretty much forgotten and overlooked, the state earlier was involved in a border dispute with the territory of Iowa. While most disputes between states over land had cost the litigants large sums of money and generated hard feelings, real violence had been absent. There was a close call, however, early in the state's history when Missouri and Iowa went head-to-head over a contested tract of land.

Although Missouri became a state in 1820, the northern boundary was never properly and legally surveyed. When the territory of Iowa was subsequently created, the southern boundary was simply defined as Missouri's northern boundary, setting up potential for the later conflict. To settle the situation, Congress authorized a joint commission to survey the Missouri/Iowa line. In the 1838 report, four lines were designated as being possible boundary lines, according to the phrasing of the 1820 Missouri boundary delineated by the United States Congress.[2]

Robert Lucus. (Author's collection)

The real trouble occurred in the summer of 1839 when Governor Robert Lucas of Iowa and Governor Lilburn Boggs of Missouri each issued proclamations warning the officers of the other's government not to extend their jurisdiction over the area claimed

34

by both. The boundary between Missouri and the Iowa Territory soon came into a heated dispute. Governor Lilburn Boggs ordered all officials of Missouri's northern counties to execute the laws of the state up to the northernmost designated line, using the militia if necessary. At the same time, Iowa's Governor Robert Lucas warned Missouri officials to stay out of the disputed border area.

The first territorial governor of Iowa, Robert Lucas, was not about to turn the other cheek. Born at Shepherdstown, Jefferson County, Virginia, on the first of April 1781, he received his education under a private teacher and became a surveyor. His father was an officer in the Revolutionary War who, in 1800, liberated his slaves and removed to Scioto County, Ohio.

When the War of 1812 broke out, Robert was appointed captain in the regular army and, as the war progressed, attained the rank of colonel. He served nineteen years in the Ohio legislature and, during that period, was presiding officer of both House and Senate. In 1832 he was president of the Democratic National Convention that nominated Andrew Jackson for president. In the same year, he was elected governor of Ohio, and in 1834 he was reelected, serving four years. On the seventh of July 1838, he was appointed by President Martin Van Buren governor of the new Territory of Iowa.[3]

Governor Lucas, of Iowa Territory, already had passed through a similar contest, when he was governor of Ohio, between Ohio and Michigan Territory, and had come out with flying colors. Lucas was something of a military man, and at once interested himself in an effort to organize a territorial militia. He called for the Iowa militia to stave off what promised to be an invasion by Missouri. Lucas had difficulty in many of the counties in getting them to take any interest in the matter, but the military spirit showed itself quite early in Louisa County.[4]

On January 19, 1839, Governor Lucas granted militia appointments, all of them being of the First Regiment of the First Brigade of the Second Division. These appointments appeared to many Missourians as an act of aggression in connection with the controversy between the state of Missouri and Iowa Territory over the location of the southern boundary of the territory.

This incident was called the "Border War," or the "Puke War." It was also referred to as the "Iowa War" or quite appropriately, the "Honey War." The state of Missouri claimed that the northern boundary of that state extended far enough north to include a great part of Iowa's Van Buren County. The constitution of Missouri, in defining the boundaries of that state, had defined her northern boundary as the parallel of latitude which passes through the rapids of the Des Moines River.

The boundary line dispute was the scene of at least three surveys and a near war before it was settled. The misunderstanding came about over the phrase, "rapids of the River Des Moines," found in the enabling legislation of March 6, 1820, that authorized the people of the Missouri Territory to form a constitution and state government. Subsequent surveys made to correct problems in the original survey could not find the rapids. The citizens of Iowa claimed they were in the Mississippi River where the Des Moines River joined the Mississippi near Alexandria. Missourians placed the rapids in the Des Moines River near Athens. The area in dispute was sparsely settled and approximately nine to eleven miles wide across Missouri.[5]

In the Mississippi River, a little above the mouth of the Des Moines River, were the rapids, which had been known as the Des Moines Rapids, or the Rapids of the Des Moines River. Just below the town of Keosauqua, in Van Buren County, there were also rapids (though very slight and inconsiderable) in the Des Moines River. The Missouri authorities claimed that the latter rapids were referred to in the definition of her boundary, and insisted on exercising jurisdiction over a strip of territory some eight miles in width, which Iowa claimed as being a part of her territory.[6]

When Missouri had become a state in 1820, her constitution defined her northern boundary as the parallel of latitude that passed through the "rapids of the River Des Moines." The land along this parallel was then in the possession of the Indians, but as soon as the Indian title expired, Missouri took steps to establish her exact limits. In 1836 Missouri appointed a commission to locate this boundary. The United States and the Territory of Wisconsin were invited to have representatives on the commission but failed to respond. Missouri went ahead alone.[7]

Relations among settlers in the disputed border area between Iowa and Missouri grew strained and hostile. When a Missourian had the audacity to cut down three bee trees in the contested area, the Iowa owner brought charges against the bee tree thief before an Iowa territorial judge. The honey hunter got back to Missouri with his load of honey, but a judgment for $1.50 was rendered against the said criminal and, according to tradition, the Iowa authorities with a strong posse awaited his return to collect the money.

Nothing could get settlers riled up more than somebody messing with their honey supply. The trees were valuable both for honey, which sold for a handsome thirty-seven cents a gallon, and for beeswax, which was used in various ways. And so, in the fall of 1839, Missouri and Iowa mobilized their ragtag militias and prepared to start killing each other over three trees of honey, the value of which totaled $1.50. The "Honey War," as the brief but rowdy conflict was called, had begun.

The incident inspired John I. Campbell to write a poem titled "The Honey War." Sung to the tune of "Yankee Doodle," it was a favorite in Missouri during the 1840s:

### The Honey War
by John I. Campbell

Ye freeman of the happy land
Which flows with milk and honey,
Arise! To arms! Your ponies mount!
Regard not blood or money.
Old Governor Lucas, tiger-like
Is prowling 'round our borders,

But Governor Boggs is wide awake—
Just listen to his orders.
Three bee-trees stand about the line
Between our state and Lucas.
Be ready all these trees to fall,
And bring things to a focus.
We'll show old Lucas how to brag,
And seize our precious honey!
He also claims, I understand,
Of us three-bits of money!
Conventions, boys, now let us hold
Our honey trade demands it;
Likewise the three-bits, all in gold,
We all must understand it!
Why shed our brother's blood in haste,
Because "big men" require it.
Be not in haste our blood to waste,
No prudent men desire it.
Now, if the governors want to fight,
Just let them meet in person,
And when noble Boggs old Lucas flogs,
T'will teach the scamp a lesson.
Then let the victor cut the trees,
And have three-bits in money,
And wear a crown from town to town,
Anointed with pure honey.
And then no widows will be made,
No orphans unprotected.
Old Lucas will be nicely flogged,
And from our line ejected.
Our honey trade will then be laid
Upon a solid basis,
And Governor Boggs, where'er he jogs,
Will meet with smiling faces.
(Sung to the tune of "Yankee Doodle")[8]

An infuriated Missouri Governor Boggs ordered Uriah Gregory, sheriff of Clark County, "to go get the taxes on those Iowans' property and that included bee trees." On November 20, 1839, during the height of the honey harvest, Sheriff Gregory was arrested by the sheriff of

Iowa's Van Buren County for collecting taxes in what he and Governor Boggs claimed to be Missouri. He was taken to Burlington, capital of the Territory of Iowa, where he was charged with "usurpation of authority" and was imprisoned for a brief time.[9]

Gregory later reported that the Iowans treated him pretty well and even let him roam around town. But they wouldn't let him go home. Still, he apparently enjoyed his enforced vacation and seemed relieved to have his problems solved for him, even though the courts of Clark County, Missouri, wanted their sheriff back. The court members asked the state for help in springing Sheriff Gregory from the Iowa jail and in enforcing the laws.

Public meetings were held in the northeastern Missouri counties, and resolutions were adopted encouraging county officials to enforce the laws in the disputed strip at all costs. One writer observed that the meetings "were managed by aspirants for political gain, anxious to stir up trouble, and be on the side of the war party, knowing full well that the troubles would be settled without danger to themselves."

Missouri Governor Lilburn Boggs brought the matter to a crisis by sending another officer into Iowa to collect taxes. This officer, David Doose, was also arrested and put in jail in Van Buren County. At the first court held in Farmington, Van Buren County, in April 1839, by David Irwin, judge of the Second Judicial District of Wisconsin, an indictment was found against Doose for exercising the office of constable in Van Buren County under authority of the State of Missouri. Governor Boggs of Missouri issued a fierce proclamation and called for a thousand volunteers. Governor Lucas responded with a much bigger proclamation and called for 120 troops.[10]

William L. Toole, referring to this incident in his article on Louisa County history in the *Annals of Iowa for 1870* penned: "Louisa County, like its adjoining counties, had for its early settlers a people patriotic and spirited, as was fully shown at the time of our border war; for, although then but few in number, they eagerly and freely attended to the call to repel the invaders."[11]

Public meetings were held in Iowa and patriotic speeches delivered and resolutions made to stand ready for a move against the intruders from Missouri. The display of patriotism was not confined to the males, but the wives and daughters were also zealous in their patriotism.

Maximilian Eastwood, justice of the peace, blacksmith, and tavern keeper in Toolesborough, Iowa, was a man of considerable local note and influence, and his cabins were places of public resort. On the occasion of one of these "war meetings," Mrs. Eastwood, who was a favorite among the people, "assisted by her female friends, prepared a free dinner for all assembled, and enough for all. The dinner was made notable because of the huge johnnycake she prepared for the occasion; it was fourteen feet long and about one foot wide, baked on a board before a fire fixed along a large log, and perhaps the largest cake ever made in Iowa."[12]

The Missourians tried to raise 2,200 militiamen, but less than half showed up. However, it was reported they came armed with an assortment of fighting technology. One resourceful volunteer showed up with a sausage stuffer as his weapon. It was December, snowy and bitterly cold. The Lewis County, Missouri, Militia was sent into the disputed area without tents, with few blankets and only partially armed. They did, however, have plenty of whiskey.

Meanwhile, Governor Lucas had called out the Iowa territorial militia for war in what he termed "the seat of excitement." His inspiring words were reported to have been, "Death to the pukes!" He prophesied wrongly as it turned out, that the dispute "might ultimately lead to the spilling of blood." About 1,200 men answered his battle cry, and they, too, came with an ample supply of booze.

Some three hundred Iowa men were mustered at Farmington, spies were sent out to observe the movements of the Missourians, and pickets were stationed to give the alarm if the enemy (Missourians) crossed the Indian boundary. A public meeting in Farmington sensibly resolved that the Iowans would act on the defensive and neither "aggress nor be aggressed upon."

Other neighboring county militia groups rushed to the aid of their Iowa comrades. One prominent Iowan, Mrs. Sarah Hurley, remembered the Wapello Cavalry quite well, that it was in the habit of drilling out west of town and that her uncle, David Clark, who at that time lived in Muscatine and had been commander of a militia company back in Indiana, came down occasionally to drill the boys.

This company of militia from Muscatine marched into Louisa County to aid its brethren, as did a company from Johnson County, which came as far as the bluff south of Wapello. Upon learning that there would be no war, the men from both counties returned home.

Several militiamen from Schuyler County stepped forward to battle the enemy, although most were unsure as to who the enemy was, before and especially during the Civil War. Although Missouri was a free state, enlistments in Schuyler County were almost evenly divided between Union and Confederate forces. Neighbor no longer trusted neighbor, and families were divided in loyalties. Bushwhackings and skirmishes occurred throughout the area. Some families left, unable to live under such stress.[13]

One of the results of the "Puke War" was the first review of the Iowa militia. When the call was issued by Governor Lucas for troops to repel invasion by Missouri, the Iowa militia had hardly been formed, and was much inferior to the troops from Missouri. Governor Lucas hurriedly appointed commissioned officers in the localities where companies were to be raised. Couriers were sent out on horseback to various points to request all able-bodied men to meet at some locality for the purpose of enlistment. Usually a blacksmith shop or a schoolhouse was selected as a convenient rallying place.

The recruits were ordered to bring with them what weapons they possessed or could procure. Outlying districts did not even know why a militia was wanted, but the response to Governor Lucas' appeal was earnest and loyal. The troops were armed with rifles, shotguns, pistols, and other firearms of a variety of forms. Some of the officers had trailing dragoon swords; some had straight dress swords; some had no swords. No two men were attired or armed alike. The Iowa Territorial militia of the winter of 1839-1840 was a strange sight.

Granted, 1,200 men enlisted under Governor Lucas' proclamation, yet this militia never was paid for its services. Neither were the persons who furnished supplies recompensed for their efforts. Soon after the hostile demonstrations on the border had been quieted, a review of the Border War Army of Iowa Territory was ordered, to take place at Burlington. The governor wished to ascertain the condition and the numerical strength of the troops. Many of the soldiers hoped the review was ordered so that a payroll might be made up, and were deluded into vain rejoicings.

The territorial militia was very green, having had comparatively no drill. The men were hastily instructed by Colonel Temple, the commanding officer, so that they might make as presentable an appearance as was possible, under the conditions. In particular, they were impressed with the idea that to be military they must look stern.

The reviewing party consisted of the governor, his aides, and Lieutenant Ruggles, of the regular army, the inspecting officer. All were on horseback. Governor Lucas wore a blue jeans coat, long, and buttoned closely about his body; his trousers were tucked into high, stout boots; his hat was by no means new. Lieutenant Ruggles was immaculate, for the army uniform of those days was brilliant with lace and glitter.

His frock coat was of the regulation blue, richly adorned with gold lace and gilt buttons. The collar was a tall stock, which tightly enclosed his throat like a vice. His boots had buff tops. Huge epaulets were on his shoulders, and on his head a chapeau with two long plumes waving from it. The settlers stared at him in admiration.

In marching in review, the militia traversed a field. The ground was uneven, and covered with stumps, hazel brush, and the limbs of trees. Every few moments a soldier would stub his toe and fall. Then his companions, or an officer, would swear at him. When the order, "Present arms," was given, the line showed a medley of rifles and shotguns.

The settlements in Iowa Territory at this time, the latter part of 1839, were scattered, and the militia was poorly organized. But within a short time after the call to arms, numerous Iowans, under orders from Major-General Jesse Browne, were encamped in Van Buren County, and directly opposite were 1,000 Missourians, under General Allen. The two forces were glaring at each other, anxious for a fracas.[14]

The plan of the Missourians during the Puke War, however, was to send the sheriff with militiamen as his posse into the disputed strip to collect taxes. If resistance was met, there would be a fight "and the blood of the slain would be upon Iowans and not upon Missourians, who would be simply enforcing the law."

Two days after ordering the sheriff to resume his tax collecting duties, the Clark County officials drew back, possibly because they saw that Iowans were ready to call the Missourians' bluff, if such was really the case. Instead, the Missourians appointed a committee to confer with the Iowa territorial legislature "to procure, if possible, an amicable adjustment of the border difficulties." Neither the Missouri general assembly nor the governor knew of this committee's intentions.

The determined committee of five made its way to Burlington, where the Iowa legislature was in session. The territorial legislature received the overtures of the Missourians "in the kindliest manner and most generous spirit." Both sides came up with a classical political solution. They dumped the problem in the lap of the federal government and sent the troops home.

Meanwhile, Iowans had considered it best to send peace commissioners to Missouri with a view of adjusting the difficulties. General A.C. Dodge, of Burlington; General Churchman, of Dubuque; and Dr. Clark, of Fort Madison, were appointed and proceeded to discharge the duties of their mission.

When they arrived, they found that the county commissioners of Clarke County, Missouri, had rescinded their order for the collection of taxes in Iowa, and the governor of Missouri had sent messengers to Governor Lucas with a proposition to submit an agreed case to the

Supreme Court of the United States. Both Iowa and Missouri petitioned Congress to authorize a suit to settle the question.

The verbal terms of the agreement between the two sides stated that Sheriff Gregory would be released. Missouri should continue to collect taxes in the contested strip. If the Congress and court went against Missouri, the collected money would be refunded to Iowa.

Missouri's Governor Boggs, who had spent $20,000 and had put his reputation on the line in the "Honey War," strongly disapproved of the peace terms on the grounds that he had no power to suspend the enforcement of laws in any part of the state, including the nine-mile strip in question, and that Congress had no power to take one inch of Missouri's declared limits.

Boggs, therefore, ordered that "no suspension of civil or military functions under the laws of Missouri be allowed within its rightful limits" and directed all civil and military officers to do their duty. During the next ten years, the few Missouri officials who tried to exercise authority in the disputed strip were arrested by Iowa authorities, detained for a while and finally sent home.

Iowans were increasing in numbers, and they boldly looked upon the Missouri intrusions as merely "flea bites." As long as the boundary question remained unadjusted, people did not care to invest in "Chaldea," or Centerville, as the town would later be called. After all, Missouri's boundary claim ran right through the railroad junction at Chaldea. If Missouri's claim should be established, Appanoose County would move its county seat further north. Because the people did not want to be considered Missourians, the growth of the town could not continue until the boundary issue was resolved.

While the "Puke" or "Honey" War was being waged in Missouri and Iowa, Robert Sallee James was a student at Georgetown College where he met Zerelda E. Cole, a resident at a Georgetown convent. Zerelda's father, James Cole, had been killed in a horse accident when Zerelda was only two years old. Her mother, Sallie Lindsay Cole, then married Robert Thomason in 1838 and moved to Missouri, leaving young Zerelda in Kentucky with her uncle, James Lindsay.[15]

On December 18, 1841, Robert James and Zerelda Cole were married in Kentucky, and, a few months later, they moved to Missouri. The following children were born to them in Clay County: Alexander Franklin James, 1843; Robert R. James, 1845 (Robert lived only thirty-three days); Jesse Woodson James, 1847; and Susan Lavenia James, 1849.

During 1845 and 1846, while Robert James began working his newly acquired 247-acre farm in Kearney, Missouri, that state, the Territory of Iowa, and Congress finally agreed to let the United States Supreme Court decide the whole issue of the border dispute. On February 13, 1849, the Supreme Court handed down its ruling. The court held that the old Indian line marked the true northern limits of Missouri. Iowa was given all the territory it had had before the contest.[16]

In addition to the boundary ruling, the justices under an order of the Supreme Court of the United States, appointed William G. Miner, of Missouri, and Henry B. Hendershott, of Iowa, as acting commissioners to survey and establish the boundary line. The commissioners were instructed to mark the line between the two states and to erect iron pillars, one on each end of the line, and to place iron or stone posts at intervals of ten miles along the border. "MISSOURI" was to be inscribed on the south side and "IOWA" on the north side of each post.

After work was completed on January 3, 1851, the Supreme Court approved the report of the commissioners and then ordered the total cost of $10,880.41 to be divided equally between the two states. The commissioners discharged the duties assigned them, and peace was restored.

Centerville citizens were absolutely ecstatic over the court's ruling. Besides being freed from what they imagined to be Missouri's tyranny, Centerville would have the distinction of being the Appanoose County seat. Putnam County's citizens were also delighted about the settlement. The Missouri county of Dodge, which had been created only months before the Supreme Court's decision, was now smaller than the state constitution allowed. The Dodge County part remaining in Missouri became part of Putnam County, angering those who wanted to maintain the status quo.

Perhaps somewhat inebriated and disappointed that their pay for active duty would end, some officers openly denounced those who had agreed to settle the conflict peacefully. But the enlisted had enough of the war. The men, who had been reluctant to leave home in the first place, had been marching in deep snow and camping in the bitter cold. Consequently, their joy at being able to return home was mixed with contempt for those responsible for the "war."

Holding the two governors responsible for the unnecessary trouble, Missouri troops expressed their disgust by cutting a haunch of venison into two parts, labeling one "Governor Lucas of Iowa" and the other "Governor Boggs of Missouri," hung them up, and used them for target practice. After the men reached home, some of them wore their coats wrong side out as a badge of their distinguished services in and safe return from the Honey War.

Though the officers and men had returned to pick up their lives, the entire dispute eventually had passed through the halls of Congress and ended up in the Supreme Court of Congress of the United States. Peace reigned once more, at least for a couple of years when Missouri and Kansas fought it out in what was to become the prelude for the War Between the States.

When the Civil War officially began in April 1861, Jesse's brother, Frank, joined the Home Guard to resist the Union invasion and then joined Confederate General Sterling Price's army at Lexington. Frank fought in the Battle of Wilson's Creek in August 1861 and eventually fell in with an infamous band of guerrilla fighters who served under William Clarke Quantrill and "Bloody Bill" Anderson.[17]

Missouri's old nemesis, Iowa, and conspicuously among them, Louisa County, still smarting from its Congressional victory in the Puke War, dispatched hundreds of men to fight for the Union against Frank James at Wilson's Creek. According to the report of Adjutant General Baker, made in 1866, the quota of troops to be furnished by Louisa

County, Iowa, for the suppression of the rebellion under the calls made by President Lincoln in 1861 and 1862 was five hundred, and the number of troops furnished by the county under these calls is given by the same report as eight hundred forty-two. This gives the county a surplus over the call of three hundred and forty-two.[18]

Louisa County furnished nearly the whole of the following companies: C of the Fifth Infantry; K of the Eighth Infantry; F and G of the Nineteenth Infantry; F of the Twenty-fifth Infantry, and F of the Thirty-fifth Infantry. It also furnished quite a number in Companies C of the Eleventh; C of the Eighth; E of the Fourteenth; C of the Fourteenth; I of the Sixth; E of the Sixteenth; D, G, and H of the Seventeenth, and one or more in the following companies: A, C, and E of the First Infantry; Companies A, G, and H of the Second Infantry; G of the Fifth; A and I of the Seventh; H and I of the Eighth; A of the Ninth; F, G and II of the Eleventh; K of the Thirteenth: K of the Fourteenth; H of the Fifteenth; C of the Sixteenth; C of the Eighteenth; C of the Nineteenth; D, E, and I of the Twenty-fifth; C of the Thirtieth; A and D of the Thirty-fifth; B and G of the Thirty-seventh; C of the Forty-first, and B, F, and H of the Forty-fifth; and Companies A, B, C, D, and E of the First Cavalry; A, H, I, and K of the Second Cavalry; K and L of the Fourth Cavalry; M of the Seventh Cavalry; D, E, F, H, K, L, and M of the Eighth Cavalry; and A of the Ninth Cavalry. There were also some Louisa County soldiers in the following commands: Engineer Regiment of the West, the First Battery Iowa Light Artillery, the Fourth Veteran Infantry, Fifteenth United States Regulars, the Sixteenth Illinois, and the Fifty-fifth Illinois.

A fair idea of the patriotism of Louisa County and her devotion to the Union can be gained from the fact that by the Census of 1860, the county had a population of but 10,370 and that she furnished during the war 1,217 soldiers. This means that practically fifty percent of the men of Louisa County enlisted in the federal army.

During the spring of 1863, federal militia, hunting Frank James and other irregulars, stopped at the James farm demanding information. Fifteen-year-old Jesse, who was plowing the field, was beaten and left

James Farm. (Courtesy Library of Congress)

in the field for dead by the angry federals. His step-father, Dr. Reuben Samuel, was tortured and hanged, although he survived, and Jesse's mother and sisters were tossed into jail.

A year later, Jesse joined the guerrillas, and on September, 27, 1864, he is believed to have participated in a massacre of unarmed federal troops at Centralia, Missouri. Jesse allegedly killed the commander of the pursuing federal troops, Major A.V.E. Johnson. The *Missouri Democrat* shocked its readership with its sensationalistic headline: "Guerrilla Atrocities. Butchery of Soldiers and Citizens on the North Missouri Railroad—Maj. Johnson's Command of Militia Ambuscaded and Almost Annihilated—Maj. Johnson Killed, but Twenty-five of His Whole Command Escaped."[19]

According to the early reports, Major A.V. E. Johnson's federal command of about 150 men were in pursuit of Bill Anderson's band of guerrillas, numbering about 175 men. The guerrillas had been chased out of Monroe County and were on their way South when they rode into

Centralia, on the line of the railroad. They entered the town about eleven o'clock, dressed in federal uniforms, well armed, mounted and equipped.

The citizens believed they were state militia. Shortly after their arrival, a gravel construction train came along, which was seized and stopped. A few minutes later, the passenger train from St. Louis arrived and was also seized. Three civilians, who offered resistance, were shot in the cars and either killed or wounded. The other passengers, including between thirty and forty soldiers, were all ordered out of the cars, and robbed of all their money and valuables.

Suddenly, the guerrillas began firing upon the unarmed soldiers, some of whom attempted to escape by running into the houses and into the fields, but they were pursued and shot. Twenty-four soldiers were murdered, seven of whom were of the First Iowa Cavalry stationed at Mexico, Missouri, and ten of whom were discharged soldiers, veterans returning to their homes from Atlanta. It was also reported that the dead were beaten, their heads cut off and hacked with swords, and every possible indignity inflicted on them. A torch was applied to the depot, and the train containing the three wounded civilians was fired and started on its way up the road.

Anderson's men galloped away once the carnage was completed. In an hour, they were pursued by Major Johnson and his command. Anderson hid his men in the bushes and awaited his pursuers about two or three miles beyond Centralia, in Boone County. Major Johnson, approaching the ambush, was fired upon. He immediately withdrew his command, dismounted them, and formed in line of battle. The guerrillas burst from the bushes with fierce yells and rapid firing. Major Johnson's horses took fright and left him and his men to wage the unequal contest on foot. They had delivered but one volley when the guerrillas were upon them, shooting, hacking and slaying to the right and left. The militia made no stand, and scattered and fled in all directions.

The previous month, Bloody Bill had penned a letter to a local newspaper, which was later reprinted in the August 4, 1864, edition of *The New York Times*. The spelling, punctuation and grammar errors are his own:

To the editors of the two papers in lexington to the Citizens and the community at large General Brown and Col McFairran and his petty hirelings such as Captain Burris the friend of Anderson. Mr editors in readding Both your papers I see you urge the policy of the citizens taking up arms to defend their persons and property, you are only asking them to sign their death warrants do you not know Sirs that you have some of Mosouries proudest Best and noblest sons to cope with Sirs ask the people of Mo. who is acquainted with me if Anderson ever robed them or misstreated them in manner all those that speaks the truth will say never. . . . But listen to me, fellow citizens. Do not obey this last order. Do not take up arms if you value your lives and property It is not in my power to save your lives, if you proclaim to be in arms against guerrillers. I will kill you I will hunt you down like wolves and murder you. You cannot escape. It will not be Federals after you. Your arms will be no protection to you. 25 of my men can whip all that can get together it will not be mulishia sutch as McFairrons But regulars that has Been in the field for three years that is armed with from 2 to four pistols and sharps rifles. I commenced at the first of this war to fight for my country not to steal from it I have chosen guerriller warfare for to revenge my self for rongs that I could not honerably avenge other wise. . . . the Yanks sought my life but failed to get me revenged theirselves by murdering my father destroying all my property, and have since that time murdered one of my sisters and kept the other two in jail 12 months But I have fully glutted my vengeance I have killed many I am a guerriller. . . . I have tried to teach the people of Mo. that I am their friend. . . . take up arms against me and you are federals, your doctrine is an absurdity and I will kill you for being fools. Beware men Before you make this fearful leap. . . . Let the federals know that Mo sons will not be trampled on I have no time to say anything more to you be careful how you act for my eyes are uppon you . . .

Yours respectfully W. ANDERSON Commanding Kansas First gurillers[20]

In April 1865, with the war finally ended, Jesse was badly wounded when he attempted to surrender. He was nursed back to health by his cousin, Miss Zerelda Mimms, who eventually became his wife. With surrender impossible for former guerrillas, the Jameses and the Youngers began robbing banks. Jesse and Frank James, Cole and Jim Younger, John Jarrette, and Clell Miller were all former guerillas.

The boys committed the first peace-time, daylight bank robbery in American history on February 13, 1866, at Liberty, Missouri, when they relieved the Clay County Savings Association of $60,000. Jesse James, still recovering from his wounds sustained in attempting to surrender, did not participate in the hold-up. Those believed to have pulled off the robbery are Frank James, Cole Younger, John Jarrette (who was married to Cole's sister Josie), Oliver Shepard, Bud and Donny Pence, Frank Greg, Bill and James Wilkerson, Joab Perry, Ben Cooper, Red Mankus, and Allen Parmer (who was married to Jesse's sister Susan). George Wymore, a student on his way to school was killed by the robbers outside.

As many as twelve strangers rode into town on that fateful afternoon. Two of the men dismounted and entered the Clay County Savings Bank, and asked the clerk to change a ten-dollar bill. As the clerk started to do so, the robbers pointed revolvers at him and his father, Greenup Bird, the cashier, and made them stand quietly while they proceeded to rob the Bank.[21]

Upon gathering all the money they could find, they locked the clerk and cashier in the vault, and no doubt thought they had locked the door. The men went out with their stolen treasure, mounted their horses and were joined by the balance of their gang, and commenced shooting in the air. S.H. Holmes, a local citizen, had two shots fired at him, and young George Wymore was shot and killed while standing on the opposite side of the street at the corner of the old Green House. According to eye witnesses, the killing was a deliberate murder, without any provocation whatsoever, for young Wymore, nor any of the citizens of town, previous to the shooting, knew anything of what had taken place. Had the robbers succeeded in locking the bank vault on the clerk and cashier, and had retired quietly, it would likely have been some time before the robbery would have been discovered. But such was not the case.

Pandemonium reigned in the streets, and as many men that could procure arms and horses went in pursuit, but up to this writing nothing is known of the result. Many of the town's citizens, as well as the officers of the bank, concluded that the robbers were a gang of old bushwhacking desperados from Jackson County. The *Liberty Tribune* proclaimed: "But it makes no difference who they are, or what they claim to be, they should be swung up in the most summary manner. Desperate cases require desperate remedies, and we believe our people are in a humor to make short work of such characters in the future."

The gang next robbed Alexander Mitchell and Company Bank in Lexington, Missouri, on October 30, 1866, eight months after the Liberty holdup. Frank and Jesse James, Cole Younger, John Jarrette, and perhaps one other were the robbers who took part, and the take was $2,011.50. Five men rode into Lexington that day and visited the banking house of Alexander Mitchell and Company. The bank was deserted except for Cashier J.L. Thomas, since it was the noon hour.[22]

Two of the five men walked slowly toward the bank. The watching cashier stepped behind the counter when one of the two strangers presented a fifty-dollar bond and asked if he could change it. The cashier opened the cash drawer and was fumbling for change when he looked up to see four big revolvers pointed at his head. Two more men had appeared in the doorway, and the man who had asked for change demanded the cashier turn over all the bank's money.

Thomas did as he was told, and the robbers tossed the loot into a wheat sack. The gunmen backed to the door, placed their guns into their pockets, and moved swiftly but quietly to their horses. All five quickly rode out of town. As soon as the horsemen had disappeared, Cashier Thomas spread the alarm. A posse was organized, but no trace of the five men was found.

Four months later, another robbery was attributed to the gang, although there is no evidence linking them with it. At noon, on March 2, 1867, five horsemen rode into Savannah, Missouri, and hitched their horses near the private bank of Judge McLain. The judge and his son saw them and, remembering the Lexington affair, where four of the five men entered, Judge McLain did not wait to be told to hand over the money. He seized a pistol and began firing. The four men drew guns and returned his fire. Judge McLain fell, shot through his breast.

Meanwhile, his son had dashed into the street, spreading the alarm. The robbers fled from the bank and galloped out of town. Although none of the outlaws was injured, they had not obtained a cent from the McLain bank. Again a posse failed to find any trace of the bandits. In addition to the James boys, Samuel Pope, and William (Bud) McDaniels were suspected. The two latter men were arrested but released when they presented alibis. Judge McLain recovered from his wound and became a local hero.

Three months later, fourteen men invaded the town of Richmond, Missouri, in Ray County, close to the home of the James brothers. They rode into town shouting the guerrilla yell. Six of the men halted at the Hughes and Mason Bank, the doors of which had been closed and locked when the shouts were heard. The six broke into the bank, looted it of about $4,000, which they put into a Missouri grain sack, and joined their companions outside.

Meanwhile, citizens had gathered, prepared to give fight. Mayor Shaw started firing briskly. The guerrillas punctured him with four bullets, and he fell dead. In the nearby county jail were several prisoners, said to have been confined because of their Southern sympathies. The guerrillas attempted to liberate them, killing B.G. Griffin, the jailor, and his son, a boy of fifteen.

The fourteen robbers galloped out of town. Posses were immediately organized, and a fund was subscribed to capture the robbers. Warrants were issued for eight former guerrillas: John White, James White, Isaac Flannery, Andrew McGuire, Payne Jones, Richard Burns, Thomas Little, and Allen Parmer. Little and Burns were hanged, but the others managed to escape. The Jameses and Cole Younger were sought, but they presented alibis, while keeping discreetly under cover.

The gang waited a year and a half after the Lexington holdup before their next confirmed robbery on March 20, 1868. Frank and Jesse James, Cole Younger, Oliver and George Shepard, Arthur McCoy, and John Jarrette robbed the Nimrod Long Banking Company in Russellville, Kentucky, of $14,000 in the process.

A man calling himself Thomas Colburn, and claiming to be a cattle dealer, offered to sell Bank President Nimrod Long a note of $500 denomination. As none of the coupons had been cut off, and the stranger, who pretended to be from Louisville, where the notes were worth a premium, offered it at par and allowed interest, Long became suspicious and refused to accept it.[23]

On March 18th, Colburn returned again with a friend and asked Long to change a $100 bill. Suspecting the note to be counterfeit, Long again declined. He was still suspicious of Colburn, and the man accompanying him made him ill at ease.[24]

On the 20th, about 2:00 P.M., as Mr. Long, Mr. Barclay (a clerk in the bank), and Mr. T.H. Simmons, a farmer living near Russellville, were sitting behind the counter, Colburn and another man rode up to the door, hitched their horses and entered the bank. Three companions remained outside. They asked for change for a $50 note. Mr. Long pronounced it counterfeit, when Colburn drew a revolver, placed its muzzle against his head, and cried out, "Surrender!" Mr. Long wheeled around and sprang toward the door leading into a room in the rear of the banking office. He hoped thus to make his exit from the building and give the alarm. One of the robbers, however, intercepted him at the door, placed a pistol within six or eight inches of his head and fired, without uttering a word. The ball did no greater injury than graze Long's scalp for about two inches, tearing away the hair and flesh, but not fracturing the skull. Long grabbed hold of the weapon, and made an effort to wrench it from his assailant, but the robber succeeded in regaining possession of his pistol. He immediately commenced to beat Long over the head with the butt, and, after a few furiously dealt blows, knocked him to the floor.[25]

The latter, however, sprang to his feet and again got hold of the pistol, just as the robber was about to cock it and shoot him. During the scuffle, Long managed to reach the back door of the rear room. Here he concentrated his almost exhausted strength into a final effort, freed himself from the clutches of the robber, sprang through the door and closed it after him. He rushed towards the front of the building, screaming for help.

Upon reaching the street, he found two men sitting on their horses behind some trees at the intersection of Main and Bethel Streets.[26] They were both armed with Spencer rifles and pistols, and were shooting up and down the street at all citizens who came within range. As Long ran by, they also fired twelve or fifteen shots at him, but without effect.

Inside the bank, Hugh Barclay and Thomas H. Simmons were confronted by Colburn and the other bandit with cocked revolvers and threats of instant death in case they resisted. After Long made his retreat out the back door, the other robber returned. One robber stood guard over Barclay and Simmons, while Colburn and the other took over nine thousand dollars in currency from the cash drawer.[27]

From the vault, the door of which was standing open, they took several bags of gold and silver. Several private boxes which were on a shelf in the vault and contained bonds were broken open, but none of the bonds were taken. Two robbers kept guard outside, and, although the alarm had spread, they kept the citizens at bay until a local man, O.C. "Matt" Owens, had the courage to begin firing upon them with a pistol. Owens was shot in the side but not dangerously wounded. Finally the sentinels became alarmed and called for their accomplices inside to come out. They quickly complied, bringing with them saddlebags crammed with gold and greenbacks.

The robbers leaving the bank were greeted with a heavy volley by a squad of citizens advancing up the street. At a signal from Colburn, the outlaws dashed at full speed out of town along the Gallatin Pike. Many shots were fired at them, but outside of a report that one had his arm broken, none of the shots took effect.

Ten minutes later, some forty citizens, mounted on such animals as they could collect from buggies, wagons, and hitching posts, started in hot pursuit. All the advantage, except in point of numbers, was with the robbers. They rode splendid horses and were as completely armed and equipped as the most daring and accomplished highwayman could desire.

The outlaws appeared to be riding towards Bowling Green, Kentucky, where they were seen by some farmers, before turning westward towards Glasgow. They apparently split up, with one of the groups riding towards Gainesville.[28] Only five miles from Russellville, their trail was lost in the woods, nor was anything heard of Colburn and his men until March 21st, when a dispatch was received stating that he and his band had crossed the Louisville and Nashville Railroad early in the morning near Mitchellsville.

This time, however, the outlaws had been seen a little bit more clearly than in past holdups and a somewhat detailed description of some of the robbers was given to the Logan County sheriff following the robbery. A local newspaper described the robbers as "very good looking, stout young men."[29]

Nimrod Long asked Louisville detectives D.T. "Yankee" Bligh and John Gallagher to investigate the robbery. Bligh determined that George Shepard was in Chaplin, Kentucky, and three days after his arrest in a Chaplin store, he told the detective that he had been away trading horses and was nowhere near Russellville at the time of the robbery. Bligh told him that a piece of paper which had been in the robbers' custody, mentioned his name. Shepard was taken to Russellville where he was identified as one of the robbers and was tried and sentenced to three years in prison. Oliver Shepard was tracked to his father's home in Missouri and was shot and killed while resisting arrest.[30]

Rumors circulated that the robbery was planned to get enough money to send Jesse on a sea voyage. He was still suffering from his lung wound. Shortly after the holdup, he did take a voyage around to California where he met his brother Frank, and they allegedly stayed for some time with an uncle who was a doctor. It was several months before the Jameses returned to Missouri. And when they did, their names were definitely linked for the first time with the new wave of crime.[31]

Several lawmen, however, especially detectives like Bligh and Gallagher refused to call off the hunt for Frank and Jesse James. With things heating up, the gang took a couple of years off, although they continued to be in the limelight because of sensation-seeking journalists. In 1868, newspaper reporters found their headline when, according to family members, John Jarrette and his wife, Josie, were ambushed by enemies. The Jarrette home was set on fire while the couple and their two young children, Margaret and Jeptha, were sleeping inside. Cole and Jim Younger were able to rescue the children, but John and Josie perished in the fire.[32]

## Notes

[1]Benjamin F. Gue, *History of Iowa from the Earliest Times to the Beginning of the Twentieth Century*, Volume Four, New York, Century History Company, 1903.

[2]Missouri State Archives, Soldiers Database, Records Services, Abstract of Wars & Military Engagements.

[3]Benjamin F. Gue, *History of Iowa from the Earliest Times to the Beginning of the Twentieth Century*, Volume Four, New York, Century History Company, 1903.

[4]Arthur Springer, *History of Louisa County, Iowa, from Its Earliest Settlement to 1912*, Volume I, The S.J. Clarke Publishing Company, 1912, Chapter XII, pp. 177-208.

[5]Dwight Weaver, "Missouri's Historic Border Battles," *Missouri Resources Magazine*, Summer 1999.

[6]*The History of Polk County, Iowa*, Union Historical Company, Birdsall, Williams & Company, 1880.

[7]Henry Sabin, L.L.D. and Edwin L. Sabin, *The Making of Iowa*, Chicago & New York, A. Flanagan Company, 1900.

[8]This poem was first published in *The Palmyra Whig* on December 26, 1839. It was written by John I. Campbell, a local satirist from Marion County. Campbell became a founding member of the Missouri State Historical Society.

[9]*The History of Polk County, Iowa*, Union Historical Company, Birdsall, Williams & Company, 1880.

[10]Arthur Springer, *History of Louisa County, Iowa, from Its Earliest Settlement to 1912*, Volume I, The S.J. Clarke Publishing Company, 1912, Chapter XII, pp. 177-208.

[11]"Annals of Iowa for 1870," William L. Toole article on history of Louisa County, Iowa.

[12]Arthur Springer, *History of Louisa County, Iowa, from Its Earliest Settlement to 1912*, Volume I, The S.J. Clarke Publishing Company, 1912, Chapter XII, pp. 177-208.

[13]"Brief History of the Founding and Early Growth of Scuyler County," compiled from Caywood's 1888 *History of Adair, Putnam, Sullivan & Schuyler Counties*, The 1878 Atlas of Schuyler County, information collected by the Office of Historic Preservation, files of Schuyler County newspapers and personal interviews as reported by Nelle George.

[14]Henry Sabin, L.L.D. and Edwin L. Sabin, *The Making of Iowa*, Chicago & New York, A. Flanagan Company, 1900.

[15]Phillip W. Steele, Jesse and Frank James: *The Family History*, Gretna, Pelican Publishing Company, 1987, pp. 31-35.

[16]Dwight Weaver, "Missouri's Historic Border Battles," *Missouri Resources Magazine*, Summer 1999.

[17]Robert L. Dyer, *Jesse James and the Civil War in Missouri*, Columbia & London, University of Missouri Press, 1994, pp. 23-26.

[18]Arthur Springer, *History of Louisa County, Iowa, from Its Earliest Settlement to 1912*, Volume I, The S.J. Clarke Publishing Company, 1912, Chapter XII, pp. 177-208.

[19]*Missouri Democrat*, September 29, 1864; *New York Times*, October 2, 1864.

[20]*New York Times*, August 4, 1864.

[21]*Liberty Tribune*, February 16, 1866

[22]*St. Clair County Courier*, May 6, 1976.

[23]*Nashville Banner*, March 22, 1868.

[24]*Louisville Courier*, March 24, 1868.

[25]*Nashville Banner*, March 22, 1868.

[26]*Louisville Daily Journal*, March 21, 1868.

[27]*Nashville Banner*, March 22, 1868.

[28]Marley Brant, *Jesse James: The Man and the Myth*, New York, Berkley Books, 1998, p. 70.

[29]*Louisville Daily Journal*, March 21, 1868.

[30]Marley Brant, *Jesse James: The Man and the Myth*, pp. 70-71.

[31]*St. Clair County Courier*, May 13, 1976.

[32]Marley Brant, *Jesse James: The Man and the Myth*, p. 71.

# Chapter Three

# Corydon Bank Robbery

*"I am aware that my name has been connected with all the bank robberies in the country; but positively I had nothing to do with any one of them. I look upon my life since the war as a blank, and will never say anything to make it appear otherwise. The world may believe as it pleases."*     —Cole Younger[1]

AMERICA IN 1869 WAS ON THE MOVE and was swept up in a whirlwind of change and progress which benefited most of its citizens. Ulysses S. Grant had just become president in 1869, and on May 10th, the Union Pacific-Central Pacific Transcontinental Railroad was completed as the two lines met at Promontory Point, Utah. Wyoming passed the first woman's suffrage act; Susan B. Anthony was elected president of the American Equal Rights Association, and Elizabeth Cady Stanton president of the National Woman Suffrage Association, which demanded federal voting rights for women.

Elizabeth Cady Stanton. (Courtesy Library of Congress)

Susan B. Anthony. (Courtesy Library of Congress)

Although the Indian Wars in the West would continue for another two decades, the First Sioux War had ended with the Treaty of Fort Laramie, and the United States government agreed to abandon Forts Smith, Kearney, and Reno. Change affected the legal system as the number of justices on the Supreme Court

Ulysses S. Grant. (Courtesy Library of Congress)

increased from seven to nine. Earlier in the year, Jay Gould and Jay Fisk attempted to drive up the price of gold and corner the market while on "Black Friday," President Grant released four million dollars and drove the price down, an action that caused a stock-market panic.

Americans were reading Mark Twain's, *The Innocents Abroad*, Louisa May Alcott's, *Good Wives* (*Little Women II*), *Oldtown Folks* by Harriet Beecher Stowe, and Bret Harte's *Tennessee's Partner* and *The Outcasts of Poker Flat*. Harte was passionate about the treatment of minorities, and he was particularly disgusted with the influence civilization was having on the West. He wasn't pleased with the effects that the railroad was having on the West either, nor was he pleased with the way the white man was taking advantage of minorities—Indians, Chinese, and Mexicans—to help settle the West. Both of these themes are shown throughout his works. Although Bret was appalled at these events, writing about them in the weekly newspaper helped to make him popular.[2]

On December 7, 1869, more than twenty months after the Russellville raid, three men rode into Gallatin, Missouri. Two of them dismounted and entered the Daviess County Savings Bank, while the third remained with the horses as lookout. One of the men produced a hundred-dollar bill and asked Captain John W. Sheets if he could get change. The other man offered to buy the bill and began whispering to the other customer. Captain Sheets started to open the cash drawer when one of the outlaws thrust a Colt navy pistol toward him, and demanded that he give him the keys to the inner doors of the safe. The outer door already stood open. The bandit held Sheets captive while the accomplice took about $700 from the safe and cash drawer.[3]

One of the men, believed to have been Jesse James, stared at the unarmed Sheets for a moment and then suddenly shot him twice. One bullet entered his head near the bridge of his nose and the other lodged in his heart, killing him instantly. In the excitement of the robbery Jesse apparently was suddenly struck by Sheet's resemblance to S.P. Cox, whom he claimed had been one of those responsible for the death of Bloody Bill Anderson and decided to avenge the death of his old comrade.

An attorney, William A. McDowell, was in the bank transacting business, and he was shot in the arm while fleeing from the building. The alarm had been given, and armed men were gathering on the street. The lookout called to his companions to hurry. They rushed for their horses, and the man carrying the money and the lookout galloped away. But the murderer of Sheets had bad luck. His spirited horse plunged and snorted. The rider had one foot in the stirrup and was dragged several yards. He managed to release himself, and the horse trotted away. One of the bandit's companions looked back, saw the plight of the dismounted man and hurried to his rescue.[4]

After the companion scooped the man up, the double-laden animal started after the third companion. Citizens fired at the fleeing bandits, but none of their bullets took effect. However, a mounted posse was formed, confident that they could overtake the heavily burdened horse. A mile from town, the fugitives encountered a farmer named Daniel Smoot and robbed him of his horse and galloped away. Near Kidder, Missouri, they forced a preacher to guide them around the town.

Jesse James was definitely linked with the robbery. His horse was captured and identified. Jesse and Frank circulated alibis, as usual, and so did Cole Younger, who was said to have been the lookout. Cole was a big man, weighing about 200 pounds, and could easily be recognized by his distinguished appearance. Jesse was a "slender stripling of a man, rarely weighing more than 150 pounds, even when in good condition." Frank was slightly taller and a little heavier.

The murder of Sheets crystallized the public opinion that something should be done about those "wild young James boys."

Following their December 7, 1869, hold-up of the Daviess County Savings Bank of Gallatin, Missouri, and the killing of cashier John W. Sheets, the members of the James-Younger Gang hid out in Texas and various sites in Jackson County, Missouri. Mr. Sheets had been a highly respected man, having served two terms as county sheriff, six years as circuit clerk, four years as recorder, as well as county commissioner.[5]

In June 1870, Jesse James penned a letter to Missouri Governor Joseph W. McClurg, denying any involvement in the holdup and killing. McClurg had represented Missouri in Congress for three terms, before being drafted into the governorship from 1869 to 1871. While he was in Washington, D.C., rebel raiders destroyed his store in Linn Creek, causing financial reversals from which he never recovered. McClurg, however, was an intensely religious man and was looked upon as fair and just.[6]

Jesse's letter to McClurg read:

I and my brother Frank are charged with the crime of killing the cashier and robbing the bank at Gallatin, Missouri, December 7, 1869. I deny the charge. There is not a word of truth in it. I can prove by some of the best men in Missouri, where I was the day of the robbery and the day previous to it, but I well know if I was to submit to an arrest, that I would be mobbed and hanged without a trial. The past is sufficient to show that bushwhackers do not have any show in law in Missouri. Several bushwhackers have been arrested in Missouri since the war, charged with bank robbery, and they must all have been mobbed without trial. I will cite you to the case of Thomas Little of Lafayette County. A few days after the bank was robbed at Richmond, in 1867, Mr. Little was arrested in St. Louis, charged with being one of the party who perpetrated the deed. He was sent from St. Louis to Warrensburg under a heavy guard. As soon as the parties arrived there they found out that he (Mr. Little) could prove, by the citizens of Dover, that he was innocent of the charge. As soon as these scoundrels found out that he was innocent a mob was raised, which broke in the jail, took him out and hanged him.

Governor, when I think I can get a fair trial, I will surrender myself to the authorities of Missouri. But I never will surrender to be mobbed by a set of blood-thirsty poltroons. It is true that during the war I was a Confederate soldier, but since that I have lived a peaceable citizen, and obeyed the laws of the United States to the best of my knowledge. The authorities of Gallatin say the reason that led them to suspect me, was that the mare left at Gallatin by the robbers was identified as belonging to me; that is false. I can prove that I sold the mare previous to the robbery. It is true that I fought Deputy Sheriff Thomason, of Clay County, but was not my brother with me when I had the fight? I do not think that I violated the law when I fought Thomason, as his posse refused to tell me who they were.

Three different statements have been published in reference to the fight that I had with Thomason. But they are all a pack of falsehoods. Deputy Sheriff Thomason has never yet given any report of the fight that I have seen. I am personally acquainted with Oscar Thomason, the deputy's son, but when the shooting began his face was so muffled up with furs that I did not recognize him. But if I did violate the law when I fought Thomason I am perfectly willing to abide by it. But as for them mobbing me for a crime that I am innocent of, that is played out. As soon as I think I can get a just trial I will surrender myself to the civil authorities of Missouri, and prove to the world that I am innocent of the crime charged against me.[7]

On July 5th, the *Liberty Tribune* published another letter from Jesse James in which he declared he would soon prove an alibi by witnesses of unimpeachable veracity: "Since my letter to you of June, I have been influenced by my friends to prove an alibi and to let those men know who accused me of the Gallatin murder and robbery that they have tried to swear away the life of an innocent man.

"Governor, the testimony of my witnesses will be published through the columns of the *Kansas City Times* in two or three weeks, and it will be such as you and all men can believe."[8]

Jesse's letters to the governor were corroborated by an article in a Clay County newspaper which read:

It will be remembered that the bank at Gallatin, Daviess County, in this state, was robbed on the morning of December 7th, 1869, and the cashier, Captain Sheets, killed. The author of the double crime made his escape, leaving behind him, however, a bay mare which was traced to Jesse W. James, living in Clay County. It was supposed that James was the robber and murderer, and the party in pursuit went directly to his house and demanded his surrender. James refused to surrender and made his escape, and has not been seen by anyone who could arrest him since. A short time ago, however, there appeared in a Kansas City paper a letter from him avowing his innocence of the crime, and stating as the reason for his flight, his fear that the pursuers would have hung him on the spot without proof of his guilt. Since then there have appeared several affidavits from James's friends and relatives, which, if truthful, prove an alibi for him. John S. Groom swears that on the evening of December 6th, twelve hours before the murder, Jesse James was in his store in Clay County, seventy miles from Gallatin. James M. Grow swears that on the morning of the 6th, the day before the murder, the accused was at his house in Kearney, Clay County. A.B. McGinnis swears that on the 8th, the day after the murder, he saw James at Mrs. Fox's in Clay County. Miss Susie James, a sister of the accused, swears that her brother Jesse and herself attended preaching in Greenville, Clay County, on Sunday, December 5th, and after their return Jesse sold her bay mare Kate (the one left by the murderer at Gallatin) to a stranger who said he was from Topeka, Kansas. She further testifies that her brother was at home on the 7th, the day after the murder. Zerelda Samuel, mother of the accused, swears that her son Jesse was at home December 6th, 7th, and 8th, and that he sold his sister's mare to a man from Topeka, Kansas, for five $100 bills on Sunday, the 6th. Reuben Samuel, stepfather of the accused, testifies to the same thing.[9]

Jesse James moved about under the name of Charles Lawson; Cole Younger as Arthur H. Bishop of Kansas City. They read the newspapers closely, attended church on Sunday, and contributed liberally to the offering plates.[10]

As the boys became short of change, they decided to pull off another robbery. Secretly returning to Missouri in the latter part of 1870, the boys were chafing under their prolonged idleness.[11] In the past, they had confined their activities to Missouri and, more recently, to Kentucky. It was Jesse James who came up with the idea to rob a "Republican" state, and Iowa was quickly chosen. Corydon was a flourishing little town just over the border where a considerable amount of business was transacted.[12]

The year 1871 was a very important one to Wayne County, [recalled Corydon citizen E.A. Rea several years later]. The Southwestern Railway Construction Company built the railroad that afterward became the Rock Island, through the county, and the towns of Seymour, Kniffin, Grainville (afterward changed to Harvard), and Allerton were established. The Missouri, Iowa and Nebraska Railroad was built to Centerville, in the fall of 1870 or spring of 1871. General F.M. Drake of Centerville was president of it and had asked the people of Wayne County to raise one hundred thousand dollars to assist in building the road through Wayne County. They made surveys through the county, going through Promise City, Corydon, Lewisburg, and on to Leon. The first bank in Wayne County had been opened in Corydon in the fall of 1870 by Ocobock Brothers in a one-story frame building located on the corner. . . . A.W. Ocobock and Frank Boies of Chicago operated it.[13]

Wayne County had been remarkably free from crime. It had not had the experience of several other counties in the state in dealing with a population of miners, most of whom were foreigners. However, a bank robbery in Corydon would change all this and attract the attention of people all over the state. The fact that a band of robbers could come into a town in broad daylight, rob a bank, and then escape, was sufficient to alarm bankers across the country.[14]

On the way to Corydon, the gang rode east of Lineville towards the "old Duff" place. They stopped at the Hines farm and allegedly talked Mr. Hines into trading one of his horses for one that was winded from the long ride from Clay County. Jesse selected a mare and gave the farmer a little money to boot. Hines had no inkling that his visitors were noted outlaws.[15]

Mr. Hines informed Jesse that he had to take the colt too as it was not weaned yet. Jesse agreed, and he and his party rode off. Hines turned to one of his hands and remarked, "I believe we will soon hear a shot." Sure enough they did. The two men walked down the old Clio Road and crossed the creek. There lay the poor little dead colt. Jesse and his boys couldn't be bothered with it, as they were on their way to Corydon to make an unauthorized withdrawal from the local bank.

Four of the outlaws probably spent the night of June 2nd at the Alcorn family farm near Allerton and a handful of miles from Corydon. When the boys left the following morning, heading north towards

Corydon, one of them gave the Alcorn's son Miles a silk handkerchief as a token of their appreciation.[16]

Another account states that the boys visited the Condra farm and rode towards Corydon to look around on a trial run. Although this is highly speculative, two of the robbers were said to cut off to come in from the south to join the others at the Eagle Tavern, a two-story frame building at the east end of the south side of the square. Upstairs of the tavern were three rooms where the proprietors lived. Downstairs was one large room, with probably a kitchen area at the rear, chairs and tables here and there, and a bar running along the east wall. After mingling with the locals to obtain information they might require, the gang could have lunched there or strolled a short block north to Baker's Hotel and Stage Shop if they did visit Corydon at all before the robbery.[17]

On June 3, 1871, about one o'clock in the afternoon, Jesse James, Frank James, Cole Younger, and Clell Miller—well mounted and armed—rode slowly into Corydon from the south, where a meeting was in progress in the public square. The railroad meeting had been called to induce the people to vote a tax in aid of the building of a line of the M.I. & N. Railroad through Corydon, and it was largely attended by the people of the town. The town's leading businessmen had already raised several thousand dollars, and the money had been deposited at the Wayne County Treasurer's Office. Although the strangers were seen coming into town, they were paid little heed, as strangers often came to Corydon, and none of the men looked suspicious.[18]

None of the people who had gathered outside the church were thinking robbery as most were totally immersed in the first big organized effort to bring a railroad to town. Without the train, Corydon could neither hope to continue as the county seat or perhaps survive at all. Only two months earlier, Locomotive Number 150 had pulled her first train through nearby Allerton which, growing by leaps and bounds, would shortly threaten to declare itself the county seat. Corydon had to acquire railroad connections of its own, or die.[19]

The threat of impending financial loss and inconvenience to Wayne County's northern population were matters of profound concern to many who came to town that day in droves. Others, less concerned, came to be entertained by the verbal fireworks of the celebrated orator. And most came early to get business out of the way, thus leaving them free to attend the Methodist Church. From about ten o'clock in the morning, Corydon was a beehive, its normal population of about 625 swollen perhaps to 850.

There was a great deal of noise. Children playing marbles, mumblepeg, or tag were shrieking in the courtyard. Hard leather souls and heels were clattering at their noisiest along the east and north sides of the square in the heart of Corydon's business district.

E.A. Rea remembered: "Henry Clay Dean, who lived just over the Missouri line south of the town of Dean, which was named for him, came to Corydon in the summer of 1871 to make a railroad speech in order to help complete the money raising campaign. Mr. Dean had a good reputation as an orator, and also as a man that hated soap and water and was generally spoken of in the newspapers of that day as the great unwashed [sic]. The railroad meeting was held in the old frame Methodist Church that stood back about thirty feet from the street on the lot where the present church stands. The building was full [with] crowds standing at each window and in the yard to hear the speech. Nearly all the business houses were closed and the merchants had gone to the meeting."[20]

Jesse and his men approached the northeast corner of the square and the Wayne County Treasurer's Office. The office was full of money from recent tax collections. As a ploy to get into the safe, the leader of the gang asked the lone clerk if he could get change for a hundred dollar bill. The junior clerk informed him that the safe was locked and the treasurer had gone to the town meeting. Trying to be helpful, the clerk directed them one block west to the town's bank.[21]

Quietly mounting their horses, the riders rode down the street and dismounted in front of the Ocobock Bros. Bank, located near the northwest corner of the public square. It is alleged that the men pretended to be engaged in a horse trade when one was to pay the other the difference of ten dollars between the value of the two horses. He drew out a twenty dollar bill and asked if anyone could change it.

One of the riders took charge of their horses while another was stationed as a watch or guard in front of the bank. The other two outlaws entered the bank and found no one inside but the cashier, Oscar Ocobock. The cashier suddenly looked up the barrel of a large Colt revolver, which he later described as being loaded with a barrel eight or ten inches long. It was held by a thick-set, well-built but not very tall, sunburned man. The outlaws bound him hand and foot, obtained the keys to the safe with no trouble and made off with between six and ten thousand dollars.[22]

According to the *Kansas City Journal*, this was the first time a bank officer had been tied by them, "as their usual method of killing the cashier answered their purposes better, and why this was made an exception to their rule is still a mystery."[23]

After emptying the loot into a sack, they emerged from the bank, mounted their horses, and with masks covering their faces, rode over to the political meeting being addressed by Henry Clay Dean. As they passed the church, there being a large number of men standing outside, the church not being sufficiently large to hold the crowd, the robbers flourished their revolvers. Jesse apologized for interrupting the speech and with the other bandits by his side, said:

"Well, you've been having your fun and we've been having ours. You needn't go into hysterics when I tell you that we've just been down to the bank and robbed it of every dollar in the till. If you'll go down there now you'll find the cashier tied and then if you want any of us, why, just come down and take us. Thank you for your attention."[24]

Upon the conclusion of Jesse's remarks, the riders let out a wild yell, tipped their hats, and sped off in a southern direction. Initially the crowd thought the little speech was merely an attempt to break up the meeting. It took the citizens a few minutes to recover and comprehend the situation, many of them pointing towards the cloud of dust revealing the direction the riders had taken. Once they checked out the bank, a posse was hastily organized under the direction of Captain Little, and they rode away after the robbers.[25]

> Mr. Ocobock, the bank, did not have any property in the town and had refused to subscribe or take any part in the attempt to raise the money for the railroad, [stated E.A. Rea]. He did not go to the railroad meeting, but while the meeting was going on the James Bothers, Clell Miller, and one of the Younger brothers rode into town, hitched their horses at the north side of the square, went over to the bank and secured a contribution of between $6,000.00 and $10,000, which did

Mr. Henry Clay Dean, of Iowa, had published in 1868 a book of 512 pages, entitled *Crimes of the Civil War*, and stated in his introduction, "I am a Democrat; a devoted friend of the Constitution of the United States; a sincere lover of the Government and the Union of the States." Later, in August 21, 1883, when the Winston robbery case went to trial, Frank James was represented by a group of distinguished attorneys; ironically, one of them was this same Henry Clay Dean. The great orator had always had his suspicions that Frank was involved in the Corydon robbery but he never said anything publicly about it. In fact, he claimed that Frank had even invited him to participate in the crime. Other members of the defense team, however, considered him to be a bit unstable and a potential liability, so he was excluded from all their conversations and decisions.[27]

"THE HOUSE BEGAN TO BREAK INTO APPLAUSE."

not go to help the railroad cause. It might have been better for Mr. Ocobock to have gone to the railroad meeting. I was clerking in a grocery and meat market, owned by Brant & Dillion on the south side of the square. They left me to keep store while they went to the meeting. There wasn't anyone on the square.   I was sitting out in front of the store and saw these men get off their horses and go to the bank.  They soon came back, got on their horses and rode west past the church and I was told they called out to the crowd, "We robbed the bank, catch us if you can." The eloquence of Henry Clay Dean could not keep his audience after this, and the public square was soon full of people and I learned the bank had been robbed.  There was great excitement. A company of men was soon organized and they started in pursuit, but did not succeed in capturing them.[26]

Adam Ripper, a young boy who would later become Justice of the Peace in Corydon, was walking along the boarded sidewalk towards his father's blacksmith shop, when he became startled in seeing four men on horseback galloping down the dusty street towards him. He realized the men were strangers in town—tall, good-looking fellows wearing broadbrimmed hats and carrying guns. As they swept past him, one of the men yelled, "We've robbed your bank! Catch us if you can!" The others whipped out their revolvers and fired "ringing" shots into the air.[28]

The boy ran to the safety of the blacksmith shop, and from the doorway, watched the outlaws as they galloped away. Ripper later stated in an interview: "One or two writers have told in their stories that [one of] the robbers threw me a silver dollar as they passed. But that couldn't possibly be true—there were no silver dollars at that time. Anyway those fellows weren't throwing any money away after they'd gone to so much trouble to get it!"[29]

Along the way, the posse came upon a place where they discovered evidence that the robbers had stopped to divide the money taken from the bank. They found strips of paper which had likely been used in wrapping the different packages of the loot, the amounts appearing on each wrapper.

According to one account, Mary Woods-Bright of North Lineville, Iowa, was boiling clothes in an old iron kettle when seven men in dusters rode up out of the cornfield. Her husband, Sam Bright, had gone into Lineville to get some cottonwood logs so he could rebuild a chicken coop. Mary asked the men what they wanted and "the tall skinny one with a scraggly beard" told her they would like something to eat. She fixed them some cold biscuits and warmed up some gravy left over from breakfast, then fried up some fat back for them.[30]

She had no coffee but one of the seven did. Mary boiled the coffee, and the men ate heartily. As they left, the leader allegedly flipped her a ten-dollar gold piece—the most money she and Sam had had since they sold some shoats the year before. When Sam Bright pulled up with his wagon load of lumber that night, he told her the bank at Corydon had been robbed by Jesse James and his boys. Mary laughingly related she had had breakfast with Jesse James.

A farmer named Tom Stevens reported to the sheriff in Corydon that the gang had passed through the town of Woodland, near Lineville and halfway between the robbery site and the Missouri border. According to Stevens, someone had "exchanged" a heated horse for one of his, which he had left tied to a hayrack near his road. The mare, which was stolen, had a colt and it must have followed the mare during the theft. Another farmer reported that he found several ponies under a tree in his grove.[31]

The robbers had good horses and were thoroughly armed, and the Corydon posse failed to overtake them. In a few hours, the outlaws crossed the Missouri state line, and as darkness set in, it became impossible for the posse to trace them. Having headed west towards Decatur County, the outlaws camped just out of rifle range over on the Missouri side. They cooked some stolen chickens over a hastily made fire where they ate and rested.[32]

One of the men from the quickly formed Corydon posse had to go into Davis City to obtain legal papers allowing them to follow the robbers into Missouri. Jesse and the boys timed it perfectly and were gone before the man returned with the papers from a judge.

As many as ninety men followed the gang south to the Missouri line. Some took each trail leading south, many rode east to the railroad at Allerton, and still others investigated south to Princeton and Trenton, Missouri. The C&SW Railroad was under construction and would not be completed to Cameron until late in September.[33]

However, some members of the posse continued on, and reaching a certain point between Pattonsburg and Cameron, they discovered that a party of men had stopped at a farmhouse for dinner and were still there. The posse proceeded to make enquiries about them, but one of the pursuers flushed the game by firing his gun before arrangements could be made to surround the house. If the robbers were there, they had escaped.[34]

One small group of the posse followed the trail to Leon, Iowa, on Saturday, then to Pleasant Plains and Eagleville, Missouri, on Sunday. They trail led to Bethany, and after following them until noon of the second day after the robbery, five of the posse men overtook the outlaws at Civil Bend in Daviess County, Missouri, where they were resting. A gunfight erupted.[35]

The posse in pursuit was led by Iowa farmer John A. Corbit. He was followed by Corydon officer Charles R. Wright, hotel owner James D. Coddington, and two Missourians, Carter and Slater. Coddington had seen two of the robbers who had stayed at his hotel in Corydon on Friday night and identified Clell Miller as one of the men.[36]

The fight took place about noon on Monday, June 5, 1871, at the Civil Bend School (School No. 4) and the school stable. The posse arrived from the north and spotted the gang of four men sitting, resting with their backs against the school building. Money wrappers were left at this spot, so the gang may have been dividing the loot in order to split up. The gang jumped up and ran for the stable, where they had left their guns and horses.

Farmer John A. Corbit later testified that the day was cloudy and rainy. He maintained that the schoolhouse was four or five rods west of the north-south road and that the stable stood about 180 steps southwest of the school. Officer Wright went with Coddington to the west of the stable in a wheat field. They made it to within sixty yards of the stable. Corbit was 120 steps to the east of the stable on the road.

According to Corbit, the gang started shooting once they reached the stable. Coddington offered the bandits a chance to surrender, but one strong, fine voice called out from the stable, "We cannot see it." The gang mounted their horses in the stable and fled south after about twenty gunshots were exchanged. At least one shot took effect, killing a posse man's horse.

A linen coat, a pair of gloves, four or five large revolver holsters, and a large revolver with "W and W" engraved on the butt were found at the school stable. The posse caught up with the gang again about two and one-half miles south of the Freeland Boyer farm near Cottonwood Creek. There an accidental early shot fired by a posse member resulted in another escape before the posse was in position to prevent it.

The fleeing outlaws stopped at Freeland's well to water their horses. When the Iowa posse got there, the outlaws, with fresh horses, decided to fight it out. The tired posse, however, declined and turned back. Not surprisingly, posse members told a different story about their loss of interest in overtaking the gang after a long chase.

Another posse was organized on June 12th and placed in the charge of a Pinkerton detective, and they proceeded to make another effort to follow and capture the robbers. They passed through Princeton, Trenton, Cameron, Kearney, and Kansas City, but failed to find any trace of the bandits.[37]

Others took up the hunt and followed the outlaw's trail into Clay County before it disappeared in Jackson County. A Liberty newspaper declared: "The pursuing party is now very large, it having been constantly added to its number since it left the town in which the depredation was committed, and it is to be hoped that the miscreants will soon be captured. The bank offers one thousand dollars reward for their apprehension and arrest."[38]

Kansas City detectives also continued to search for the robbers. Two months after the robbery, a Pinkerton agent named Westphall arrested Clell Miller in Clay County and took him back to Corydon to stand trial. He was finally tried on November 10, 1872, the trial lasting all week. Because of the contradictions in identifying him as one of the robbers, and the testimony of several of his friends from southern Missouri presenting him with an alibi, he was set free. Frank and Jesse, meanwhile avowed their entire innocence of any participation in the raid on Corydon, and of having anything to do with bank robberies on moral principles, yet at the same time they were enjoying a great deal of solid comfort from their share of the loot. Claiming to be with friends in Clay and Jackson counties at the time of the hold-up, there were several parties eager to vouch for them.

Following Miller's acquittal, Jesse penned the following letter to the *Kansas City Times*:

> I have just seen in the *Lexington Register*, copied from the *Caldwell Sentinel*, charging myself and my brother Frank with robbing a bank in Iowa of seventy thousand dollars. And as I believe the editors of the *Kansas City Times* to be honest men and inclined to do justice to everyone, I have concluded to drop a few lines to them for publication.
>
> As to Frank and I robbing a bank in Iowa or anywhere else, it is as base a falsehood as ever was uttered from human lips. I can prove, by some of the best citizens in Missouri, my whereabouts on the third day of June, the day the bank was robbed, but it is useless for me to prove an alibi. One year ago I proved an alibi by some of the best citizens of the State, and proved enough to satisfy every honest man that I was innocent of the killing of Captain Sheets, at Gallatin, but the degraded Radical party criticized my alibi and insinuated that I was a robber as not; but they don't think so, they know it is false when they say so.
>
> As to Frank and I defying the civil authorities, it is perfectly absurd. We have never defied the civil authorities. I have no doubt but the authors of some of those pieces published against Frank and I are the perpetrators of the crimes charged against us.
>
> From what I can learn, I have been indicted at Liberty for resisting the civil authorities on the 11th of December 1869. If times ever get so in Missouri that I can get an impartial trial, I will voluntarily go to Clay County and stand my trial. But I am satisfied that if I was disarmed at present, that those brave Radical heroes in Missouri would try to mob me.[39]

Missouri Governor Silas Woodson, however, paid Jesse's letter little heed. On October 13th, he posted a $2,000 reward for the arrest and delivery of Jesse and Frank James to the sheriff of Daviess County, Missouri.[40]

Jesse James sightings were many following the raid and each generation passed on its connection. John Caldwell of Caldwell, Iowa recalled:

> I remember my father telling me a story that his grandfather had told him, when I was maybe eight years [old], about Jesse James robbing a bank in Corydon, Iowa. It's well known that Jesse stopped briefly at the church on the way out of town after robbing the bank and interrupted the minister to announce that "some riders" had just robbed the town's bank. "You folks best get down there in a hurry." The way I remember the story was that Jesse and at least his brother, Frank, came to the farm of a relation after robbing the Ocobock Brothers' Bank of approximately $6,000 on the 3rd of June 1871. Apparently this relative made no connection of these riders to the James Gang, or perhaps the news of the robbery had not yet made its way to all the outlying farms. It was told that the riders came to the farm in the evening, looking for a place to rest. The lady of the house allowed them to stay the evening in the barn, and offered to share her evening meal. She apologized for the meal not being much, explaining that times had been hard on the farm recently, but that they were welcome to share in what she had. When she awoke the next morning the riders had gone, leaving behind a nice little sum of cash in gratitude for her kindness.[41]

On April 29, 1872, five men robbed the Bank of Columbia at Columbia, Kentucky. They followed the James-Younger strategy of splitting the party with two men coming from one direction and three from another. At the corner of Burkesville Street and Frazer Avenue, two of the riders turned into Jefferson Alley and dismounted, hitched their horses, and entered the bank. A third rider entered the alley, dismounted, and held the bridles of the three horses, while the remaining two bandits took up positions outside the front of the bank.[42]

Inside the bank, the robbers confronted the cashier, R.A.C. Martin, who had recently moved with his wife to Columbia from

Shelbyville to take advantage of work in the new bank. Four other men sat and talked at a large round table near the front door. They were: Judge James Garnett, president of the bank; Major T.C. Winfrey; James T. Page; and W.H. Hudson.

Martin was busy at the cashier's desk in the rear of the bank. One of the strangers approached him, another went to Judge Garnett, and the third walked toward Hudson. When the strangers pulled out Colt .45s, Judge Garnett cried out, "Robbers! Bank robbers!" The bandit who had approached Judge Garnett moved toward him, gun in hand. Hudson seized a chair and struck out at the gunman, who dodged, his finger on the trigger. With remarkable quickness of thought, Judge Garnett struck the man's hand just as the gun went off; the bullet hit his hand, causing an injury that years later necessitated the amputation of the hand.[43]

As the third robber glanced toward the commotion, Martin went for the gun he kept in a desk drawer. But the robber, believed to have been Frank James, returned his attention to the cashier in time to shoot Martin. Hudson and Judge Garnett grappled with the large gunman, later allegedly identified as Cole Younger, who had shot the judge. Winfrey and Page took advantage of the confusion to run outside and spread the alarm. Seeing them run out of the bank followed by one of the robbers, the two mounted bandits began shooting at anything that moved. Page made it to safety, but Winfrey was slightly wounded when he started through the door of Kemp's Drug Store and a bullet hit the doorframe, sending splinters into his face.

Inside the bank, Judge Garnett and Hudson finally managed to throw their antagonist to the floor and escape. The other two remaining robbers took what money they found in the cash drawer but were unable to get into the locked safe. They apparently dragged the unconscious and bleeding Martin to the safe, intending to force him to open it—not realizing he was mortally wounded.

Out on the street, the three robbers jumped on their horses and headed out of town amid a fusillade of gunfire. Hearing the cries of

"Bank robbers!" a young man named Montgomery Craven, working in the hardware store, grabbed the gun kept in a drawer and ran outside, taking cover behind a barrel. He shot at the bandits, but missed his targets.

Another account identified the young man as Isaac Cravens, a clerk at Phillips and Bradshaw Company. He got off a shot, but the riders returned the fire and drove him back inside. One bullet lodged in the door sill just above his head.[44]

The robbers rode out of town along Jamestown Street with only $600 taken from the bank. Their use of the side roads showed they had thoroughly planned their escape route. At Petite's Fork, they turned up the creek and followed it past Conover's Mill. Arriving at a gate that led onto another road, they encountered William Conover, who, with a field hand, was working in a field along Glens Fork. The heavily bearded leader of the gang, later identified from Conover's description as Jesse James, ordered him to open the gate, but Conover refused. However, when the rider leveled a pistol on him, Conover turned to his helper and told him to comply.

The bank offered a $2,500 reward. A posse, formed by James R. Hindman, a Civil War captain, took off after the bandits but lost the trail of the robbers near the Russell County line. The gang was thought to have worked its way north through Taylor and Marion counties to their hideout in Nelson County.

The gang, however, had outwitted a large posse by riding straight away for several miles and then circling the town. Detective Bligh was certain that Cole Younger was the leader of the band and that Frank and Jesse James participated in the heist. He and others also were convinced that the outlaws had been in the area for at least a week prior to the raid, with Frank James staying with a wealthy farmer.[45]

According to another account, the five strangers rode into Columbia on fine horses and stayed at the home of Green B. Acres several days before the robbery. They represented themselves as livestock buyers and were very amenable as they rode about the community, apparently seeking cattle to purchase. In reality they were learning the lay of the land, so they would know the best routes out of town for a quick getaway. No suspicion, then or later, was attached to Acres. He was as astonished as everyone else when he discovered that he had unwittingly hosted five members of the infamous James outlaw gang.[46]

The Kansas City Fair was drawing big crowds, and on September 26, 1872, three mounted men rode up to the gate in front of an estimated ten thousand people. One of the men dismounted, walked up to the cashier, and said: "What if I was to say I was Jesse James and told you to hand out that tin box of money—what would you say?" The cashier replied: "I'd say I'd see you in hell first."

"Well, that's just who I am—Jesse James—and you had better turn it over pretty damned quick or . . ." The robber pointed a navy revolver at the startled cashier, who immediately handed him the tin box containing almost $10,000. Jesse James was believed to be the man who grabbed the box.[47]

Stories about this robbery, however, are conflicting. Another version states that one of the bandits walked up to the gate without saying a word, grabbed the tin box, and emptied the contents into his pocket. Ben Wallace, the ticket-taker, ran out and began wrestling with the man. Another robber fired at Wallace, but the bullet hit a small girl in the crowd and inflicted a large flesh wound in her leg. The three outlaws mounted their horses and dashed off into the woods with loot totaling but $978.[48]

On October 15th, the following letter, believed to have been penned by Jesse James, was published by John Newman Edwards, who tended to glorify the outlaw, comparing him to one of the Knights of the Round Table:

> To the *Kansas City Times*:
> As a great deal has been said in regard to the robbery which occurred at the Kansas City Exposition grounds, I will give a few lines to the public, as I am one of the party who perpetrated the deed. A great many say that we, the robbers, deserve hanging. What

have we done to be hung for? It is true that I shot a little girl, though it was not intentional, and I am very sorry that the child was shot; and if the parents will give me their address through the columns of the *Kansas City Weekly Times*, I will send them money to pay her doctor's bill. And as to Mr. Wallace, I never tried to kill him. I only shot to make him let go my friend. If I had been so disposed, I could have shot him dead. Just let a party of men commit a bold robbery, and the cry is hang them, but Grant and his party can steal millions, and it is all right. It is true, we are robbers, but we always rob in the glare of the day and in the teeth of the multitude; and we never kill only in self-defense, without men refuse to open their vaults and safes to us, and when they refuse to unlock to us we kill. But a man who is d--d enough fool to refuse to open a safe or a vault when he is covered with a pistol ought to die. There is no use for a man to try to do anything when an experienced robber gets the go on him. If he gives the alarm, or resists, or refuses to unlock, he gets killed, and if he obeys, he is not hurt in the flesh but he is in the purse.

Some editors call us thieves. We are not thieves—we are bold robbers. It hurts me very much to be called a thief. It makes me feel like they were trying to put me on a part with Grant and his party. We are bold robbers, and I am proud of the name, for Alexander the Great was a bold robber, and Julius Caesar, and Napoleon Bonaparte, and Sir William Wallace—not old Ben Wallace—and Robert Emmet. Please rank me with these, and not with the Grantites. Grant's party has no respect for anyone. They rob the poor and rich, and we rob the rich and give to the poor. As to the author of the letter, the public will never know. I will close by hoping that Horace Greeley will defeat Grant, and then I can make an honest living, and then I will not have to rob, as taxes will not be so heavy. Very respectfully,

JACK SHEPHERD, DICK TURPIN, CLAUDE DUVAL

P.S.—We expected the money would go from the gate to the Secretary's office at the Fair Grounds, and when Mr. Wallace started, we thought he had all the money. We expected to get about $15,000 when we robbed the till, or we would not have taken the chances. Our watch that we had set at the gate let the money go without seeing it pass,

JACK SHEPHERD[49]

Two new recruits joined the gang, Robert Younger, twenty, and Bill Stiles, more commonly known as Bill Chadwell. Frank James and Jim Younger were said to have gone out to Cheyenne, Wyoming. In their absence, the others rode down to Ste. Genevieve, Missouri, on May 27, 1873, where the Ste. Genevieve Savings Association ordinarily had about $100,000 in cash on hand. But the bank was in the process of liquidation, and the robbers got only about $4,000, mostly in silver coins, which were heavy. The bandits are said to have dropped the loot several times and once enlisted a stolid Dutchman to help catch a horse and pick up the coins.

## Notes

[1]Cole Younger, October 20, 1880, letter to J.W. Buel, printed in J.W. Buel, *The Border Outlaws*, Syracuse, Alvord & Sleight, 1883.

[2]Henry L. Golemba, Wayne State University, Bret Harte, DLB 74, *American Short-Story Writers Before 1880*; Charles A. Fleming, Oklahoma State University, Bret Harte, DLB 79; Dottie Webb, *Local Color: Nineteenth Century Regional Writing in the United States*, Bret Harte: Popularity, Poetry, and Performance, 23 August 1998; Victoria Henderson, Bret Harte: 1836-1902, Internet.

[3]Homer Croy, *Jesse James Was My Neighbor*, New York, Duell, Sloan & Pearce, 1949, pp. 53-55; *St. Clair County Courier*, May 13, 1976; Marley Brant, *Jesse James: The Man and the Myth*, pp. 74-75.

[4]*Kansas City Daily Journal of Commerce*, December 9, 1869.

[5]*The History of Daviess County, Missouri*, Kansas City, Missouri, Birdsall & Dean, 1889, p. 496.

[6]Draper-McClurg Family Papers, 1838-1981 (C3069), Western Historical Manuscript Collection, Columbia, Missouri.

[7]*The History of Daviess County, Missouri*, Kansas City, Missouri, Birdsall & Dean, 1889, pp. 500-501; *Liberty Tribune*, June 21, 1870.

[8]*Liberty Tribune*, July 5, 1870.

[9]*The History of Daviess County, Missouri*, Kansas City, Missouri, Birdsall & Dean, 1889, pp. 500-501; *Liberty Tribune*, July 22, 1870.

[10]Henry Dale, *Adventures and Exploits of the Younger Brothers, Missouri's Most Daring Outlaws, and Companions of the James Boys*, New York, Street & Smith, Publishers, The Secret Service Series—No. 32, 1890, p. 138.

[11]*Kansas City Journal*, April 4, 1882.

[12]Henry Dale, *Adventures and Exploits of the Younger Brothers, Missouri's Most Daring Outlaws, and Companions of the James Boys*, pp. 138-139.

[13]Excerpt of a letter written by E.A. Rea, Corydon, dated August 15, 1929. Author's Collection.

[14]Wayne and Appanoose counties, Iowa, Biographical and Historical Record, 1886, in collection at Prairie Trails Museum, Corydon, Iowa.

[15]"Jesse James and the Colt," F. Eugene Barber Papers, in collection at Prairie Trails Museum, Corydon, Iowa.

[16]Marley Brant, *Jesse James: The Man and the Myth*, p. 83.

[17]Dave Stirling, untitled document in collection at Prairie Trails Museum, Corydon, Iowa.

[18]Theodore M. Stuart, *Past and Present of Lucas and Wayne Counties*, Volume I, 1913, p. 274; Henry Dale, *Adventures and Exploits of the Younger Brothers, Missouri's Most Daring Outlaws, and Companions of the James Boys*, p. 138.

[19]Dave Stirling, untitled document in collection at Prairie Trails Museum, Corydon, Iowa.

[20]Excerpt of a letter written by E.A. Rea, Corydon, dated August 15, 1929. Author's Collection.

[21]"Historical Account of the Ocobock Bank Raid," in collection at Prairie Trails Museum, Corydon, Iowa.

[22]Henry Dale, *Adventures and Exploits of the Younger Brothers, Missouri's Most Daring Outlaws, and Companions of the James Boys*, p. 138; *Gallatin North Missourian*, April 4, 1993, article by David Stark.

[23]*Kansas City Journal*, April 4, 1882.

[24]J.W. Buel, *The Border Outlaws*, p. 157.

[25]Wayne and Appanoose counties, Iowa, Biographical and Historical Record, 1886, in collection at Prairie Trails Museum, Corydon, Iowa; William Lee Burton, "Adam Ripper, Corydon Resident for 62 Years, Tells of Town's Thrilling History," 1932, in collection at Prairie Trails Museum, Corydon, Iowa.

[26]Excerpt of a letter written by E.A. Rea, Corydon, dated August 15, 1929. Author's Collection.

[27]Ted P. Yeatman, *Frank and Jesse James: The Story Behind the Legend*, Nashville, Cumberland House, 2000, p. 283.

[28]William Lee Burton, "Adam Ripper, Corydon Resident for 62 Years, Tells of Town's Thrilling History," 1932, in collection at Prairie Trails Museum, Corydon, Iowa.

[29]Ibid.

[30]"Breakfast with Jesse James," F. Eugene Barber Papers, in collection at Prairie Trails Museum, Corydon, Iowa.

[31]*Osceola Republican*, June 8, 1871.

[32]"Jesse James and the Colt," F. Eugene Barber Papers, in collection at Prairie Trails Museum, Corydon, Iowa.

[33]*Gallatin North Missourian*, April 4, 1993 , article by David Stark.

[34]Wayne and Appanoose counties, Iowa, Biographical and Historical Record, 1886, in collection at Prairie Trails Museum, Corydon, Iowa.

[35]*Liberty Tribune*, June 16, 1871.

[36]*Gallatin North Missourian*, April 4, 1993 , article by David Stark.

[37]Wayne and Appanoose counties, Iowa, Biographical and Historical Record, 1886, in collection at Prairie Trails Museum, Corydon, Iowa.

[38]*Liberty Tribune*, June 16, 1871.

[39]*Kansas City Times*, October 1872.

[40]Marley Brant, *Jesse James: The Man and the Myth*, p. 87.

[41]John Caldwell letter to author dated December 9, 2004.

[42]Lorena Farris Jackson, "James Gang Quietly Invaded Downtown Columbia in 1872," *Columbia Magazine*, September 2002.

[43]James Hines, "Robbery," *Kentucky Living Magazine*, June 2002.

[44]Lorena Farris Jackson, "James Gang Quietly Invaded Downtown Columbia in 1872," *Columbia Magazine*, September 2002.

[45]William A. Settle, Jr., *Jesse James Was His Name*, Lincoln & London, University of Nebraska Press, 1966, p. 44.

[46]James Hines, "Robbery," *Kentucky Living Magazine*, June 2002.

[47]William A. Settle, Jr., *Jesse James Was His Name*, Lincoln & London, University of Nebraska Press, 1966, pp. 44-45.

[48]*Kansas City Times*, September 27, 1873.

[49]*Kansas City Times*, October 15, 1872.

*Chapter Four*

# Adair Train Robbery

*"In all the history of medieval knight-errantry and modern brigandage, there is nothing that equals the wild romance of the past few years' career of Arthur McCoy, Frank and Jesse James, and the Younger boys. Their desperate deeds during the war were sufficient to have stocked a score of ordinary novels, with facts that outstrip the strung-out flights of fantasy. Their fierce hand-to-hand encounters . . . their long and reckless scouts and forays, and their riotous jollity . . . all combined to form a chapter without a parallel in the annals of America . . ."*
—The *Lexington Caucasian*[1]

J ESSE JAMES, SLOWLY BECOMING THE LEADER of the notorious James-Younger Gang, took an especial interest in the increasing number of train robberies being committed in the United States. Although many historians have mistakenly credited the James-Younger Gang with committing the first train robbery, nothing was further from the truth. The Reno Gang, a band of outlaws that terrorized the Midwest committed the world's first peacetime train robbery on October 6, 1866, nearly seven years before the James-Younger Gang held up its first train at Adair, Iowa. The Reno brothers netted $13,000 from the heist.[2]

Ironically, America's second train robbery occurred in the same town of Seymour, Indiana, a little less than a year later on September

28, 1867. The robbers this time were not members of the Reno Gang but two men living in the immediate area. Although they took $7,000 from the train, both men were captured and hanged.[3]

The Reno's fared little better. On November 17, 1864, several gang members raided the treasurer's office at the Daviess County Courthouse, in Gallatin, Missouri, and made off with $23,618 in cash and bonds. John Reno was positively identified as one of the robbers, and the Pinkertons were hot on his trail.[4] On December 4, when John went to the Seymour railroad station, one half-dozen Pinkerton men

Jesse James. (Courtesy of the Library of Congress)

hopped off a train and arrested him with the help of either the Daviess County sheriff or by "Captain Ballinger and Woodruff" of Daviess County in Indianapolis.[5]

John Reno stood trial in Gallatin and pleaded guilty on January 18, 1868, as a lynch mob formed outside the courthouse. He was sentenced to twenty-five years in the Missouri State Penitentiary in Jefferson City. He had been the leader and brains of the Reno Gang, but his older brother, Frank, and the others carried on without him.

On the night of December 12, 1868, a hundred vigilantes wearing scarlet masks and armed with revolvers and clubs, descended upon the Pearl Street Station, overpowered the sheriff and his men, and attacked four prisoners, all members of the Reno Gang. One by one, the doors to the individual cells were opened and the terrified prisoners were pulled out. Frank Reno was first on the death list. A pre-knotted noose or halter was placed over his head, then secured to an iron pillar near the stairwell leading to the second-floor cells. The oldest Reno brother was then pushed from the landing. William, the youngest of the brothers, was next, and he was hanged beside Frank. When the vigilantes entered the cell of Simeon Reno, he fought madly, but they overpowered him and strung him up in the southwest corner of the jail, his feet barely grazing the ground. It took him almost half an hour to strangle to death. Last was Charlie Anderson, who had to be hanged twice, as the first rope broke.

John was released from prison in February 1878 and returned to Seymour, but his three criminal brothers were dead. Seven years later, John was sentenced to three years in the Indiana State Prison at Michigan City for passing counterfeit bills. John Reno died at his home in Seymour on January 31, 1895. As for the bandit Reno brothers— Frank, John, Simeon and William—they were later overshadowed by the James brothers and others, but they had left their mark on outlaw and railroad history.[6]

The early train robberies caused a panic all through the country. The advent of the railroad in the place of the stagecoach eliminated the road agent from the perils of travel; however, here was the same old thing in an aggravated form.[7]

Would-be robbers had established a pattern of hanging around isolated train stations awaiting the night express. While the train loaded and unloaded passengers, these men would slip away, only to emerge from the shadows once the train had started up, usually just behind the tender, at the front of the express car. Within seconds, they would thrust revolvers into the ribs of the engineer and fireman and let it be known they were taking over the train. For several years, nearly every robber climbed aboard at this "blind baggage," windowless front of the express car.[8]

Adair, Iowa, in 1873, was a quiet little town named in honor of General John Adair, an officer in the War of 1812 and sixth governor of Kentucky. The town was laid out during the previous summer by George C. Tallman of Brooklyn, New York, on property that he owned. On August 20, 1872, the plat of the town was filed in the Recorder's Office of Adair County. Prior to the official naming of the town, the site was referred to as Summit Cut because it was the high point on the

Rock Island Line in Iowa and because the ridge forming the watershed divided the Mississippi River and the Missouri River.[9]

The Rock Island Railroad had been extended through Adair in 1868-1869. The Section House was built in 1869 and used as headquarters for engineering corps who were making the survey for the Main Line of the Rock Island Railroad and for the Robert Grant family to live. The section house was the first building in Adair. Grant had been dispatched to Adair in 1870 to maintain this section of the railroad.

Mrs. Grant was the first woman to live in Adair. She later owned the house south of the water tower on Fifth Street. The southwest part of Adair, called Tallman's Addition, was laid out in 1872. John Ewing started the first grist mill, and later W.R. Turner and Claus Huss and Sons operated a mill. T.D. Louge became Adair's first doctor in 1873.

Early in July 1873, members of the James-Younger learned that $75,000 in gold from the Cheyenne, Wyoming, area was to be carried through Adair on the recently built main line of the Chicago, Rock Island & Pacific Railroad. Some of the boys had visited Cheyenne and had obtained the information from reliable sources. The band made immediate plans to profit by the information.[10]

It had been only two months since the robbery of a Ste. Genevieve, Missouri, bank, called "one of the boldest bank robberies on record," had been attributed to them.

> If there is any operation in which the audaciousness of pure deviltry ever be displayed, it is in the exercise of robbing a bank in broad daylight, [declared the *St. Louis Weekly Globe* on May 30, 1873]. Situated upon the corner of Merchant Street and Main stands a two-story brick house, formerly occupied as a dwelling but now used as a banking-house by the Ste. Genevieve Saving Association; General F.A. Rosier is president and O.D. Harris, Esq., cashier. When halfway in the room the cashier happened to turn his head and was startled at [the] sight of two pistols pointed at his temples, and was most thoroughly aroused to the delicacy of the situation, as he felt the cold muzzles quickly pressed to them. The force used by the robbers was so great that for hours afterwards one of his temples showed the mark of the pistol barrel. Before he could

remonstrate he was saluted with a stirring command, "Open the safe or I'll blow your d—d brains out." Harris hesitated about opening the safe, which being observed, caused the robbers to level their pistols at Rozier, threatening to shoot him if he should run. But Rozier broke away and was confronted by the two other men on horseback, who were concealed from observation.

The robbers speedily released Mr. Harris, mounted their horses, and the four commenced firing in all directions in intimidate pursuers. Above the report of shots was heard a wild "Hurrah! For Sam Hildebrand, catch the horse-thieves if you can," and the rapid hoof beats of the retreating horses showed that the "job" was finished. Two of the robbers slept the night before at a farm house two miles out. They knew that General Rozier, the president, whose room was on the same floor with the bank room, was absent. The robbery, one of the boldest on record, did not pan out very handsomely, as the booty amounted to only $3,600.[11]

The *Ste. Genevieve Fair Play* stated curtly on May 29, 1873, that "Tuesday morning at [ten] o'clock . . . Four men rode into town on horseback and hitched their horses in the vicinity of Mr. Anderson's store, they walked leisurely up to the bank; two of them stopped outside and two of them started into the bank. Each one drew a pistol and presented it to Mr. Harris' head and said, 'Open the safe, damn you, or I will blow your brains out.'"[12]

Less than two months later, these very same outlaws—most likely including Cole Younger's brothers Jim and Bob—planned to strike the eastbound train outside Adair. The idea was probably Cole Younger's. The boys held a conference at one of their old rendezvous in Jackson County where Cole proposed his new scheme.

The plan met approval immediately and several rail lines including the Hannibal & St. Joseph Railway were discussed as possible victims. Cole, however, suggested another strike in Iowa, and all the bandits were in agreement. Large sections of northwestern Iowa, along with most of southern Minnesota and southeastern Dakota Territory, were being devastated by swarms of Rocky Mountain locusts while relief committees struggled to aid the impoverished. With the farmers busily engaged in battle against the grasshopper hordes, no one would expect a train robbery.[13]

The boys held a second meeting, this time at the home of a friend in Clay County and the final arrangements were made.[14]

Jesse had begun to realize that with changing times his outlaw activity had to expand farther and farther from home. In the past, one of his men could walk into a bank, ask to have a $100 bill changed, and then draw a pistol, but those "easy" days were coming to a close. Strange men and horses in the streets had made citizens suspicious, although the long linen dusters the men wore seldom attracted atten-

tion. The loose-fitting dusters were necessary, as they concealed the guns the robbers carried on their hips and in their pockets. Jesse had on at least one occasion carried six pistols on him, plus belts of ammunition and loose cartridges in his pockets.[15]

While some gunmen flirted with double-action revolvers, men like Jesse James relied upon the single action because of its accuracy and reliability. The self-cocking double action was less accurate because of its heavy double-action trigger pull. Men who lived by their guns needed what worked best for them in a given situation. Although the

Jesse James. (Courtesy of the Library of Congress)

outlaws probably did not plan on killing anyone, they required a weapon that could meet any situation since their lives depended upon it. Jesse was partial to the Smith and Wesson Schofield .45. The hammer had to be drawn back with the thumb to cock the pistol. This separate action turned the cylinder and brought a loaded chamber around into position. Jesse needed but to touch the trigger to release the hammer.[16]

Some of the gang members preferred the Colt .45. Although some models had undergone alteration, no changes mechanically had been required internally with the Colt. One of the most popular hand guns on the frontier was the 1851 Navy Revolver, referred to as the "Old Model Belt Pistol," or the "Colt's Navy." The Colt was manufactured with a 7.5-inch barrel, and in the hands of a skilled gunmen, the six-shooter could be emptied into its target in a matter of seconds. Because the revolver weighed only a little over 2.5 pounds, it was not unusual for a well-armed pistolero to carry two of them.[17]

In 1873, United States Ordnance adopted the Colt for the service. According to Captain John R. Edie: "I have no hesitation in declaring the Colt revolver superior in most respects, and much better adapted to the wants of the Army than the Smith and Wesson." The same report stated, "This pistol, for efficiency, safety, simplicity, and lightness, is far in advance of any military pistol that has yet appeared."[18]

On July 12th, the party of about seven men left their sanctuaries and rode off toward Council Bluffs. They rode into Adair about July 18th and, posing as businessmen, picked up information about the train schedule and also explored the rails. On July 21, they encamped near a blind curve along the line.[19]

Frank James and Cole Younger hurried to Omaha to find out when the gold shipment would reach Adair while Jim and Bob Younger, Clell Miller, and Bill Chadwell remained with Jesse James at an encampment outside Adair in the hills. When Frank and Cole returned, they immediately made their arrangements for wrecking the train that same afternoon.[20]

Also nearby was the town of Casey, which had been founded on 12 January 1869 by an Irish Railroad foreman. The town was first used as a waiting place for those who wanted to live in the new, but not officially designated, county seat, Dalmanutha. But Dalmanutha never really got off the ground, and Casey grew rapidly to over a 1,000 residents. Gradually, the boom subsided, but Casey continued to be a stable community with a caring group of residents.

With Casey situated but seven miles west of the intended robbery site, Jesse's men visited the town and purchased a rope at Valentine's Hardware Store to be used to derail the train. In addition to buying the rope for use in the robbery, the boys requested services from a local blacksmith livery stable to care for their horses.

The outlaws allegedly stopped at the farmhouse of Abner Sisson about a mile south of the robbery site where they were given supper and a place to sleep in the haymow. The boys were "ever so polite," and when they departed, they told Sisson's teenage daughter to visit them if she and the family were ever in Missouri.

In Council Bluffs, Iowa, Cole and Frank learned that the No. 2 train of the Rock Island Lines would be carrying up to $100,000 or more in gold through Adair on July 21, 1873, for eastern banks. Upon their return to the Adair-Casey hideout, they related the information to Jesse and their fellow gang members. The date was set for the afternoon of July 21st.

That same afternoon, the outlaws called at the section house and were given pies and other foods from Mrs. Grant. Shortly after, they broke into a handcar house, purloined a spike-bar and hammer with which they pried off a fish-plate connecting two rails and extracted the spikes at a curve of track near the Turkey Creek Bridge. The men quickly tied a rope on the west end of the disconnected north rail, passing the rope under the south rail to a hole they had cut in the bank in which to conceal themselves.

About 8:30 p.m., Rock Island Lines passenger train No. 2 climbed a steep grade and approached a sharp curve. The train, made up of two Pullman sleeping cars, five coaches and an express-baggage car was about four miles west of Adair, between the Mississippi and Missouri rivers. Near the end of the curve the outlaws lay ready with their rope tied to the rail they had pried loose. As the train rounded the curve, the engineer, John Rafferty, saw the rope tied to the rail and immediately reversed his engine and applied the air brakes.[21]

91

Adair Train Robbery picturing derailed train. (Courtesy of the Library of Congress)

During the confusion and commotion, the rail was jerked out of place and the engine plunged into the ditch, along with two baggage cars, and toppled over on its side. The woodwork and considerable machinery were wrecked and nothing but splinters remained of the cab. The tender lay on top of the engine, bottom side up, and on top of the tender was heaped a baggage car. The other baggage car lay on its side on the bank, the floor inclined at a steep angle. While both baggage cars were seriously wrecked, one was totally destroyed. The forward wheels of the first passenger coach jumped the track but the other coaches suffered no damage.[22]

Fireman Dennis Foley later recollected: "Left Council Bluffs at 4:53 P.M., Monday. . . . There was no one on the engine but myself and Rafferty. We left Anita on time, 7:39 P.M. About six or seven miles this side of Anita the engine left the track, and I looked up toward the engineer and asked him what that cracking sound was. I now believe the sound to have been pistol shots. He made no answer. I looked around and could see nothing. In a few minutes the engine was on her side."[23]

Aboard the train were twenty-eight Chinese students, "selected from the better class of Chinese citizens," on their way from Hong Kong to the Chinese educational mission at Springfield, Massachusetts. The boys, ten to fifteen years of age, were under the special charge of Wong Shing, and General Agent S.S. Stevens did all in his power to make the visitors comfortable. The splendid palace car, *City Leavenworth*, was placed at their disposal, and a special agent detailed to accompany them. Their baggage occupied an entire car.[24]

The great weight of this car was undoubtedly a favorable circumstance for the balance of the train as it broke the sudden jar at stopping. There was no one in the car. In the second car were Superintendent Royce, Conductor Smith, the express agent John Burgess, Luggage-master Albert Fick, and the Registered Letter Carrier, O.P. Killingsworth. The Chinese students were in the rear car.[25]

The robbers jumped out of the bushes firing their guns in the air, causing pandemonium among the terrified crewmen and passengers. Bullets whizzed by Mr. Royce, and one grazed the head of Fick. The violent concussion of the wreck caused the express car to be lifted at one end, shoved forward, then careened at an angle of forty-five degrees. Packages pounded against the lower side of the car. The men in the car were knocked about as well. Engineer John Rafferty of Des Moines was killed; the fireman, Dennis Foley was seriously injured, along with numerous passengers.[26]

The engineer Rafferty lay with his neck broken, caused by falling at the time of the crash. He was also wounded by a pistol shot in the thigh. At first it was supposed that he had been shot dead, but such was not the case. When Fireman Foley came to his senses, he found himself lying on the floor of the cab, with the dead body of the engineer on top of him.[27]

Dragging the body onto the track, Foley began to alarm the others on the train, but he was compelled to turn back by the robbers. Extinguishing the furnace fire, he let the water out of the boiler, thus preventing an explosion. As he was doing so, the outlaws fired several shots inside the train, and William Smith, the conductor, had two bullets sent through his clothing.

Foley, however, recalled:

> I looked out and saw four or five fellows who were firing seem-
> ingly in the express car. I was on the deck. I tried to raise up, and
> as I raised up, Rafferty fell off my back. I took hold of him and
> spoke to him but he made no answer. I asked him if he was dead.
> He made no reply. I took him up in my arms and carried him away
> from the engine, fearing that the engine might explode, and hoping
> that he might still be living. I stopped to rest a bit. When I raised
> him up, one of the four or five masked men said, "Stop or I will
> shoot you." I laid John down in the ditch and went to conductor
> that John was dead. As I passed around in front of the engine, two
> shots passed by my hat. I met the conductor about four car lengths
> back from the engine. I cannot describe the men, except that they
> were roughly dressed, wearing low hats and with masks over their
> faces. I met the conductor on the north side of the train. I did not
> see any masked men on that side till I came to the conductor. The
> passengers were outside and the conductor was trying to get them
> to go back. Two of the masked men went to the express car.[28]

The two outlaws, presumed to be Frank and Jesse James,
climbed into the express car with cocked .44s. One of these men,
believed to have been the leader, removed his mask upon entering. A
rail employee said he appeared to be dressed like a laborer. This man,
with a "vicious countenance," did nearly all the talking and shouted,
"Give us those keys—give us those keys, or I'll blow your brains out!
Give us the money, or I'll blow you to hell! We want money! Where's
them safe keys—quick, or some of you'll get killed."[29]

At the same time, he pointed his pistols at the heads of several
frightened crew members and yelled, "Where's the bullion? Give us the
bullion." Then he turned to his own men and screamed, "Rush in and
help! Come on! Such a set of robbers as you are—rush in and help."

The two gunmen quickly forced John Burgess, the guard, to
open the safe. He did as he was told before being tied and thrown into
a corner. Pistols were also held at the heads of the registry clerk and Mr.
Rice, assistant superintendent of the road who were also in the car, and
had hardly recovered from the shock of the concussion when the rob-

bers entered. But in doing so, the startled outlaws discovered the safe held but $2,000 in currency and no gold. In the car as well were two boxes of registered letters which the pair did not touch. At the last moment, the gold shipment had been changed to a later train![30]

"I saw two of the robbers enter my car," remembered John P. Burgess. "They ordered me to open the safe and give them the money. They pointed three large revolvers at my head, one man holding two, and the other one, threatening to shoot me if I did not comply. I felt myself bound to do so in order to save my life."[31]

The passengers, some slightly injured in the accident, were confronted by armed men; all but one masked in full "Ku Klux Klan" garb, and were guarded so that no one could offer any resistance from the cars. At the first shock, the passengers had been thrown forward, and after the recoil many had started forward to the scene of the wreck, but were driven back by threats, mingled with occasional shots. Panic set in with women and children screaming and crying and men hiding their cash, watches, and jewelry. The outlaws collected another thousand dollars by relieving the passengers of their watches, cash, and jewelry. All the loot was dumped into bags. Other members of the outlaw band stood on either side of the train, and every time a passenger showed his head at the window, he was fired upon. Superintendent Royce, Billy Smith, Flick the baggage man, and several others managed narrow escapes. Smith's pants and coats were cut by bullets, and Flick's head was grazed.[32]

The outlaws aimed to keep all the passengers in the cars and to drive the train employees in as well. One passenger, a Chicago man, stepped out of the car and begged the robbers not to shoot the women and children. The men allegedly shouted they were "no damn common robbers" and only took from the rich to give to the poor. At the same time, they ordered him back in the car and fired several shots in his direction.

During the raid, the Chinese students lay flat on the floor of their car, many of them screaming. When the bandits reached the coach where these students were and demanded they hand over their valuables, they merely stared at the grain sack, as none of them understood English and what was being asked of them. One of the bandits made signs of emptying his pockets, but the Chinese did not have pockets, only sleeves. In disgust, the bandits left without their contributions.[33]

The *New York Times* commented on these frightened young men occupying the two sleeping coaches in an editorial dubbed "Civilized Travel," the editor lamenting that Iowa had not followed the example of Maine and Connecticut in making the willful wrecking of a railroad train a felony of the first order. At least then, eluding to the following excerpt, when the Chinese visitors wrote home of their inhospitable reception, they could add that it was promptly and properly avenged:

> It may have occurred to more than one of those young men that a country where such practices are possible, was hardly the best fitted for the instruction or edification of youth. And if, in addition, they had heard anything of the treatment of their countrymen on the western coast of our great Republic, they may well have begun to doubt whether, to associate with this sort of neighbors, it was worthwhile casting down their immemorial wall.[34]

After concluding their plundering, the robbers went to their horses, which had been tied a short distance away. The robbers rode away to the south, uttering a rebel yell characteristic of the Civil War period. They disappeared as quickly as they had come, the raid, from the ditching of the train to their departure, taking only about fifteen minutes.[35]

Levi Clay, employed by the railroad in Adair as a brakeman, leaped from the rear car when the train crashed and hastened to Anita on foot where he spread the alarm. According to Clay, the train had been thrown off the track by fifty to seventy-five men, who were robbing and murdering all the passengers. Townspeople armed themselves with rifles, shotguns. Revolvers, and clubs, and headed out to the crash site determined to rescue survivors.[36]

The local telegrapher sent word to Des Moines and Omaha, and soon the news was carried throughout the nation. A train loaded with armed men left Council Bluffs for Adair and dropped small parties of men off along the route where saddled horses were waiting.[37] Frank Cox, the road master, dispatched a mounted troop of forty men in pursuit of the bandits.

A special Iowa detective was hired by the railroad and express companies to ferret out the thieves and bring them to justice. The official at once organized a band of eleven men to go with him after the outlaws. Having heard that the James boys had been living in both Ray and Lafayette counties in Missouri, the lawmen were joined by the Lafayette County Vigilance Committee. Picking up the outlaws' trail, they found a magnificent mare they believed had belonged to Jesse James. The mare was sent to Dubuque.[38]

Learning that the posse was getting close, the gang escaped from Lafayette County. Their trail was lost for a time but the detective received information that the robbers had gone to stay with the Youngers at their home near Johnson City, a village in St. Clair County, some eighty-five miles from Sedalia, and fifteen or sixteen miles south of Montrose.

The Vigilance Committee arrived in Sedalia on August 27th, and officers of the Missouri, Kansas, and Texas Road furnished them with a special train. The official in charge had orders to take the party to any point on the road that might be deemed necessary to further their project. A stop was made at Montrose where the committee left the train and took wagons to Johnson City, which they reached about midnight. They left the wagons and teamsters by the roadside to make it appear as if they were hauling lumber, while the main party took to the woods and made their camp. Scouts were sent out to ascertain whether the robbers were in the area.

At nine o'clock in the morning, one of the scouts came in and said the Youngers had put up for the night in their home near Johnson City. The teamsters were called into camp with the wagons and a plan of attack was quickly decided upon and the party started for the house. All the posse members were instructed not to make any noise until daylight, but one over-anxious recruit lost his memory and yelled, "Close in upon it!" This brought matters to a climax and the entire party advanced to the house, their guns pointed at the doors and windows.

The outlaws were ordered to surrender and come outside, but when no signs of fight were visible, it was soon ascertained that the only occupants of the building were women and children, the outlaws having escaped. The women were very frightened and said that the robbers had not been seen in the vicinity. They later claimed to have been grossly abused by some of the Vigilants and one member of the family went to Jefferson City to report the incident to Governor Woodson. The committee returned to Sedalia very much chagrined and hungry, several of them complaining they had been covered with chiggers and ticks. The following day, they took a train, disbanded, and went home.

O.P. Killingsworth, of Omaha, an agent of the Post Office Department, was aboard the train which was robbed, and gave a lengthy interview to the *Davenport Gazette*. According to Killingsworth, the express run that night from Omaha was very light, and before the robbery, Messenger Burgess had told him he had the smallest amount in his safe he had carried in months. However, he maintained there were three tons of bullion—gold and silver bricks—on the floor of the car.[39]

After the outlaws had gone, there was a general outpouring of passengers from the crippled train. Some of the ladies who had been frantic with terror, emerged pale and trembling, and many of them wept when they learned of the fate of the engineer and how he had bravely stood his post.

As soon as word reached Chicago, the company offered a reward of $5,000 for the discovery of the bandits. To this the government added the highest amount permitted by law. The whole southwestern part of Iowa was aroused, and the line of the Burlington and Missouri River Road was heavily guarded. Special trains with armed men departed from Council Bluffs in parallel lines to intercept the robbers, and a large scouting party left Atlantic, some fifteen miles south of the disaster.[40]

One newspaper stated in an editorial:

The hot pursuit to which the dastardly wreckers of the train on the Chicago, Rock Island and Pacific Railroad are being subjected will do more than anything else to discourage this species of robbery. The people of broad sections of country have voluntarily enrolled themselves by the enormity of their crime. When intending railroad robbers discover that the hand of every man is certain to be raised against them, they will probably feel disposed to turn their talents into less perilous, even if also less profitable, channels.[41]

But the James-Younger Gang felt nothing of the kind, and, in fact, marveled over how easy it was to rob a train. The fleeing outlaws paused after a few hours' ride, divided the spoils, and separated into pairs to meet again that night. They rode toward Missouri, split up again, and singly went into their hiding places. Separating after a robbery had become a James-Younger trademark and proved successful for the elusive band. Other outlaw gangs stayed together, believing in the old adage, "there is strength in numbers," but this ploy left them highly recognizable and they were frequently captured.[42]

Unlike the others, Jim Younger regretted his participation in the robbery. Killing and harming innocent people had not been part of their plan but the others argued that Rafferty's death and Foley's injuries were the result of an error in judgment not planned or anticipated. He informed his brothers that he wanted nothing more to do with train robberies and declined his share of the money when it was offered to him. Bob Younger realized that his brother was right; after all, this was not the war, but Jesse told him that because the engineer and fireman were railroad employees, they were fair game.[43]

Five miles south of the robbery site, the trail of five horsemen had been struck, and followed to the Nodaway River, some thirty-eight miles southward. A full description of the horses was obtained and the general consensus among Iowans was that the robbers could not escape. Most citizens agreed that the crime was committed by the same band of Missouri guerrillas that had robbed the bank in Corydon two years earlier.[44]

Some of the posses picked up their trail again and followed it to the Missouri River, where there was unmistakable evidence that the robbers swam the stream with their horses. Picking up the trail on the opposite side of the river, the outlaws were followed into Jackson County, where, as always, every trace disappeared. A party of detectives went to Monegaw Springs in search of the bandits and sighted Jesse James and two of the Younger brothers. They made no effort to arrest the fugitives, however, and quickly rode away thankful they had escaped with their own lives.[45]

Since it was obvious the train could not be righted, train officials decided to walk the passengers into the nearest town, which was Anita. Utter chaos followed as the rail men shouted and badgered the confused passengers who were finally organized and sent walking down the track behind the brakeman with a lantern. An emergency telegraph set had been hooked up and cut in on the regular line. Word was eventually dispatched requesting a wrecking crew and reporting the robbery.[46]

The train crew tried to organize local farmers in the area to pursue the robbers, but the farmers had no love for the iron horse men and refused, saying they hadn't lost any money and the railroad men could go chase them themselves. Agents along the line, however, were contacted and told to organize posses.

William A. Smith, conductor of the ill-fated train, later testified at the coroner's inquest on the body of John Rafferty, the engineer:

> I was in the smoking car near the front end. From the noise I thought the engine was in the ditch, with one or two cars piled upon it. I was thrown under the seat in front of me. Don't remember which side of the car I got out, but know that I reached the engine on the north side. I went forward to see what was up. The first person that I met was one of the masked men, near the baggage car door, who pointed a revolver in each hand toward me and told me to get back, firing at me at the same time. I backed down as far as the sleeping coach before I felt I was out of his way. There I met Dennis Foley, the fireman, who said "Bill, Jack is dead." The passengers were in a hubbub, and the women and children were cry-

ing. I told the passengers that I thought the masked men were trying to rob the baggage car and tried to borrow a revolver but failed.

I could still see the man from where I was. I saw another passing up and down the opposite side of the train. I think he was firing at me, also. Some of the passengers asked me to get into the train as these men were firing at me and I would be the cause of some of them being killed. I then went into the sleeping car at the rear, still trying to get a revolver, urging the passengers to keep quiet, as these men were robbing the baggage car. I went out of the ladies' car, up the back and thence to the engine.

Two balls passed through my clothing while I was on the bank. These shots came from the south side of the train. I did not see a man on the north side then; did not see or hear anything more of the masked men. After the passengers got quiet, I went forward to investigate the cause of the wreck. At the hind truck of the smoking car I found a fish-plate had been removed from the rail at the west end and the rope was passed under the south rail across the ditch and up on to the bank. A piece of the rope was also found which seemed to be taken from the other. It was a new rope, the size of a common bed cord. The west end of the rail, when I saw it, was only a few inches from the south rail. The hind trucks of the smoking car were still on the track. We had been running [eighteen to twenty miles per hour].[47]

The *Daily Iowa State Register* reported on Tuesday morning, July 22nd, that "[the train] due here in Des Moines from the west last night at 10:30 o'clock did not arrive on time, and about [eleven] o'clock the news spread over the city that it had been attacked, ditched and sacked by a masked gang of robbers, half-way between Anita and Adair, [sixty-one] miles west of Des Moines. The first dispatch received was about 10:30 o'clock, from Superintendent Royce (who fortunately happened to be on the train sent from Casey)."[48]

The article claimed that there were at least seven robbers, possibly eight—all masked—and they took off south on horseback leaving Engineer John Rafferty dead, the engine on her side in a ditch, one of the baggage cars up on the bank, and the other "upset on the side."

But the scene of the tragedy was located in the "wildest" area between Council Bluffs and Des Moines at a sharp curve on a steep grade, four miles from the nearest telegraph. There were no houses for miles, and the land was broken up into ravines and sloughs that were nearly impassable except to persons familiar with the area. According to the *Register*, the spot was well chosen—the plot well laid and well executed, the only mistake made, seemingly, being the failure to cut the telegraph wire.

The United States Express Company offered a reward of $500 each for the arrest of the railroad bandits. This made a total of $12,000 to be paid to the man who produced the arrest and conviction of the villains. A total of $5,000 was put up by the railroad company, $3,500 by the state and $3,500 by the express company.[49]

The robbers had not been identified since only one had showed his face during the holdup. He was described as "a large bushy, red-faced man." Speculation focused upon some three-card-monte men from Council Bluffs and Omaha, who hated Conductor Smith for his prohibiting them on his train. Another view conjectured that the perpetrators of the raid were the same men who had recently robbed a Missouri bank in broad daylight.[50]

At least two of the men had ridden "trailed and bloodied racers." Most of the horses were subsequently identified as having been shod at Atlantic, Iowa, a few days prior to the raid. One local blacksmith claimed he had shod one of the mounts with shoes made from watch springs and another with steel shoes.

A Mr. and Mrs. Stuckey, who lived in the house where the robbers ate dinner in Ringgold County on July 22nd, came forward with descriptions of five robbers. They stated that the man who appeared to be the leader stood about five feet seven or eight, had light hair, blue eyes, heavy sandy whiskers, broad shoulders, a straight and tolerably short nose that was slightly turned up, tolerably high broad forehead, and was intelligent looking. According to the Stuckeys, this man, probably thirty-six to forty years old, looked too well educated to be a working man.[51]

The second robber was tall and slender, light complexioned, and somewhat delicate looking. He had a high, not very broad, forehead, very long light brown hair and whiskers, "inclined to be sandy," was near six feet tall with long slender hands and looked as if he had never done any work in his life. With a little Roman nose and blue eyes, he, too, seemed well educated, was very polite, not inclined to talk much, also about thirty-six to forty, and he was dressed in light clothes.

The third man was rather slender, five feet nine or ten inches tall, sandy haired although it might be considered light brown, with a Grecian nose, not at all refined but somewhat sarcastic, hard with a bad countenance, brown eyes, looked to the Stuckeys as an intemperate man, he wore a dark wool hat with a stiff rim, dark clothes, and was perhaps from thirty-five to thirty-eight years of age.

The fourth outlaw was dark complexioned, dark-haired, had no whiskers, he had a broad and tolerably high forehead, five feet seven or eight, heavy set, straight, and rather intelligent looking countenance, black eyes, and straight Grecian nose. Attired in light pants and a vest, dark coat, and light wool hat, he appeared to be thirty-four to thirty-eight years of age.

The fifth man possessed a fair complexion, blue eyes, light brown hair with chin whiskers, a little sandy, stood about five feet nine or ten, was large and portly, but not very fleshy, broad shoulders, was intelligent looking, with a large Roman nose. He was perhaps thirty-six to thirty-eight years old, was dressed in light clothes, and "made quite a pleasant appearance."

These descriptions described Frank and Jesse James, Clell Miller, and Jim and Bob Younger, but the other two robbers had not been seen by the Stuckeys. Jack Bishop accused Ike Flannery of being one of the band in the *Kansas City Times*, but because Bishop had had some kind of falling out with Flannery, his remarks were not taken seriously by the law.[52]

Confusion as to the identity of Frank and Jesse James on the part of the law played a huge role in their escaping detection. Reports over the years had been wildly inconsistent as to height, weight, the shape of their faces, and color of their hair and whiskers. In most cases, descriptions of the brothers had been formed after a brief glance by a casual observer during a time of great excitement. Because of this, law officials could not easily obtain their true identities, which allowed the two gunmen complete freedom to move about in Missouri and other states.[53]

Jesse James was often considered moody—easy to get along with when things were going well but "cruel, demanding and dangerous" when they were not. Because he knew no fear, he was a natural leader, despite his often being reckless.[54] Jesse was popular with Southerners because they saw him and his gang as a means of extracting revenge on those who had supported the Union during the Civil War. There was a great deal of animosity in the South toward the banks and railroads Jesse robbed. These same institutions charged high interest rates and steep freight charges. And, of course, many Missourians knew that these same bank owners had supported the Northern cause.[55]

Allan Pinkerton's son, William (known as Billy), later gave an interview to the *Chicago Times* and said of Jesse James:

> Jesse is too restless and improvident a man ever to be anything else than an outlaw. He has been bred to the business of crime, and it is second nature to him to murder and rob. Although he has made a large sum of money by his famous robberies, he has not been able to retain any of it, and parties who have seen him in and about Kansas City during the past few months say he was "down at the heel," and in bad shape financially. He is an inveterate and a hard gambler, and diligent pursuit of that line of business has reduced him to penury almost. . . . The gang was made up originally of Jesse James, Frank James, Cole, John, and Jim Younger, Tompkins, McDaniels, Clel Miller, and Arthur McCoy. They had acquired an appetite for plunder and crimes during the war, when they served under Quantrill, Mundy, Anderson, the Swamp Fox, and other noted guerrilla leaders of the Missouri valley. After the war they kept on with their lawless work. . . .
> The first connection we had with the gang was after the Corydon, Iowa, bank robbery, which followed upon the heels of the St. Genevieve [Gallatin] episode. There was a political gathering of some kind at Corydon, when the gang rode into town, captured the

bank and about $10,000 in currency, and took their departure with the utmost coolness, cursing the "d—d Yanks" for cowards as they left. Robert A. Pinkerton was dispatched to the scene, and together with a number of citizens, followed the raiders to the Missouri line. The Iowans abandoned the search at this point, and Robert went on alone. [He actually was accompanied by the sheriff, and had a brief gunfight with the gang at Civil Bend, in Daviess County.] He traced them to Blue Mill ferry over the Missouri, on the border of Clay County, and spent several days in the vicinity, acquainting himself with the history of the men who were engaged in the expedition. During the progress of his investigation he visited the house of Mrs. Samuels, the mother of the James brothers, and called on several persons who were more or less intimately connected with the gang. He failed to get hold of much information of value. While looking about he ran across an old woman who warned him that he was being shadowed by a tall, powerful man with red whiskers, who intended to kill him if he got troublesome. Robert was a young fellow then and quite boyish in appearance, a fact which warmed the old woman to him. The tall man turned out to be Arthur McCoy, one of the most ferocious of the James Gang. Soon afterward the bank determined to give up the hunt, and Robert returned home. This was in 1871, I believe. The plunderers soon after the Corydon exploit turned road agents, and a series of stage robberies in southern Missouri and Arkansas were laid to their credit.[56]

Frank, on the other hand, was the best-educated member of the gang. He often carried a volume of Shakespeare in his pocket. Tall and thin, with a sharp, aquiline nose and high-pitched voice, he did not resemble an outlaw.

According to a James Gang associate, George Shepard, the brothers were not at all alike. Said Shepard: "Frank is the most shrewd, cunning and capable; in fact, Jesse can't compare with him. Frank is a man of education, and can act the refined gentleman on all occasions. Jesse is reckless, and a regular dare-devil in courage, but it's Frank that makes all the plans and perfects the methods of escape. Jesse is a fighter and that's all. Why, he can't hardly read or write, and these stories about his writing to the Kansas City papers and the *Nashville Banner* is all stuff. If any letters were ever written, FRANK WROTE THEM."[57]

Shepard stated that Jesse took all the credit for the robberies because Frank was "quiet and gentlemanly, and would rather not be known, so he directs Jesse and Jesse directs the crowd. He likes notoriety and always takes care to let the people on trains know that he is the leader, and he always enjoyed the reading of his exploits in the papers. Jesse was full of dramatics and basked in the limelight."[58]

Frank, according to Shepard, would pass anywhere for a man of wealth. "He has pleasant manners, is very quiet, and talks low. He has light blue eyes, light sandy hair, and wears a close cut reddish sandy full beard, is about five feet eight inches high and weighs about 145 pounds. Jesse is larger and coarser than Frank, weighs 160 or 175 pounds, has dark brown hair and hazel eyes."[59]

Cole Younger was described as being all of six feet, four inches in height, possessing a commanding voice, and known to all he as "a friend of the South." And in every section of the Southland, he had friends who would always swear by Cole Younger."[60] One acquaintance later recalled: "During my years on the frontier, and later in the Oklahoma oil fields, I have known many men with a command of profanity—freighters, cattle drovers, muleskinners, bullwhackers, and pipeliners. But none could approach Cole Younger's brand of invective. Nor was there anything lacking in his personal courage."[61]

Jim Younger had been born on Cole's birthday and was four years younger than his brother. He was a quiet, well-mannered man, and considered more of a listener than a talker. Although Jim could always be counted upon to respond to his family's needs, the role of an outlaw had never suited him.[62]

Bob Younger, the youngest member of the gang at nineteen, was also a soft-spoken, well-liked young man. Bob, forever itching to attain his independence from his brothers, looked toward Jesse James as his role model. Bob and Jesse had become good friends after Bob visited Jesse and Zee on their honeymoon in Texas. Jesse seemed to enjoy playing father to the young man, and Bob was proud of his "father."[63]

Bill Chadwell was a small man whom many persons thought had too many teeth. Bill was the spokesman for the group, and he always seemed to have an answer for everything. No stranger to pomposity, he was once referred to in a St. Paul newspaper as "the man who fought the bulldog on Third Street a short time ago." This same newspaper reported how he dived from the steamer *Alhambra* to a depth of thirty feet to hitch a hawser to a shaft in the bottom of the river. Bill was described as the most noted diver on the Mississippi River and a person who had jumped into the river from a St. Paul bridge for a considera-tion.[64]

Clell Miller, the oldest of five sons, was born McClelland D. Miller on January 17, 1850. One relative described Clell as a fun-lov-ing boy, who idolized Jesse James. Family stories state Clell sometimes hid out in Kentucky, and at other times, made trips with the James brothers to Texas and California. It was also alleged the various gang members visited the Millers in Gentry County. The gang would race their horses around a tree, shooting at it until the tree toppled. On one occasion, Clell visited with a relative, William Miller and his family. After hanging his hat on the end of the bed, he was half asleep, when he noticed his hat in the moonlight. Clell, apparently thinking it was someone who had come to arrest him, shot at it and hurriedly dressed and left the area. The three holes in the hat could be covered with a sil-ver dollar.[65]

Arthur McCoy was also a former Confederate guerrilla and had served as a captain in General Jo Shelby's cavalry division. On March 3, 1861, the night before Lincoln's inauguration day, "The Minutemen"—Arthur McCoy, Rock Champion, Basil W. Duke, Colton Greene and James Quinlan—climbed the dome of the federal court-house on Market Street in St. Louis and removed the national flag, replacing it with the state flag. Above the Berthold mansion, headquar-ters of the Minutemen, a banner was raised that Colton Greene described as "a nondescript conceit—a red field, emblazoned with a white cross, star and crescent—made by Arthur McCoy's wife."[66]

Following the war, McCoy was allegedly involved in the killing of a Pinkerton agent and was identified as one of those who participated in the robbery of the Russellville, Kentucky, bank in 1868.

A St. Louis newspaper stated:

> This last man described was one of the railroad robbers. His name is Arthur McCoy, and will be remembered by some of the readers of the *Times*. Before the war he was a painter in this city and lived on Morgan Street. He was mixed up in an express robbery on the plains three or four years ago, but slipped away and was hidden away in a little place near Ste. Genevieve for a year and a half. Then he disappeared and was not seen until he came with the gang on the bank expedition.
>
> McCoy, after leaving Ste. Genevieve, got a place in Montgomery County about three miles south of Florence, on the St. Louis, Kansas City & Northern Railroad and ten miles of Herman, on the Missouri Pacific. He was in St. Louis a few weeks ago, but by the barest accident escaped falling into the hands of the police, slipped off and joined the band for this northern trip."[67]

Pursuit of the robbers commenced as special trains were dispatched by the Northwestern and B & M Railroads loaded with men hoping to intercept the robbers trying to escape across either of these lines. A posse led by a Mr. Ford left Atlantic early Tuesday morning, followed by another later in the day.

The outlaws, meanwhile, rested in some timber on land owned by a family named McCall. Digging into the stolen mail bags, they divided up the money they had appropriated, and split up.[68] Mrs. Jennie Bang later reported the following:

> The McCall boys found the mail sacks which had been looted and which contained unwanted mail as well as some jewelry. They brought the sacks and contents to our place as my father was keeping the post-office in our home. . . . My father proceeded to get the mail in circulation by sending it to Summit post-office, now Adair, and from there the mail was carried on foot to Casey by Levi Clay.[69]

One of the McCall boys retrieving the mail was reputed to have been Jack McCall, who later went to Deadwood, Dakota Territory, slipped into the No. 10 Saloon, walked to within three feet of Wild Bill Hickock and shot him in the back of the head with a .45 he pulled from his coat pocket. The bullet passed through Wild Bill's skull and exited his right cheek before lodging in the wrist of another poker player.[70]

Another account states that during the morning, Ford and his posse found a valise beside the road that had been taken from the express manager, and soon after, an express company envelope that had been torn open, robbed of its contents, and discarded. Ford picked up their trail and followed it to the Nodaway River where it vanished. One report surfaced that "the villains are surrounded on all sides and that their capture is anticipated."[71]

Three days later, the *Rock Island Daily Argus* reported:

Des Moines, July 23. - Nothing entirely reliable in regard to the pursuit and capture of the railroad robbers has been received at this place today. It is thought that they have crossed into Missouri and are making for the wilds of Mercer County in that state. The total amount taken by the robbers from the train in now known to be twenty-three hundred and thirty-seven dollars.

The latest advices from the railroad robbers is that last evening between Creston and the State line, [they were] pushing for Missouri with the utmost speed. They passed a farm house last evening, about dark, their horses being well jaded. The company divided, one-half going in another direction. Dispatches received from the officers in pursuit, this morning, state that they have got between them and Missouri, whither the robbers are going. They are evidently regular Missouri guerrillas, who understand the business they are in. The country is all alarmed and hundreds are in pursuit and it seems impossible for them to escape although they are mounted on horses of racing stock.

The engines on the Rock Island road are draped in mourning for the death of Rafferty, the engineer killed at the railroad robbery. The robbers were too wily for those in pursuit and headed for their hideout in the hills of western Missouri where they were fairly safe from lawmen among their friends and relatives.[72]

The *Rock Island Daily Argus*, July 25, 1873, stated that law enforcement agents formed a posse and went in pursuit of the bandits.[73] In September, the Lafayette County Vigilantes Committee,

traced the train robbers to Johnson City, St. Clair County, and surrounded the house where they were supposed to be hiding, but the birds had flown. The band consisted of three Youngers and the James brothers. [Arthur] McCoy was not with them. There was a reported fight between the robbers and vigilantes and the wounding of one of the Youngers. It was believed that the robbers had started for Texas. A telegram from Wells, Fargo & Co., at San Francisco, California, fixes the sealed package taken by the robbers at $637, making the total amount secured by the robbers $2,337. Of that, $950 belonged to the CRI & P Company, and was being transported for them.[74]

A Council Bluffs newspaper ran a story from the *St. Joseph Herald* regarding the robbers:

Two of the gang are the James boys, of Clay County, Missouri, the same party which robbed the Chariton and Clarendon banks; one of them is of the Rambo party, which attempted to rob the Chillicothe bank, and the other two are supposed to belong to Pattonsburg or Chillicothe.

The James brothers crossed the Hannibal and St. Joseph Railroad at Kidder last Friday morning on their way south, evidently going to their mother's house. In the evening they stopped at the farm house of Mr. Bacon and wanted to stay all night. He refused, but told them of a house further on where they could stop. They rode on and passed over the ridge, but not seeing them ride over the ridge beyond he became uneasy and slept very little during the night.

Next morning he arose and immediately went in the direction they did and soon found where they had lain in the brush, and also where they had picketed their horses. He followed the tracks of their horses some distance in a southerly direction towards Clay County and then returned home. He says all the members of the party had fine horses, but they were much jaded and looked as though they had traveled a long distance with little care or food. When the riders jumped off, the horses began to eat smartweed with an apparent relish.

This Jesse James is known to be a chief of a gang of robbers which is a terror from their headquarters in Clay County to Sherman, Texas. Indeed when it is known they have committed any depredations, everyone gives up further effort to capture them.

The two other suspected parties, which belong to the same gang, and who separated from the James brothers at a more northerly point, crossed the Rock Island branch Saturday morning at [eleven] o'clock near Jamesport and went in the direction of Pattonsburg. Special detectives are in front of them awaiting their appearance, and others were not more than an hour behind them at the last accounts, and in all probability will be captured.[75]

The outlaws' trail led straight into Missouri. Several people in the area of the robbery said that two of the outlaws looked like Frank and Jesse James.

## Notes

[1]*Lexington Caucasian*, September 5, 1874.
[2]William Bell, "The Reno Gang's Reign of Terror," *Wild West Magazine*, February 2004.
[3]Homer Croy, *Jesse James Was My Neighbor*, New York, Duell, Sloan and Pearce, 1949, p. 74.
[4]William Bell, "The Reno Gang's Reign of Terror," *Wild West Magazine*, February 2004.
[5]*North Missourian*, December 19, 1864.
[6]William Bell, "The Reno Gang's Reign of Terror," *Wild West Magazine*, February 2004.
[7]Charles Michelson, "The Trade of Train Robbery," *Munsey's*, February 1902.
[8]Richard Patterson, *Train Robbery: The Birth, Flowering, and Decline of a Notorious Western Enterprise*, Boulder, Johnson Books, 1981, p. 113.
[9]*Adair News*, July 28, 1922.
[10]J.W. Buel, *The Border Outlaws*, Syracuse, Alvord & Sleight, 1883, p. 169.
[11]*St. Louis Weekly Globe*, May 30, 1873.
[12]*Ste. Genevieve Fair Play*, May 29, 1873.
[13]William Watts Folwell, *A History of Minnesota*, Volume III, St. Paul, Minnesota Historical Society, 1969, p. 97.
[14]Henry Dale, *Adventures and Exploits of the Younger Brothers, Missouri's Most Daring Outlaws, and Companions of the James Boys*, p. 153.

[15]Homer Croy, *Jesse James Was My Neighbor*, New York, Dell Publishing Company, Inc., 1960, p. 93.

[16]Kenneth Ulyatt, *Outlaws*, Philadelphia and New York, J.B. Lippincott Company, 1976, p. 41.

[17]Captain William R. Orbelo, "Colt Model 1851 Navy Revolver," *Western Frontier 1980 Annual*, Summer 1980, p. 33.

[18]R.L. Wilson, *Colt: An American Legend*, Artabras, New York, London, Paris, Abbeville Publishing Group, 1985, pp. 175-179.

[19]Homer Croy, *Jesse James Was My Neighbor*, p. 75; Donald L. Gilmore, "When the James Gang Ruled the Rails," *Wild West Magazine*, August 2000.

[20]*Adair News Special Addition*, Summer 2003.

[21]*Rock Island Argus*, August 7, 1985, James and Lucille Sampson, "Jesse James got his start on Rock Island Lines."

[22]*Daily Iowa State Register*, July 23, 1873.

[23]Ibid.

[24]*Council Bluffs Nonpareil*, July 22, 1873.

[25]*Daily Iowa State Register*, July 23, 1873.

[26]*Davenport Gazette*, July 25, 1873; *New York Times*, July 26, 1873; *Adair News Special Addition*, Summer 2003; *New York Times*, July 30, 1873.

[27]*New York Times*, July 23, 1873.

[28]*Daily Iowa State Register*, July 23, 1873.

[29]*New York Times*, July 26, 1873.

[30]*New York Times*, July 23, 1873; *Adair News Special Addition*, Summer 2003.

[31]*Daily Iowa State Register*, July 23, 1873.

[32]Ibid; *New York Times*, July 23, 1873.

[33]Homer Croy, *Jesse James Was My Neighbor*, pp. 76-77.

[34]*New York Times*, July 25, 1873.

[35]*Daily Iowa State Register*, July 23, 1873.

[36]*New York Times*, July 29, 1873.

[37]*Adair News Special Addition*, Summer 2003.

[38]*New York Times*, September 12, 1873.

[39]*Davenport Gazette*, July 25, 1873; *New York Times*, July 26, 1873.

[40]*New York Times*, July 23, 1873.

[41]*New York Times*, July 27, 1873.

[42]Frank Triplett, *The Life, Times and Treacherous Death of Jesse James*, New York, The Swallow Press, 1970 reprint of the 1882 edition, pp. 74-75.

[43]Marley Brant, *The Outlaw Youngers: A Confederate Brotherhood*, Lanham, New York, London, Madison Books, 1992, pp. 122-123.

[44]*New York Times*, July 23, 1873.

[45]J.W. Buel, *The Border Outlaws*, Syracuse, Alvord & Sleight, 1883, pp. 169-170.

[46]Homer Croy, *Jesse James Was My Neighbor*, p. 77.

[47]*Rock Island Argus*, August 7, 1985, James and Lucille Sampson, "Jesse James got his start on Rock Island Lines."

[48]*Daily Iowa State Register*, July 22, 1873.

[49]*Rock Island Argus*, August 7, 1985, James and Lucille Sampson, "Jesse James got his start on Rock Island Lines."

[50]*Daily Iowa State Register*, July 23, 1873.

[51]*Council Bluffs Nonpareil*, July 25, 1873.

[52]J.W. Buel, *The Border Outlaws*, Syracuse, Alvord & Sleight, 1883, pp. 170-171.

[53]William A. Settle, Jr., *Jesse James Was His Name*, Lincoln and London, University of Nebraska Press, 1966, p. 99.

[54]Homer Croy, *Cole Younger: Last of the Great Outlaws*, Lincoln and London, University of Nebraska Press, 1956, pp. 82-82.

[55]Robert L. Dyer, *Jesse James and the Civil War in Missouri*, Columbia and London, University of Missouri Press, 1994, p. 66.

[56]*Kansas City Evening Star*, July 21, 1881

[57]*Good Bye, Jesse James*, Liberty, The Jesse James Bank Museum, 1967, pp. 24-25, first printed in the *Kansas City Daily Journal* in 1882,

[58]Donald L. Gilmore, "When the James Gang Ruled the Rails," *Wild West*, August 2000, pp. 41-42.

[59]*Good Bye, Jesse James*, pp. 24-25.

[60]*Terrell* (Texas) *Transcript*, April 26, 1907.

[61]Albert S. Gilles, "Jesse, Frank and Cole," *Frontier Times*, September 1969, p. 47.

[62]Homer Croy, *Last of the Great Outlaws*, New York, The New American Library, 1956, p. 82.

[63]Marley Brant, *Jesse James: The Man and the Myth*, New York, Berkley Books, 1998, p. 161.

[64]Emmett C. Hoctor Collection, Plattsmouth, Nebraska.

[65]Ruth Coder Fitzgerald, *Clell and Ed Miller, Members of the James Gang*, 1987, pp. 2-12.

[66]Anthony Monachello, "Struggle for St. Louis," *America's Civil War*.

[67]*St. Louis Daily Globe*, July 23, 1873.

[68]Marley Brant, *Jesse James: The Man and the Myth*, p. 101.

[69]*Adair News*, April 22, 1954.

[70]T.D. Griffith, "Aces, Eights and Number 10," *Historic Traveler Magazine*, November 1996.

[71]*St. Louis Daily Globe*, July 23, 1873.

[72]*Rock Island Daily Argus*, July 24, 1873.

[73]*Rock Island Daily Argus*, July 25, 1873.

[74]*Rock Island Argus*, August 7, 1985, James and Lucille Sampson, "Jesse James got his start on Rock Island Lines."

[75]*Council Bluffs Nonpareil*, July 29, 1873.

*Chapter Five*

# Accusations and Denials

*"Clell Miller, Tom McDannial, William McDannial, Jack Kene, and Sol Reed are the five men who robbed the Muncie, Kansas, Railroad train that 8th of December 1874. . . . When those scondrals robed the train at Muncie they took a horse and rode it to Clay County and turned it out to leave the impression that it was the James boys."*
—Jesse James[1]

I N RESPONSE TO THE ACCUSATIONS published in the *St. Joseph Herald* and the *Council Bluffs Nonpareil*, Jesse James wrote the *St. Louis Dispatch* from Deer Lodge, Montana Territory, on December 20, 1873, denying the brothers' complicity in the Adair train robbery and other recent crimes:

> Will you permit me a little space in your columns to say a few words on my own behalf, and in that of my brother, Frank? I know that we are outlaws, and that there is big money on our heads; but even though we were to be hung tomorrow, a newspaper that wanted to give a man a fair chance to put himself right before those he cared for, would not hesitate to let him print the truth.
>
> I see from the newspapers of Missouri that one of the Jameses was recognized with the party who robbed the store in Cass County

some weeks ago, and that later, at Monagaw Springs, when the prisoners were captured, a James said to a prisoner, "Do not look at me, damn you, for if you go away and report on me I will follow you up and kill you if it take[s] me a year."

Perhaps nothing that I might say in way of denial would change any man's opinion of me, either one way or the other; but this I do say, that neither Frank nor myself have been in Missouri since the third day of October 1873, nor any nearer Missouri than Denver City. Neither of us was in Cass County at the time mentioned, nor any time within the past year. I am as guiltless in this Cass County store robbery as a child unborn, and knew nothing whatever of it until I saw it in the newspapers.

This proposition, however, do I make, and will stick to it. I made this to McClurg when he was governor, and he said it was fair and manly, although he did not pay attention to it, and now I make it to Governor Woodson, who has offered a large reward for my head. If he will guarantee me a fair trial, and Frank also, and protect us from a mob, or from a requisition from the Governor of Iowa, which is the same thing, we will come to Jefferson City, or any other place in Missouri, except Gallatin, surrender ourselves, and take our trial for everything we have been charged with. I do not know that Governor Woodson can do this thing, but if he can and will, we are ready to surrender ourselves. All he will have to do is give us his word that we shall not be dealt with by a mob, as we would most certainly be if the militia of Daviess County could get their hands upon two of Quantrill's and Anderson's best men, or if the Iowa authorities could get us for a crime that we never committed.

If everything said about a man who had a positive character was true, all the jails and penitentiaries in the country would be full. We have many enemies in Missouri because of the war—many who want to see us killed if they can get other people to do the killing; but for all that, if the governor of our state will guarantee us a fair trial, we will surrender. If we do not, then let public opinion brand us as highwaymen, and do it truthfully, for I will never again write a line to defend myself. But surely we should have a little credit in trying to put ourselves right, and in seeking to have protection while doing it.

We have been charged with robbing the Gallatin bank and killing the cashier, with robbing the gate at the Fair Grounds at Kansas City, with robbing a bank in Ste. Genevieve, with robbing a train in

Iowa and killing an engineer, with robbing two or three banks in Kentucky and killing two or three men there; but for every charge and on every charge we are willing to be tried. If Governor Woodson will just promise us protection before we can prove before any fair jury in the state that we have been accused falsely and unjustly. If we do not prove this, then let the law do its worst. We are willing to abide by the verdict. I do not see how we could well offer anything fairer. We do not mean to be taken alive, and those who know this will believe this, even if we do say it ourselves; but we would delight in having a fair trial, and having this sleepless vigilance on our part broken up. Any communication addressed to me at Deer Lodge, Montana Territory, will be attended to.[2]

Cole Younger later also denied any participation in the Adair train robbery:

It was immediately following the Rock Island robbery at Adair, Iowa, that there first appeared a deliberate enlistment of some local papers in Missouri to connect us with this robbery. New York and Chicago as well as the St. Paul and Minneapolis papers did not connect the Youngers with the crime, and three days after the robbery these papers had it that the robbers had been followed into Nodaway County, Missouri, while we were at Monegaw Springs all that time. Besides those mentioned in my 1874 letter, Marshall P. Wright's affidavit that he showed Jim and me at Monegaw Springs the morning paper containing the account of the robbery the next morning after it took place, was presented to Governor David Clough of Minnesota in 1898.

It is 250 miles or more and no cross lines of railroad existed to facilitate our passage, so it would have been impossible for anyone to have made the trip. The shortest rail lines are roundabout, via St. Joseph and Kansas City, so it would be apparent that I could not have been at the Rock Island wreck.[3]

This same Cole Younger, however, intimated in a separate interview that he was there and that they had expected the train would stop when the locomotive left the tracks. Instead, it plowed ahead a few feet and toppled over, breaking the steam pipe. Engineer John Rafferty was trapped inside the cab and scalded to death.[4]

116

One week after the train robbery, a coroner's jury convened to inquire into the death of John Rafferty, the engineer. Coroner Overman had I.J. Morgan, N.M. Burtch, and James Garrity sworn in as jurors and the inquest commenced with the testimony of Dr. A.G. Field of Des Moines:

> At the instance of the coroner, I examined the body of John Rafferty today in connection with Dr. Wiley. There were a number of bruises on the chin, left side, and back of the neck and chest. Also on the small of the back on the left side, and at and below the left knee. On the back part of the right leg was a deep laceration, and a contused wound extending from the inside of the knee backward and upward about eight inches. The neck was fractured at the fourth vertebra, which injury was the immediate cause of death. The wound upon the leg had been caused by some rough, dull-edged instrument like the edge of a board, which had either fallen against him or he had fallen against it. There were no indications of gun-shot wounds. The bruises had been made about the same instant, and before life was extinct. They were all probably due to the fact of the train having been thrown from the track.[5]

The Pinkerton Detective Agency, basing its findings upon descriptions given by passengers, charged the James-Younger Gang with the crime. Newspapers across the country reviled Jesse as a merciless outlaw, causing the railroad companies to band together. They turned to Allan Pinkerton to protect their trains and put the James-Younger Gang behind bars.[6]

Pinkerton was often credited with having a third sense, an ability to identify guilty parties of crimes long before police investigators were able to come up with alleged names. He laughed at the notion he had mystical

Allan Pinkerton. (Courtesy Library of Congress)

117

powers, but credited his talent on experience. He later told an audience that "each criminal, has his or her marked, personal technique that gives them away every time. On reading a telegraphic newspaper report of a large or small robbery, with the aid of my vast records and great personal experience and familiarity with these matters, I can at once tell the character of the work, and then, knowing the names, history, habits, and quite frequently, the rendezvous of men doing that type of work, am able to determine, with almost unerring certainty, not only the very parties who committed the robberies, but also what disposition they are likely to make of their plunder, and at what points they may be hiding."

Pinkerton and his sons, having made the pursuit of criminals a professional business, took their results directly to the business public, educating them on the types of foe they faced. In the 1870s, 1880s and 1890s, Pinkerton spokespeople, usually William or Robert, offered

William Allan Pinkerton, 1846-1923, full-length portrait, seated, at desk in office. Courtesy Library of Congress.

Pinkerton Detective Agency. (Courtesy Library of Congress)

advice and preventive measures to banks, railroads, shipping offices, mail services, and other enterprises that dealt with the handling and movement of money. The Pinkerton National Detective Agency became, in sort, a teaching tool for many large city law bureaus which looked upon them as the idyllic tone of law enforcement.

Both police and business kept in touch with Pinkerton for consultation. The communication was a two-way street, for Pinkerton effected a continual flow of information to these entities in forms of wanted posters, mug shots, felons' identification cards, and pamphlets for securing such and such a business against break-ins, hold-ups, and confidence games.

The former Civil War guerillas-turned-gunmen Jesse and Frank James found the Pinkertons especially vexing. Their gang's greatest strength was the backing they received by their own southern Missouri populace. Well into the 1870s, it still rankled that the North had won the war and Missourians saw their Jesse as a modern-day Robin Hood fighting the wealthy Yankee bankers and rail men tooth and nail. The "Pinks" were considered the tools of the tycoons and were received with closed mouths when on the trail in those parts. Despite day-to-night manhunts—rides in which Allan Pinkerton himself often took part—they continued to lose the James boys, even on the flat, Iowa prairie.[7]

On August 6th, a man in Carlinville, Illinois, who had refused to give his name, was arrested by the authorities on suspicion of being one of the train robbers.[8] Two weeks later, a man named Henry Lyon, also known as "Dublin," was arrested in Omaha as a possible suspect in the robbery. Lyon hailed from the West Coast and was said to be quite wealthy, possessing a great deal of money and an interest in a San Francisco gambling house valued at $75,000.[9]

Arthur McCoy, believed to have been one of the robbers, was also from the Pacific Coast and had been implicated in a Wells Fargo stagecoach robbery in California, which netted the crooks $30,000. Lyon was a friend of McCoy and had put up money to get him out of the scrape. Within the past month, Lyon had corresponded with Mrs. McCoy and, learning that she was having financial difficulties, had sent her a draft for $100. When law officials learned of Lyon's relationship with the McCoy family, they believed he might lead them to the whereabouts and capture of the gang.

A search of Lyon's room on Farnham Street turned up other letters penned by Mrs. McCoy. Lyon was placed on $5,000 bail for his appearance at a preliminary examination which had been postponed until some necessary papers arrived from Iowa.

In September, a special dispatch was received in St. Louis stating that the Iowa train robbers had been moving about western Missouri and were all together again, except for McCoy. Detectives had information that the gang was planning another bank robbery once they were joined by McCoy. Special officers began watching certain banks closely, suspecting they were targeted for the raid.[10]

Local authorities also received a special dispatch from Jefferson City warning them that the gang was at that time in Clay County and was threatening to burn out certain parties who had been active in efforts to arrest them. Governor Woodson was reported to have declared that if the local authorities and citizens did not exhibit a stronger disposition to arrest them, he would send an armed force after them.

Since the holdup, several small southern and central Iowa towns claimed sightings of the James-Younger Gang as well. John Corridan, a member of the well-organized early law enforcement group the Union Horse Company, had tracked down many horse thieves and criminals around Hinkletown beginning in 1869. According to Corridan, the James Gang camped on Corridan land to the north of Kinross. Corridan claimed that Jesses James and his notorious bunch of outlaws were passing through the area when they reportedly stopped over for the night.

He remembered them making camp a short distance east of the Corridan home. According to Corridan, one of the gang slipped into
Wellman for a haircut and a shave.[11]

Another sighting took place in Greene Valley, one mile east of
Hinkletown:

> Sadly enough, there were a number of thieves in Greene Valley.
> One Sunday the F.M. Berry family returned home from church only
> to notice some strange men by one of their log cabins. Being very
> hospitable, they invited these men in for dinner. Just as they were
> preparing to sit down to eat, the sheriff from Marengo arrived and
> arrested the guests; the men were a group of horse thieves.
>
> There were numerous other bands of horse thieves around. A
> group of men who called themselves "the Vigilantes" was organized
> to protect the civilians and their property. The captain of these
> Vigilantes was William Popham of Yankee Lane. It was reported to
> Mr. Popham that the thieves were operating around Greene Valley
> but had their headquarters in North English or Millersburg. A Mr.
> Johnson and a Mr. Grimm both reported seeing suspicious looking
> men near Yankee Lane. Upon investigation they discovered these
> men had their camp near Greene Valley. Soon Mr. Johnson and Mr.
> Grimm missed some good horses. Mr. Popham and Mr. Grimm
> went in pursuit of the thieves, but lost their trail in some heavy tim-
> ber near Millersburg. They questioned a Mr. McCarthy, who said
> they had gone to Saint Joseph, Missouri. Mr Grimm and Mr.
> Popham then split up; Mr. Grimm followed them, and Mr. Popham
> went ahead on a train to head them off. A little after sun-up the
> next day, Mr. Grimm captured the thieves as they were attempting
> to trade off the stolen horses. Mr. Grimm turned them over to offi-
> cers who returned them to Iowa County for trial. While waiting to
> be tried, the thieves broke out of jail, never to be captured again. It
> is believed that the horse thieves in this area were a part of the
> famous, law-breaking Jesse James Gang.[12]

Still another came from Fairview:

> The Billy Hull place was a busy one. There was always a lot of
> work and a lot of people would come and go. One evening an able
> looking young man rode in on a lame horse. He asked if he could
> stay until his horse's leg healed. . . . One morning he was gone, leav-

ing a note of thanks and wishing them well. About two weeks later, William came home from where ever he had been, carrying a newspaper he had picked up. In it was a picture of their late guest and an account of a train robbery in which he had taken part and the surmise that he had not come off Scott free. It was Jesse James. No matter what others might have said or thought, the Hull Boy's always had a good word for Jesse.[13]

Another unconfirmed robbery occurred on January 15, 1874. Frank and Jesse James, Cole and Jim Younger and Clell Miller reportedly robbed the Concord Stagecoach on the road near Malvern and Hot Springs, Arkansas, of $4,000. The bandits hid in the brush about five miles east of Hot Springs. When the coach lumbered along, bearing fourteen passengers, Frank James emerged and commanded the driver to halt. The passengers were lined up and searched.

According to the story, one of the passengers had a Southern accent. "Were you in the Confederate army?" inquired one of the highwaymen. "I was," replied the passenger. "Name your regiment, company and colonel." The passenger obeyed. "So was I in the Confederate army," related the robber. "I served under General Jo Shelby of Missouri." He handed the passenger's watch and wallet back. "We never rob Southerners," he said.

Built by Abbott, Downing and Company, the Concord stagecoach was used extensively in the west due to its design in addition to being exported to Australia and Africa. The original basic model had a twelve-foot wheel base and weighed in the vicinity of 2,100 pounds. The coach itself rode on twin thorough-braces made out of rawhide strips which made a three-inch thick leather spring. The undercarriage was typically painted bright yellow, but the coach body color was the purchaser's choice. Typical colors were scarlet red and green. The door window was glazed but the side windows were unglazed. Canvas or leather curtains hung above each window which could be rolled down during bad weather. Plush interiors usually had three upholstered bench seats that allowed twelve passengers to ride inside. It was possible for passengers to ride up on top of the coach, and it is known of at least one coach that had a bench seat on the back of the stagecoach.

The gang decided to engineer another train robbery on January 31, 1874. Frank and Jesse James, Cole, John, and Bob Younger, Clell and Ed Miller, Jim Reed, and Jim Cummins robbed the Iron Mountain Railroad near Gad's Hill, Missouri, of $22,000. After taking over the station, the robbers placed the station master and others under guard and set the semaphore signal for stop so the southbound train from St. Louis would halt at Gad's Hill.[14]

When the train topped the grade, Engineer Bill Wetton knew something was amiss. He spotted a crowd of men, women, and children huddled around a large bonfire, and even more alarming, someone had opened the sidetrack, and a man was standing on the station platform waving a red flag. The train slowly switched off of the main track onto the siding.[15]

Three masked men crawled out from under the station platform and another appeared at the opposite side of the track. Conductor Chauncey Alford found himself facing the muzzle of a cocked navy revolver. Two of the bandits rushed forward and removed engineer Wetton and fireman Campbell from the train. Conductor Alford later told the press: "Some of the passengers and trainmen rushed out upon the platforms, and others put their heads out of the windows, to see what the trouble was; the fifth masked man ran along the side of the cars, and with a pistol in each hand, shouting that myself and the engineer were held as hostages for the passengers' good behavior, and if anyone attempted to fire we would be shot."[16]

This story was widely circulated by friends of the Jameses and the Youngers, who said that the outlaws were simply avenging the South by their robberies. However, they did frequently rob Southerners. Most of the activities were in Missouri, which had been chiefly Southern in sympathy.[17]

The Pinkerton detectives had been hired to capture the Jameses and the Youngers, but thus far they had enjoyed little success. But in

1874 the tide was beginning to turn. During the James-Younger Gang robbery of the Iron Mountain Railroad, Jesse James, as usual, could not resist a joke. When the bandits had completed their haul, obtaining about $5,000, one of the outlaws handed a train crew man a sheet of paper on which was written, all ready for newspaper publication, this brief account of the robbery:

> The most daring robbery on record—the southbound train on the Iron Mountain Railroad—was stopped here this evening by five heavily armed men and robbed of _____ dollars. The robbers arrived at the station a few minutes before the arrival of the train and arrested the station agent and put him under guard, then threw the train on the switch. The robbers were all large men, none of them under six feet tall. They were all masked, and started in a southerly direction after they had robbed the train. They were all mounted on fine blooded horses. There is a hell of an excitement in this part of the country.

Jesse's report was accurate enough in describing the excitement. Detectives and posse men combed the underbrush all around Gads Hill, where the robbery took place.

While the Post Office Department and the express company's detectives worked around the clock on the Gads Hill robbery, the governor of Missouri offered a $10,000 reward, the governor of Arkansas $2,500, and the Post Office Department $5,000—a total of $17,500 for the capture of the robbers, dead or alive. This staggering amount was such an incentive that probably a hundred amateurs in the detective business started for various parts of western and southwestern Missouri in search of those whom they supposed capable of committing the robbery. A few of these amateurs succeeded in finding the trail westward from Shannon County, and followed the robbers, before the regular detectives from Little Rock, St. Louis, and Chicago took over.[18]

The outlaws were eventually cornered, and took up a defensive position in the ravines of Rush Mountain, in St. Clair County, about 200 miles west of Gads Hill. A special detective employed by the Iron

Mountain Railroad Company visited the site, and "met with rough treatment." He found that the gang had hidden in the woods, and on approaching the robbers' lair, a sentinel holding a couple of revolvers forced him to halt. The detective was disarmed, his rifle and revolver confiscated, and he was searched thoroughly by the gunman, who tried to ascertain what had brought him into the woods. Luckily for the detective, there was no evidence upon him of a detective nature.

After the search he was ordered to leave the vicinity by a certain road or be shot. Several of the settlers near the hiding place reported to him that this gang would not allow anyone to go through the woods and ravine where they were.

The Pinkerton detectives knew that the Youngers had relatives in St. Clair County, Missouri, near Monegaw Springs. On March 15, 1874, Pinkerton agents Louis Lull and James Wright rode with Osceola, Missouri, Deputy Sheriff Edwin Daniels in search of the Youngers. John and James Younger, concealed in the upper story of a farmhouse, listened to the detectives asking for directions from some of their friends. Then the Youngers followed the Pinkerton men.[19]

Near Roscoe, Missouri, the Pinkertons encountered John and Jim Younger in the road. John saw them and told them to stop. Wright took off, and Jim shot his hat off as he kept on riding away. Lull and Daniels tried to pass themselves off as cattle buyers, but Lull's British Tranter revolver was the giveaway. They were too well armed to be what they claimed, and the Youngers knew better.[20]

John waved a double-barreled shotgun at the pair, and, sensing a fight, Lull pulled out a Smith and Wesson No. 2 revolver and shot John through the neck, which triggered a blast from his shotgun hitting Lull in the shoulder. Daniels caught the other barrel and fell, dying.

Lull took off and the mortally wounded John Younger gave chase, catching up with him after the detective had ridden under a low -hanging tree branch. John fired twice at the detective, the second shot striking him in the chest. John started to ride back to his brother but fell out the saddle dead. Jim took his brother home to bury him. Lull died several weeks later.

The *New York Times* described the killings:

> Yesterday, President Allen, of the Iron Mountain Railroad, received
> a telegram from Osceola, [Missouri], to the effect that on last Monday
> a couple of detectives made a forced march on the place where the
> robbers were secreted, and got into a desperate fight, which lasted sev-
> eral hours. In the fight two detectives were killed and one severely
> wounded, but no names were given. One of the gang was killed, name-
> ly John Younger, one of the famous Younger brothers, who have been
> daring bushwhackers in Missouri for several years, and are supposed
> to have been implicated in the Iowa train robbery last September. John
> was about twenty-eight years of age, five feet ten inches high, weight
> nearly 200 pounds, and was of a repulsive appearance. He was born
> in Cass County, Missouri, and during the late Civil War was in the
> Southern militia of Missouri, then in Quantrell's [sic] band, and after-
> ward served under General Shelby. His home was always in the
> woods, and he was thoroughly posted in the details of the country
> south of the Missouri River.[21]

After the death of John Younger, the remainder of the band continued to lead a charmed life. The Jameses and the Youngers appeared
out of nowhere and disappeared into the nowhere. Another Pinkerton
man was mysteriously killed, but there was no proof that the Jameses or
the Youngers committed the crime.

In April of 1874, the boys were credited with robbing a stagecoach near Austin, Texas, of $3,000, although they may have had noth-
ing to do with the holdup. Jesse was in Kansas City about this time on
a very important personal matter although he was seen by an old friend
in Galveston shortly afterwards. The acquaintance later told the press:

> Not many days ago I saw the celebrated Jesse W. James in the city
> of Galveston [Texas], talked with him, was introduced to his wife,
> and recognized in her an old acquaintance of Jackson County—a
> lady whom I had known both before and since the war, and one
> who had been of immense service to the Southern guerrillas when
> they were operating upon the border in 1862 and 1863.
> I had a long talk with Jesse. He was waiting for a vessel bound
> for Mexico, when it was his intention to go with his wife to Vera

Cruz, and from there into the interior and take him a farm. Frank was with him, and they appeared to have many friends and acquaintances in Galveston. Jesse gave me some interesting items concerning his marriage, and told me that it was his intention to keep the matter a secret as long as he could, but that before he left home the event had been talked of much, both in Kansas City and Clay County, and so now that as he was going to leave the country in a few days, he would give all the particulars concerning it . . . "On the 23d of April, 1874, I was married to Miss Zee Mimms, of Kansas City, and at the house of a mutual friend there. . . . We had been engaged for nine years . . ."[22]

In early September, the James-Younger Gang was accused of committing a bold highway robbery near Lexington, Missouri, in broad daylight, and in sight of several hundred persons. According to the press, "The perpetrators of this latest Missouri outrage were the notorious James brothers, Frank and Jesse, and the two 'Younger Boys.' These rough-riders are fair specimens of the class of ruffians who, having unwillingly surrendered at the close of the war, have since been engaged in committing all sorts of outrages from chicken-stealing to bank-stealing."[23]

About six o'clock, as the stagecoach had crossed the ferry and was approaching the railroad depot with eight passengers, three masked horsemen dashed out of the woods, brandishing revolvers. One stopped the coach's horses and sat at their heads while the other two thrust their heavy army revolvers into the windows and threatened instant death to any one who resisted.

One of them, who afterward proved to be Frank James, dismounted, while his brother Jesse held his horse and stood guard. Frank then ordered all the male passengers to get out and hold up their hands. . . . The command was promptly obeyed, and in a trice eight very disconsolate looking gentlemen were ranged in a row along the roadside, with their sixteen hands held high in the air. . . . Meanwhile another member of the gang rode off to a party who were strolling on the bank of the river near by, and ordered them to come up to the omnibus and fall into line. . . . Among these was a young lady of Lexington, who has known the James and Younger families for many years, and who

127

had placed Frank James under obligations by nursing him when he was wounded during the war. When she reached the omnibus this chivalric defender of the lost cause was just in the act of taking a watch and chain from one of the passengers, whereat the maiden spake: "Why, Frank James, I'm astonished to see you have come down to such small work. I thought you never did anything except on a big scale." He shook hands with her cordially, and said: "Well, I am a little ashamed of it myself. It's the first time we ever stooped to such small game. But," he added, "you needn't call names quite so loud here." The young lady then asked him to give Singleton [sic] back his watch. "Why," he (James) said, "is this man any kin to you?" She answered that he was, and she didn't want him robbed. James promptly handed the watch to her, but kept the chain, which is a very handsome and costly one. "No," she exclaimed, "give back the chain, too. I won't have part if I can't get all." After some little demurring, he returned both watch and chain; and, at her request, gave up another gentleman's watch, which he had confiscated before she arrived. All this goes to show that your true Missouri bushwhacker is a high-toned scoundrel, not altogether devoid of "honah, sah," and susceptible to the gentle and persuasive tones of lovely woman. But there are limits to his generous nature, for a little later, when Mr. James was stripping off another gentleman's fine coat and vest, the young lady said: "Oh, Frank, don't take that man's clothes. Your mother would be grieved to death if she knew how you are doing; I nursed you when you were wounded during the war, and now I believe I ought to have let you die." He rather sadly replied: "It's a pity you didn't," but went on with the disrobing process, saying: "I need good clothes myself, and mine will do for him to go over to town in." The told proceeds of this bold robbery were only about $250, so that we may expect to hear of another raid soon.[24]

Frank and Jesse denied any participation in the stage robbery, and it is highly doubtful they were involved in a crime of such slim pickings.

On December 7, 1874, the Tishimingo Savings Bank of Corinth, Mississippi, was stripped of $5,000 by at least four robbers. Two men entered the bank brandishing knives instead of revolvers while two accomplices waited outside. During the holdup, the cashier was slashed across the forehead by one of the knife-wielding bandits. Cole Younger was later identified as one of the bandits, but the holdup was likely another copycat crime perpetrated by another gang. The James-Younger Gang used guns, not knives, in their holdups, and few people in Mississippi had any idea what Cole Younger looked like.[25]

Five men robbed another train, the Kansas Pacific Railroad, near Muncie, Kansas, on December 8, 1874, the very next day after the Corinth Mississippi job. The men ordered some section hands to load the track with railroad ties. Once the rail workers completed their task, they were tied up in a shed, and the robbers flagged down the train.

As soon as the train came to a halt, the crewmen were commanded to decouple the baggage and express cars. The bandits, believed to have been Frank and Jesse James, Cole and Bob Younger, and Clell Miller, worked quickly and escaped with $30,000. Jesse later issued a denial, insisting that Frank and he had not been involved in the train robbery.

Bud McDaniels, the brother of Ed McDaniels, was arrested in Kansas City a few days following the robbery on a charge of public drunkenness. When he was searched, the sheriff found over a thousand dollars and several pieces of jewelry in his pockets. The jewelry was believed to be some that had been taken from the safe on the Kansas Pacific train robbed by the bandits. Charges were filed against him, but he escaped jail only to be killed by a farmer who had tried to capture him in a field.

By 1875, Allan Pinkerton had become infuriated by the agency's failure to arrest even a single member of the gang. The agency had been hired in 1871 by several bankers and railroad owners to track down the deadly James-Younger Gang. In January 1875 a Pinkerton agent, Jack Ladd, was posing as a field hand at work on the farm across the road from the James Farm. The farm, belonging to neighbor Dan Askew, served as a hideout for the Pinkerton spy. One afternoon, the agent thought he spotted Jesse and Frank at the farm house, though actually the brothers were miles away.

Missouri sympathy for the bandits peaked early in 1875. On the night of January 26th, six Pinkerton detectives, three of whose colleagues had been gunned down by the Jameses and Youngers in recent encounters, crept up to the James-Samuel home and tossed a smoke bomb into the house, in an attempt to lure them out. The Pinkertons later claimed the device was a flare lamp.

According to the report of the Adjutant General of Missouri, Dr. Samuels pushed the flaming device into the fireplace. He thought it was a turpentine ball, and it exploded, killing eight-year-old Archie Samuel and mangling Mrs. Zerelda Samuel's right arm so badly that it had to be amputated below the elbow. Neither Frank nor Jesse were present. On January 28th, Archie Samuel was laid to rest at the Kearney Cemetery. Zerelda, overcome with grief, did not attend. Funeral services were performed by the Reverend Thomas H. Graves.

The *Kansas City Times* and *Liberty Tribune* were among the first newspapers in the country to carry the story:

> As regards the throwing of the bomb into the house to destroy the innocent, we enter our solemn protest. The act we regard as not only indefensible but cowardly and barbarous. If the James boys have violated the laws capture and punish them to the full extent of the law, but do not punish the innocent for their acts. Much of this information was obtained from Captain John S. Groom, the obliging sheriff of Clay County, who was on the premises soon after the occurrence.
>
> Tuesday morning about half-past one o'clock Mr. Samuel, the stepfather of the James boys, awoke, and found Mrs. Samuels in the same condition. He said he heard a noise in the kitchen and thought he smelled fire. At this time he got out of bed and went out of the door of his room to get into the kitchen. When he got outside he discovered the west end of the kitchen to be on fire. The house is log, weather-boarded. Mr. Samuels at once went around to the fire and commenced to tear off the boards.
>
> Mrs. Samuel in the meantime had come from her room with her stepchildren—Johnnie, [fourteen]; Frannie, [twelve]; and Archie, [nine]. When she entered the kitchen she found Charlotte, her "Negro woman," there with her three children. They, too, had been wakened by the commotion and the fire.
>
> Mrs. Samuel saw a quilt on the bed afire. This she tore off and threw out of doors. She then discovered something on the floor

which she took to be a turpentine ball. It was on fire. She attempted to pick it up, but found it too heavy. She then tried to push it into the fire with her foot but failed.

At this moment Mr. Samuel came in, having extinguished the flames, and he tried to kick the supposed ball into the fire, but failed. He then took a shovel and threw it into the fireplace. As he did this it exploded. It was a bomb, or more correctly speaking, what is known as a hand-grenade, a ball about one inch in thickness and lined with wrought iron.

As it exploded a portion of it struck Mr. Samuel on the right side of the head but failed to knock him senseless; another portion struck Mrs. Samuel a few inches above the right wrist, shattering all that portion of her arm; another portion struck the little boy (Archie), under the third rib, on the left side, and penetrated his bowels. Still another piece struck the servant on the head, but did no serious injury. We are not advised as to whether any additional discoveries have been made. The details of Monday night's work are shrouded in mystery.[26]

E. Price Hall, who witnessed the bombing, was interviewed by author Homer Croy, who was at that time researching his book, *Jesse James Was My Neighbor*. Hall was eighty-seven years old at the time of the interview with Croy.

At the time of the explosion Hall was a boy, [wrote Croy]. His father's farm and the James farm adjoined. The Halls were awakened by the commotion and screaming. Young Price hurried to the James house to find out what it was all about.
"When I arrived there the stench was still in the house," said Mr. Hall. "Mrs. Samuel's hand was still clinging to her arm by a shred of skin. Dr, Samuel had boiled water and was preparing to cut the pieces of skin. Little Archie was lying in a cot nearby groaning. A fragment of the bomb had been driven into his side, and his life-blood was running out in spite of all his father could do. Dr. Samuel was trying to wait on both at once. Archie continued to groan and his voice got weaker. At dawn he died. When he was going out, his mother came and stood by his cot, sobbing—not for her arm but for her boy. It was the most dreadful scene I ever saw.
"Shortly after dawn I went out to explore the yard. There had been a light snow and there were the tracks of the men. I followed

the tracks a short way and found where the men had sat down on a log. I found the pistol one of them had lost. On the handle were stamped the letters, 'P.G.G.' This stood for Pinkerton's Government Guard. Allan Pinkerton had organized the United States Secret Service and he had official government standing. We followed the tracks to the railroad and saw where the men had stood waiting for the train. They had enough authority to stop the train. Then they got on."[27]

Other contemporary newspaper reports of the time simply reported the device as a "bomb" and the public was incensed. However, the public wasn't the only ones who were angry. On April 12, 1875, Dan Askew, the neighbor who had sheltered Jack Ladd, the Pinkerton spy, was found with a bullet in his brain at his home. Later in the same month, Jack Ladd was also found shot and killed.

On May 13, 1875, Frank and Jesse James, Cole and Bob Younger were accused of robbing a store in Clinton, Missouri, for $300. On September 1, 1875, the gang ventured far from the familiar hills of Missouri when four members of the outlaw gang—Frank James, Cole Younger, Thompson McDaniels, and Tom Webb—rode into the town of Huntington, West Virginia. Moving on up Third Avenue, they rode directly to the brick building near Twelfth Street, the Bank of Huntington. Frank James, followed by another man, entered the bank about one o'clock. Each man, displaying a pair of revolvers, ordered cashier R.T. Oney to hand over all the money. After the cashier complied at the point of a revolver and reluctantly handed the robbers twelve thousand dollars, Frank bade the cashier a courteous good afternoon, walked out of the bank, and rode away with the other riders.[28]

A pursuing party, comprised of a score of local citizens, followed the bandits through the bottoms of Ohio into Kentucky, where the bandits separated and lost their pursuers along the trail. One of the members of the gang, Thompson McDaniels, was later shot and killed by posse men near Pikeville, Kentucky. Later in Tennessee, the bandits met and divided the money between them.

During an attempted robbery in Tennessee a few days later, Tom Webb was apprehended with five thousand dollars stolen from the Bank of Huntington on his person. Although the money was returned to the bank, the remainder was never found.

> They seemed to take an artistic pleasure in the speed and certainty in which they dispatched their victims and the object of it all was robbery and theft, [proclaimed a Huntington newspaper editorial years later]. In the course of their scoundrelism they came to the city of Huntington, then in the experimental struggle of its first development, and robbed the only bank there of a large sum of money. . . . And just to the extent they are admired or tolerated by the public, will they be attractive examples of human depravity for every embryo criminal here or elsewhere. Had they a real spark of manhood or contrition they would seek the deepest seclusion for such years as are yet given them and not seek to recall to the public attention a chapter of villains wherein they were the chief actors.[29]

Frank gave an interview to the same Huntington newspaper in response to the editorial and denied any participation in the earlier raid:

> I was not in the gang that robbed the Bank of Huntington on the fourth of September 1875, nor have I ever been in this town before in my life. While I know that I have always been accused of robbing the Huntington Bank of twelve thousand dollars, and while I was warned only a few days ago, still I never had anything to do with the robbery of the bank here, nor did I know anything of the affair until I heard of it afterwards.
> I was at my home in St. Joe, Missouri, at the time. I did not know where the other members of the James band were and knew nothing of any plans to rob the Huntington bank. The first I heard of the affair was when I heard that the authorities believed that I was the leader of the band that committed the robbery and were looking for me on that and other charges.[30]

WHILE THE JAMESES ROBBED THEIR WAY across the East, a group of Indians in an act of defiance left their reservations out West in protest of white settlers continuing to invade their territory. They gathered in

Montana, under several chiefs including Sitting Bull. Two previous attempts to force them back to their reservations had failed.[31]

The army dispatched a force headed by Lieutenant-Colonel George A. Custer. On June 25, 1876, Custer located a group of Sioux braves and, ignoring his orders to wait, decided to attack before the party could alert the main group at their camp. First Custer sent a battalion under Captain Frederick Benteen to prevent an escape through the upper valley of the Little Big Horn River, and a group under Major Marcus Reno was sent to pursue the group, across the river, and then charge the Indian village. Their goal was to strike the Indian camp at the north and south ends at the same time. Reno's squadron of 175 men attacked at the north end, but found they were up against a much larger force than they had anticipated.

George Herendon, a civilian signed under Reno's command later recalled: "[Custer] advanced about a mile from the ford to a line of timber on the right and dismounted his men to fight on foot. The horses were sent into the timber, and the men forward on the prairie and advanced toward the Indians. The Indians, mounted on ponies, came across the prairie and opened a heavy fire on the soldiers. After skirmishing for a few minutes Reno fell back to his horses in the timber. The Indians moved to his left and rear, evidently with the intention of cutting him off from the ford."[32]

Soon after Reno attacked, he and his soldiers found themselves in a battle they could not win, and there was no hope of reinforcements from Custer's command. He quickly called off the charge before his men could be slaughtered.

> The command headed for the ford, pressed closely by Indians in large numbers, [stated Herendon], and at every moment the rate of speed was increased, until it became a dead run for the ford. The Sioux, mounted on their swift ponies, dashed up by the side of the soldiers and fired at them, killing both men and horses. Little resistance was offered, and it was a complete rout to the ford. I did not see the men at the ford, and do not know what took place further than a good many were killed when the command left the timber.

Just as I got out, my horse stumbled and fell and I was dismounted, the horse running away after Reno's command. I saw several soldiers who were dismounted, their horses having been killed or run away. There were also some soldiers mounted who had remained behind, I should think in all as many as thirteen soldiers, and seeing no chance of getting away, I called on them to come into the timber and we would stand off the Indians.[33]

Reno's retreat left Custer in a bad situation. He soon attacked the other end of the village, assuming Reno still had a battle going on that would keep them occupied. However since Reno's force had clearly been subdued, the large Indian force, closed in on Custer and his 210 men. Custer and all the troops under his command were killed.

Major Reno described the discovery of Custer death in his official repot of the battle:

I think it was about 10.30 a.m. when General [Alfred] Terry rode into my lines, and the fate of Custer and his brave men was soon determined by Captain Benteen proceeding to the battle-ground, and where was recognized the following officers, who were surrounded by the dead bodies of many of their men; General George Armstrong Custer, Colonel W.W. Cook, adjutant; Captains. M.W. Keogh, G.W. Yates, and T.W. Custer; First Lieutenants A.E. Smith, James Calhoun; Second Lieutenants. W.V. Reily, of the Seventh Cavalry and J.J. Crittenden, of the Twelfth Infantry, temporarily attached to this regiment. The bodies of Lieutenant J.E. Porter and Second Lieutenants H.M. Harrington and J.G. Sturgis, Seventh Cavalry, and Assistant. Surgeon G.W. Lord, were not recognized; but there is every reasonable probability they were killed. It was more certain that the column of five companies with Custer had been killed.[34]

ON JULY 7, 1876, FRANK AND JESSE JAMES, Cole, Jim and Bob Younger, Charlie Pitts, Bill Chadwell, and Hobbs Kerry robbed the Missouri Pacific Railroad near Otterville, Missouri, for $15,000. Whenever a train robbery or a bank cracking operation transpired in any portion of the United States, the James and Younger boys received all the censure. They were the first names mentioned, and all the blame, all the criminality was centered upon them.[35] Kerry was arrested after spending some of his take, and he readily identified his accomplices.

According to Kerry, his role had been to watch the horses while the other men robbed the train. He was a raw recruit and considered by most to be a "crack-brained simpleton." After making a full confession and naming every participant in the holdup, he got off with only two years in the penitentiary.[36]

The Jameses were a hot item to law officials following a train holdup at Rocky Cut near Otterville, Missouri, on the night of July 8, 1876, so the home was under observation by the law. An indignant Jesse wrote a letter of denial to the editor of the *Kansas City Times*, mailing his letter from Oak Grove, Kansas, on August 14.[37]

Zerelda James, mother of Frank and Jesse, had married Dr. Reuben Samuel on September 26, 1855, four years after the death of her first husband, Robert James, and three years following the accidental death of her second, Benjamin Simms. The brothers were in constant touch with their mother, who aided in their concealment.[38]

## Notes

[1]Letter addressed mysteriously only to "My Dear Friend." Marley Brant, *The Illustrated History of the James-Younger Gang*, Montgomery, Elliott & Clark Publishing, 1997, pp. 108-109.

[2]Donald L. Gilmore, "When the James Gang Ruled the Rails," *Wild West Magazine*, August 2000; *St. Louis Dispatch*, January 1874.

[3]Cole Younger, *The Story of Cole Younger*, St. Paul, Minnesota, Historical Society Press, 2000, pp. 62-63.

[4]Harry Sinclair Drago, *Outlaws on Horseback*, Lincoln and London, University of Nebraska Press, 1964, p. 55.

[5]*Daily Iowa State Register*, July 23, 1873.

[6]Harry Sinclair Drago, *Outlaws on Horseback*, pp. 55-56.

[7]Alan Axelrod, Alan, *The War Between the Spies*, New York, The Atlantic Monthly Press, 1992; Mark M. Boatner III, *Civil War Dictionary*, New York, Vintage Books/Random House, Inc., 1991; James D. Horan, *Desperate Men*, New York, Doubleday & Co., 1962; Sigmund A. Lavine, *Allan Pinkerton—America's First Private Eye*, New York, Dodd, Mead &

Co., 1963; Ben Macintyre, *The Napoleon of Crime*, New York, Delta Books, 1997; Jay Robert Nash, *Western Lawmen & Outlaws*, New York, Da Capo Press, 1994; Time-Life Books, editors of *The Wild West*, Alexandria, Virginia: Time-Life Books.

[8]*New York Times*, August 7, 1873.

[9]*New York Times*, August 21, 1873.

[10]*New York Times*, September 9, 1873.

[11]Scott Romine and Steve Miller, *A History of Kinross, Iowa*, 1979.

[12]Donna Miller, *A Glimpse of Greene Valley*, 1964.

[13]William Hull Family Biography.

[14]Carl W. Breihan, *The Complete and Authentic Life of Jesse James*, New York, Frederick Fell, Inc., Publishers, pp. 114-115.

[15]Ronald H. Beights, *Jesse James and the First Missouri Train Robbery*, Gretna, Pelican Publishing Company, 2002, pp. 59-61.

[16]Ibid.

[17]*St. Clair County Courier*, May 27, 1976

[18]*New York Times*, March 23, 1874.

[19]*St. Clair County Courier*, May 27, 1976

[20]Ted P. Yeatman, *Frank and Jesse James*, pp. 116-117.

[21]*New York Times*, March 23, 1874.

[22]*St. Louis Dispatch*, June 9, 1874

[23]*New York Times*, September 10, 1874.

[24]Ibid.

[25]Marley Brant, *The Illustrated History of the James-Younger Gang*.

[26]*Liberty Tribune*, January 29, 1875; *Kansas City Times*, January 31, 1875.

[27]Homer Croy, *Jesse James Was My Neighbor*, New York, Duell, Sloan and Pearce, 1949, pp. 90-91.

[28]*Huntington Advertiser*, August 10, 1903.

[29]*Huntington Advertiser*, August 3, 1903.

[30]*Huntington Advertiser*, August 10, 1903.

[31]*Chicago Tribune*, undated article by Max Rothstein.

[32]Ibid.

[33]Ibid.

[34]Ibid.

[35]*Kansas City Times*, August 18, 1876

[36]Robertus Love, *The Rise and Fall of Jesse James*, Lincoln and London, University of Nebraska Press, 1990, p. 187.

[37]Carl W. Breihan, *Outlaws of the Old West*, New York, Bonanza Books, 1957, p. 31.

[38]Carl Breihan, *The Day Jesse James Was Killed*, New York, Bonanza Books, No Date Given, p. 29-31.

*Chapter Six*

# Vanishing Act

*"The attack was made on Wednesday night by Sheriff Groom, of Clay County (Missouri), and four men. It was very dark and rainy. The posse went to the home of the boys, four miles from Fearney [sic], knowing they were there. Frank was seen, and, as he saw the posse about the same time, he fired a shot in the air, as a signal for Jesse. The sheriff and one man fired at Frank, without effect, when he returned the fire, hitting the tree behind which the sheriff was concealed. The boys then mounted their horses and then got away, shouting, 'come on, you --- ---.'"*
—*Faribault Democrat*[1]

I N JUNE 1876, JAMES BUTLER (WILD BILL) HICKOK joined the throng of fortune seekers arriving in Deadwood, Dakota Territory. With him on his Deadwood adventure were "acquaintances," Colorado Charlie Utter, Martha "Calamity Jane" Canary, and an assorted lot of shifty drifters of no other distinction whatsoever. Hickok had recently married a plain but sturdy circus performer named Agnes Thatcher. He left her after a two-week Cincinnati honeymoon to seek his fortune. In Deadwood he had one aim: to relieve well-healed miners of their gold dust at the gaming tables and provide for his new bride.[2]

On August 5, 1876, Deadwood's only newspaper reported the following tragedy: "On Wednesday about [three] o'clock the report stated that J.B. Hickok (Wild Bill) was killed. On repairing to the hall of Nuttall and Mann, it was ascertained that the report was too true. We found the remains of Wild Bill lying on the floor. The murderer, Jack McCall, was captured after a lively chase by many of the citizens, and taken to a building at the lower end of the city, and a guard placed over him. As soon as this was accomplished, a coroner's jury was summoned, with C.H. Sheldon as foreman, who after hearing all the evidence, which was the effect that, while Wild Bill and others were at a table playing cards, Jack McCall walked in and around directly back of his victim, and when within three feet of him raised his revolver, and exclaiming, 'damn you, take that,' fired; the ball entering at the back of the head, and coming out at the centre of the right check causing instant death, reached a verdict in accordance with the above facts."[3]

But the summer of 1876, beginning with the deaths of Custer and Hickok, was to have a heavy impact on the James-Younger Gang as well, as they journeyed to Minnesota to rob the First National Bank of Northfield.[4]

The idea to venture so far north may have originated with Bill Stiles, alias Bill Chadwell, a.k.a. Bill Chadwick, alias Bill Yates, alias

Northfield street scene. (Author's collection)

139

Bill Raymond. Stiles had once lived in Monticello, Minnesota, as well as in Rice County, and knew too well the fat banks in the state, which were ripe for plucking. He was very familiar with most of the roads leading in and out of many villages in the southern part of the state.[5] Stiles had once been convicted for horse theft in Minnesota and still had relatives living in the state, including a sister who taught in one of the Cannon Falls area schools.[6] Writing frequent letters to his brother-in-law in Minneapolis, he kept himself up to date with events in the state.

Jesse was an attentive listener as Stiles told stories of the rich northern banks and easy trains to rob. According to Stiles, the farmers in the rich Minnesota rural communities couldn't identify an outlaw band if it surrounded them, and the northern banks held more money than they knew what to do with. The men told Stiles that if they could get their hands on it, they would know what to do with it.[7] Minnesota was easy pickings, according to Stiles, who claimed the gang could make off with a large haul.[8]

His knowledge of the towns, roads, the rivers and lakes, the bridges, and most importantly, the banks was tempting, but initially Jesse did not like the idea. This was unfamiliar Northern land, and the men had no friends there, nor were there any friendly blacksmiths who could shoe their horses in a hurry. In the South, there were always ex-guerrillas who would hide them out but in distant Minnesota there was only the enemy.[9] And, of course, should Stiles be killed, there would be no one who could lead them out.

Stiles, who felt Minnesota needed a "shaking up," argued that his thorough knowledge of the area would get the boys safely back. He claimed to have friends conveniently located in out-of-the-way places, reliable people who would ensure an easy retreat. He added that since the wheat harvest had just been marketed, the banks would be bursting with money. Stiles finally convinced Jesse that through his knowledge of every road and by-path into and out of the state, the men would easily make it home with the spoils.[10]

Northfield, Minnesota. (Author's collection)

First National Bank, Northfield, Minnesota. (Author's collection)

Jesse James was often considered moody; easy to get along with when things were going well but "cruel, demanding and dangerous" when they were not. Because he knew no fear, he was a natural leader, despite his often being reckless.[11] Jesse was popular with Southerners because they saw him and his gang as a means of extracting revenge on

141

First National Bank, Northfield, Minnesota. (Author's collection)

those who had supported the Union during the Civil War. There was a great deal of animosity in the South toward the banks and railroads Jesse robbed. These same institutions charged high interest rates and steep freight charges. And, of course, many Missourians knew that these same bank owners had supported the Northern cause.[12]

Numerous accounts place Jesse and the gang in Iowa just prior to the Northfield robbery. According to an 1876 resident of Woodward, Iowa, who owned a general store, an implement store, a livery stable, and two farms, the gang members stopped at his home on their journey north to Minnesota: "Jesse James and his band of about eight men stayed at the Fred Miller home in Iowa for a week. They faced the benches in the house toward the windows to see any oncoming attempt at capture. Mrs. Miller refused to cook for them unless they would say 'grace,' which they then did. They paid for the food and feed for the horses and left."[13]

When Cole Younger and Bill Stiles visited Northfield just prior to their assault, they found the bank doing big business and carrying a large amount of cash. After asking about town as to whether there were any gun shops and being told there were none, the pair stopped at the town's two hardware stores. In examining the meager stock of weapons, they came to the conclusion the citizens were incapable of stopping a would-be robbery.[14]

On September 7, 1876, Frank and Jesse James, Cole, Jim and Bob Younger, Charlie Pitts, Clell Miller and Bill Chadwell attempted to rob the First National Bank of Northfield, Minnesota. Cole Younger later recalled:

> When Miller and myself crossed over the bridge, I saw a crowd of citizens about the corners, our boys sitting there on some boxes, [claimed Cole Younger]. I remarked to Miller about the crowd and said, "Surely the boys will not go into the bank with so many people about. I wonder why they did not ride straight through the town." We were halfway across the square when we saw the three men rise and walk up the sidewalk toward the bank. Miller said: "They are going in," and I replied, "If they do the alarm will be given as sure as there's a hell, so you had better take that pipe out of your mouth."[15]

The robbery did not go well. Chadwell and Miller were killed by local citizens during the gun battle in the street that started up almost immediately, and the remaining six fled the scene with numerous wounds. In addition to the two robbers, Bank Cashier Joseph Lee Heywood was killed defending his trust, and an innocent bystander, Nicolaus Gustavson, was severely wounded and died a few days later. To top it off, the gang didn't get hardly anything.[16]

In the days following, the six outlaws divided into two groups, the James brothers separating from the rest. The three Youngers and Pitts struggled through the rain-soaked Minnesota countryside for days before finally being captured near Madelia, exactly two weeks after the robbery. Pitts was killed. A St. Louis newspaper praised the spunky Minnesotans for defeating the outlaws:

> In Missouri [the James-Younger-outlaws] rode into the towns and robbed banks in broad daylight; stopped passenger trains and, after

emptying the express safe, "went through" everybody on board the cars. In the presence of more than 10,000 people, and in broad daylight, they presented their pistols at the ticket office of the Kansas City Fair Association and forced the treasurer to hand over $10,000. They murdered officers sent to arrest them, and, despite their plundering and murders, so enlisted popular sympathy in their behalf that the reward of $25,000 for their capture remained unclaimed, though their whereabouts were well known, and, in fact, instead of hiding, they paraded themselves publicly for the admiration of their fellow Missourians. And had they remained in Missouri to the end of their lives doubtless they might with impunity have gone on with their raiding of railroad trains, and have been regarded with admiring pride by their fellow citizens of that Commonwealth. But they extended their field of operations to Minnesota, made their attack on the Northfield Bank, committed their dastardly murder of Heywood, and, to their wonderment, doubtless, they were not thereon hailed as heroic fellows who had gallantly gathered fresh laurels . . .[17]

Riding a pair of stolen grays bareback, Frank and Jesse were able to make rapid progress, and at times, they assumed the role of posse men chasing the robbers. They were able to procure food along the way and obtain information from unsuspecting farmers.[18] Word quickly spread that the brothers were heading south or west in a mad dash to reach their Missouri haven, and every community dreaded the outlaws coming their way.

On Friday night the Jameses stopped about five miles south of Lamberton, a station on the Winona and St. Peter Railroad, seventy-five miles west of Madelia. About sundown, they rode to the home of a German farmer, and producing a map of Minnesota, made extensive inquiries about the roads and rivers in the area. The farmer noticed both men suffered from leg wounds. They told the farmer they had been riding in a wagon and were injured when the wagon broke down. The farmer dressed the wounds of the older man but the younger would not show his wound. The brothers spent the night at the farm; both sleeping the full night in their clothes.[19]

The Northfield newspaper printed an extra edition and included the following "report" from the Yankton area: "The two robbers seen eight miles south of here today. The previous night they stopped a squaw to inquire of her the road. It is reported that 150 Indians are in pursuit of them to see who they are."[20]

The *Sioux City Daily News* reported: "Armed companies, we learn, are watching the different roads through Southeastern Dakota, and it is hoped that the notorious robbers may fall into some of their hands and not escape across the Missouri. If they succeed in getting across the river their chances for escape will be greatly increased. They know all of the country well from the Missouri south through to Texas."[21]

The same newspaper reported on September 21 that two men believed to be the robbers were seen about eight miles from East Orange, with a posse about two hours behind them. The posse caught up to the robbers six miles away, just as they were leaving the home of a Norwegian man named Swanson, where they had spent the night. The Jameses had told the man they were laborers in search of work, and complained of being extremely tired and lame after walking a long distance.[22]

As the posse approached, Jesse and Frank ran into a nearby barn where the owner, Andrew Shuelson, was feeding his horses. When the farmer protested the intrusion, one of the robbers held a revolver close to his eyebrows. When the coast was clear, the men rode away, crossing the Big Sioux River into Iowa. The sheriff's assistant and the Worthington party gave chase.

As the Jameses ascended a steep bluff on the opposite side of the stream, two of the posse charged. The outlaws stopped and dismounted. Several shots were fired at the two pursuers. One of the bullets struck one of the horses in the neck. The shots apparently frightened the Worthington lawman and his posse, who returned to Beloit, Iowa, for reinforcements.

The *Sioux City Daily Journal* for September 21 was quick to comment: "The sheriff from Worthington, who is here, seems to think that the robbers will make back tracks for the Sioux and strike out for the Jim River country. A large force is scattered over the prairies between the Sioux and Rock rivers, and we are waiting anxiously for tidings from them. Had these men acted promptly they could have bagged their game this morning."

The *Journal* also made references to a third robber traveling with the James brothers: "The wounded man, who was with these two up to Sunday afternoon, has not been heard from since, and, as he was then scarcely able to stand, it is supposed that he probably died or has been left somewhere along the road."

Monday afternoon, the town of Canton, Dakota Territory, was thrown into a wild state of excitement by the arrival of an eight-man posse from Worthington and Luverne. The posse had pursued the fleeing outlaws to the Sioux River, north of town. The men said the outlaws had escaped through Lyon County to Beloit, Iowa, and over to the Canton area.

Three members of the Minnesota posse, with Will Miller of Canton, started south along the Sioux River to alert the people and cut off the robbers who were fleeing southward towards the Missouri River.[23] On Tuesday morning, the balance of the Minnesota party rode off for Sioux Falls but a driving rain aided the robbers.

The *Sioux Valley News*, Canton, Dakota Territory, reported the robbers would find their way to Nebraska "where friends were waiting for them, to shelter and take care of them." Arthur Linn, the editor of the newspaper, believed the outlaws would cross into Nebraska somewhere between Sioux City, Iowa, and Springfield, Dakota Territory.

According to one account, the outlaws crossed the Missouri River at Springfield and rode south and west to Columbus, Nebraska. At this point, they sold their horses and took a train to Omaha from whence they made their way home to Missouri. Rumors circulated that they continued on to Texas, and lawmen were sent out to arrest them, but came up empty-handed.[24]

More likely, however, the fugitives may have passed through the hills of the Big Sioux River and down into Joy Hollow, where they rested in a cave. On the Broken Kettle Road south of Milnerville, Iowa, one of the robbers stopped at the Prather farm and hastily devoured a plate of food. The second man waited outside watching the road. He, too, was given a plate of food. The outlaws then rode south through Stone Park.[25]

Another report alleged the James brothers never went near Canton but stopped at the farm of Reverend Krogness, a pioneer missionary and pastor of the Norwegian Lutheran Church, a mile and a half northeast of Beloit and two miles east of Canton. After the outlaws crossed the river, Reverend Krogness saw them on the bluff, and when they asked for food and lodging, he complied. The brothers looked fatigued, and Reverend Krogness was sure they were either the Jameses or the Youngers. He chose to cooperate. In the morning, they took one of the horses belonging to the reverend, apologized for doing so, and rode off, leaving one horse behind.[26]

As the robbers departed, Mrs. Krogness went to make the bed and discovered blood stains on the sheets. Reverend Krogness quickly rode to Beloit while his son attempted to follow the robbers. Sheriff Dixon of Lincoln County organized a posse but could find no trace of the outlaws. The younger Krogness did not locate the robbers either but he did find their horse near the town of Calliope, not far from Sioux City.

There were several streams in the area that the James boys were traversing, including Big Sioux, Rock and Floyd rivers; and the West Branch of Floyd, Otter and Indian Creeks. The Big Sioux River furnished water power for mills, and was bordered in many places by groves of timber, which provided cover for the outlaws. Rock River, a tributary of the Big Sioux, was a beautiful stream, with a valley of great fertility, and like the bigger stream, small groves of native timber bordered its banks. But from the valleys along the streams, the upland prairies rose by gentle slopes, and then stretched away for miles in a succession of broad undulations.[27]

It is quite probable that by early afternoon, Jesse and Frank had crossed the Des Moines River at Swan's Ford. After purchasing bread and milk from Swan, they consumed it on horseback in the yard. According to

Swan, they were gentlemanly in their address, and asked questions about the distances to different railroads. They stated that they lived in Rock County, Minnesota, and had purchased the team on account of their size and beauty. Swan added that the two men looked like brothers, and when they departed, they left in the direction of Rock County.[28]

Sheriff McDonald and half a dozen men from Sioux City, Iowa, armed to the teeth, took the Dakota Southern train west hoping to intercept the two robbers should they turn south at the Missouri River. McDonald and his men disembarked at Elk Point and began guarding the ferries across the river. Sheriff Baker, with a contingent from Yankton, established communication with McDonald and began guarding the country between Yankton and Sioux City.[29]

"McDonald says every person one meets on the cars along the St. Paul road is loaded down to the guards with fire-arms, resembling traveling arsenals," reported the *Sioux City Daily Journal*. "The greatest excitement prevails, and armed squads are moving to and fro continually. The hundreds of men engaged in the chase appear to have no head or organized leaders, and consequently the chances of catching the fleeing ruffians are growing fainter and fainter each succeeding day."[30]

As McDonald and Baker converged on the bandits, rumors began circulating that the fugitives had been seen in both LeMars and Sioux City, Iowa; another reporting they had crossed the Missouri River and were relatively safe; while still another claimed they had stolen a pair of black horses on the Jim River, some forty to fifty miles above the Missouri River.

The McDonald-Baker force faced difficult circumstances, as reported by a local newspaper: "The boys out after the robbers yesterday had a hard time of it. It rained steadily, and the traveling must have been very laborious on their horses. The robbers labored under the same disadvantages; still our sympathy does not spread thin enough to cover them, too. We shall expect to hear soon that the party who went out yesterday have caught the robbers, or that the robbers have caught the party, either of which would be stunning news."[31]

Still another report reached Sioux City that Sheriff McDonald and his posse had caught up with the bandits on the Missouri River in Dakota Territory in an area called Texas. One was reportedly killed, the other captured. The report ripped through the city like wildfire until noon when a second report received via a reliable courier disproved the story.[32]

At noon, on Wednesday, September 25, Dr. Sidney Mosher, Sr., of Sioux City, received a call to attend Mrs. Robert Mann who lived some twenty miles northeast of the city. Mrs. Mann was urgently in need of a goiter operation, so Dr. Mosher hurried to the Broadbent livery stable and hired a horse for the trip. At Broadbent's, he discovered a gathering of local residents discussing the Northfield robbers, their subsequent flight, and the reward Minnesota Governor John S. Pillsbury had offered for their capture. Dr. Mosher then mounted a little bay and started out for the Mann farm.[33]

As he rode along, he met two men on horseback near a bluff. Thinking they were locals, he raised his hand to them and called out, inquiring about the road. But the men continued on their way as if they had not heard him. Dr. Mosher, certain the men had not heard him, patted his horse and rode up to them. The pair wheeled their horses about, drew guns from under their coats, pointed them at his head, and ordered, "Hands up." No one said a word for several minutes when the smaller of the two strangers bellowed, "Well?"

The doctor informed them he was a physician on his way to attend a patient. The smaller robber called him a liar and accused him of being a detective from St. Paul out searching for the robbers. Dr. Mosher insisted he was no robber nor a robber hunter. The shorter man searched him while the other held the prisoner at gun point. But the doctor had recently purchased the new suit he was wearing and had failed to carry identification. The robber found only a pocket medicine case and a lancet in his pockets.

When the doctor told them he was unarmed, he was told he might have companions hiding near the bluff. To prove his identity, Mosher asked the robbers to ride back to the closest farm and ask the owner to describe Dr. Sidney Mosher of Sioux City and ask if there was a Mrs. Robert Mann in the area. Supposedly, Jesse rode back to a farm and confirmed Mosher's story. The outlaws assured the doctor they would not kill him, but they would have to detain him until evening. To make sure he did not make a mad dash for freedom, they exchanged horses, giving Mosher the worst spent of their two horses.

Jesse road in the lead with Dr. Mosher behind him, and Frank brought up the rear. As they rode along, Frank talked of the escape from Northfield and their "queer code of ethics." Dr. Mosher made a casual remark about the Civil War, which enraged Jesse, who, according to the doctor, bellowed, "Damn you, Doc. I'll kill you yet."

That afternoon, they stopped at a farm house and Jesse informed the owner that he was accompanying Dr. Mosher on his way to treat Mrs. Mann. Jesse said they had had a breakdown, and the doctor desperately needed to borrow a saddle. The farmer was somewhat suspicious, but did not want to test the men's patience, so he gave up his saddle. At six o'clock in the evening, they stopped at another farm and ate some food.

It was not until evening that Dr. Mosher noticed Frank had been shot. They had ceased riding, and Frank admitted he could not easily get off his horse without help. Dr. Mosher lifted him down. Jesse asked Frank to have the doctor set his leg although the wounded outlaw made no reply. Frank, however, removed his clothing and the doctor noticed the wound was a clean shot through the fleshy part of the thigh. Jesse ordered Mosher to remove his own clothing, tossed him Frank's, and the doctor put them on. Since he was a much shorter man than Frank, he had to roll up the legs of his trousers.

When it became dark, Jesse pointed to a light in a farm house a half-mile away and told the doctor to ride toward the light and not turn around or he would kill him. As he started, he became frightened, thinking he would be shot in the back. He ran as fast as he could, but his progress was slowed by Frank's bulky coat flapping in the wind, the too-large shoes of Frank James, and the shaking of his own knees.

Entering the farm yard, a group of dogs began barking and growling. Without pausing to knock at the door of the house, he burst in to confront a woman rocking before the fire. She began shouting "Robbers." Men came running from the barn, and the woman's husband carried a shotgun in his hand. Mosher quickly told his story, and a ten-year-old boy sitting by the fire recognized him as the doctor in Sioux City.

In the morning, the same boy found the little sorrel where Dr. Mosher had left her. Too tired to graze, she had dropped down and rested all night. When the farmer took Dr. Mosher into Sioux City that morning, the boy led the sorrel from the back of the wagon. Upon reaching town, he spread the alarm. Mosher said the Jameses had frankly told him they expected to be caught, but not alive and that they would fight to the bitter end and sell their lives as dearly as possible. He also carried their message to the Sioux City banks, "that when they gave this town a call, they (the bank officers) would do well to give up the vault keys peaceably, and thus avoid making martyrs of themselves."[34]

Dr. Mosher, after telling of his predicament, procured a fresh team of horses and rode off for the Little Sioux to treat Mrs. Mann. As he was leaving, Mr. Broadbent jokingly cautioned him to make a better trade next time, in case he was again held up and forced to exchange animals.

A Mankato newspaper covered the story:

> The two that escaped on Elder Rockwood's horses, were last seen about [fifteen] miles from Sioux City where they took Dr. Mosher of Sioux City, who was going out to see a patient, captive, and kept him with them for about four hours, exchanging clothes with him and taking his horse, and also sent to a house and borrowed a saddle saying it was for the doctor. About [eight] o'clock they let the doctor go, turning him around and pointing to a light, told him if he turned they would shoot him. Then they left with the three horses, but the next morning the doctor found the sorrel horse which they had and which was badly used up, on the prairie where they left him. They said they expected to be taken but not alive, as they proposed to make a bitter fight. One of them was wounded in the leg.[35]

151

While Sioux City buzzed with excitement over Dr. Mosher's return, Sheriff McDonald and his company of scouts rode into town from their fruitless search of the countryside. But the never-say-die sheriff was off in the morning in hot pursuit, riding through Portlandville in a southeasterly direction. Only seven miles from LeMars, McDonald and company stopped at a farm where the robbers had breakfasted the day before. Realizing the robbers had a day on them, McDonald returned to Sioux City via the Floyd Valley for a fresh change of horses.

"During the balance of the afternoon there was nothing but a continuous stream of reports concerning the robbers," reported the *Sioux City Daily News*. "They had been seen in the city; they stopped and drank beer at the Greenville house across the Floyd in the morning; they had been seen at [eleven] a.m. at Sergeant Bluffs, and so on. The most probable conclusion finally arrived at was that the robbers had kept right along in their southeasterly course across the country toward Denison, and in this direction Sheriff McDonald expected to start with his party last evening."

An officer was immediately dispatched to the Greenville house to check out the story of the James boys eating there. The investigator returned with the news that the presumed outlaws were only a couple of herders who had some animals with them.[36]

About ten o'clock in the morning, August Pruist, a farmer living northeast of town, arrived and confirmed Dr. Mosher's story, saying he had seen the doctor in their company. Pruist took a measure of the imprint of the shoe of one of the horses the robbers rode and Broadbent recognized it as that of his stolen mount. Pruist said that after the robbers left Dr. Mosher, they turned and crossed the Floyd River at Hungerford's, heading in a westerly direction.

Pruist's report corroborated an earlier report of the boys being seen in the Broken Kettle bluff area. McDonald divided his party, sending one unit east toward Smithland, while he led another party to the Broken Kettle bluffs. Despite the attempted encirclement of the robbers, many Sioux City residents believed the robbers were hiding out within the city.

A local attorney, C.R. Marks, walked down Third Street in the vicinity of Pierce and Nebraska on business, after hearing of reports the robbers had taken refuge in the city. As he approached a vacant lot, he was startled in seeing two persons lying in the tall weeds. Marks was certain he had stumbled upon the robbers, and in pretending not to see them, he edged closer for a better view. As he did so, he became terror-stricken. He saw one of the figures raise an arm over the weeds. The man was clenching what looked like a navy revolver.

Marks rushed for reinforcements. Within minutes the vacant lot was surrounded. As the party closed in on the presumed robbers, they found not Frank and Jesse James, but two Indians, one male, the other female, taking a rest. The extended hand clenching a revolver was nothing more than the man stretching his arms and yawning. The *Daily Journal* quipped, "Many reports circulated by parties who profess to have seen the robbers, would, if thoroughly sifted, turn out about the same way."

But more reliable news reached Sioux City when it was learned the robbers had stopped at the farm house of J.C. Thompson, near LeMars, about eleven o'clock Thursday morning. The strangers told Mr. Thompson they were hunting "the damned robbers; that their horses, a dark bay and a gray, were badly worn out from the chase, and that they would pay him well to ride two of his horses to a spot eight miles away. Thompson agreed, and after putting their horses in his barn, hitched up two of his to a buggy. Thompson was told they would be back the same evening, but, of course, he never saw them again.

The *Omaha Bee* carried the story:

> The two Northfield bank robbers who have been creating such excitement in the vicinity of Sioux City are still at large. The latest outrage committed by them occurred Thursday, when they went to the farmhouse of James Thompson, about ten miles northwest of LeMars, on the Illinois Central [Railroad], and said they wanted to go to a place called Broken Kettle, about [twenty] miles north of this city. Thompson had not returned home at a late hour, and fears are entertained that he has been murdered. Men are out trying to

trace him and team, but at last account had not succeeded. The two villains are undoubtedly the notorious James brothers.[37]

A stranger also rapped at the door of the nearby Mason home after dark. Mr. Mason answered, but a voice from outside exclaimed, "Don't come to the door. I want to know where to cross the west fork." Mr. Mason told him where to cross, the stranger left, and Mr. Mason went back to bed.[38]

On the evening of September 23, Sioux City went into a state of frenzy when a man believed to be either Frank or Jesse James was captured on the west fork. About seven o'clock, the "James" prisoner was brought down Fourth Street in a wagon, surrounded by guards with pistols, and taken to the county jail. A mob of citizens followed. The prisoner was immediately locked in a cell as two to three hundred people took turns staring at him through the little wicket in the cell door.[39]

The prisoner was observed standing in his cell, his eyes surveying the tiny room into which he had been thrust. Sitting down, he began playing cards with two other prisoners, looking very unconcerned as if he had been brought up in prison. Most of the observers were sure the man was a James brother, and if not, certainly a proper subject for a prison cell.

Dr. Mosher was sent for and asked to identify the prisoner as one of the two men who had held him captive on Wednesday evening. Mosher took a good look and declared he had never seen the man before. Sheriff McDonald permitted sheriffs Finch, Davis, and Hurd, of Minnesota, all of whom were at the jail, to enter the cell and search the prisoner. Hurd immediately strip-searched the suspect.

The prisoner was described by the sheriffs as a man of five feet nine or ten, 150 pounds, somewhat spare built, sandy complexion, whiskers and mustache, long dark hair, thin face, firm resolute expression of countenance, and piercing gray eyes..

The prisoner insisted his name was William C. McFarland and that he lived near a Mormon settlement in Crawford County. He said he came to the west fork area looking for work and was arrested while in the employ of a man named Smith. When he had arrived at Smith's, he was told his services were not needed, but he refused to leave and was eventually given work. Deputy Ames, who arrested him, said when he nabbed his prisoner, the suspect warned that if he only had his guns with him, he would defy all of Woodbury County.

Meanwhile, the incarcerated Youngers were told that one of the James boys had been killed, the other captured. Cole was considerably agitated and asked which had been killed, the larger or the smaller, and asked if anything had been said about him. When told about the experience of Dr. Mosher, Cole found the story quite amusing. Cole laughed and said, "Good boys to the last."

The capture of William C. McFarland, a suspected James brother, was initially a feather in Sheriff John McDonald's cap. One newspaper account published during

Cole Younger in his later years. (Courtesy of the Library of Congress)

his lifetime said he had the best record of any sheriff in the West, having captured and sent to the penitentiary more men than any sheriff west of the Missouri River. The account stated it was no easy job to be a sheriff.

The lawman could only get his man by going after him. To succeed he had to be a good horseman. After capture, his job was only half finished, for he often had to protect his prisoner from self-appointed lynch mobs.[40]

While poor McFarland languished in jail, two deputies returned to the west fork and picked up the James' trail to a site seven miles north of Correctionville, where the fugitives had eaten dinner. The two lawmen were told the outlaws had inquired about the way to Denison, so they followed in that direction, passing Willow Creek on the Maple River and picking up the trail again in Ida.[41]

The trailing lawmen were certain the Jameses had swum the Little Sioux River heading east, the Maple River above Silver Creek, and crossed the creek at a ford toward Sac City on the Coon River. The *Sac Sun* in Sac City reported on October 6th:

> ROBBERS IN SAC COUNTY.—Last Wednesday the news came to town that the two remaining Northfield robbers, supposed to be the James Brothers, passed through our county the week before on their way to Missouri. As soon as it was known that they were probably well out of the county and state, the warlike spirit of our people rose to fever hight [sic], and a small party immediately started west to capture them. When they got as far as Indian Creek they found it too high to cross, and so they marched right back to town.
> Some men on horseback were seen loitering near cattle herds on Indian creek, probably watching a chance to run off the stock.[42]

The Sun, despite the situation, ejected a little humor into the news of dangerous criminals being in the area in the same issue: "NEIGHBORING NEWS—Chaffee, of the *Ida Pioneer*, ran sixteen miles from a book agent, whom he mistook for one of the Northfield robbers."

Two weeks later the *Sac Sun* ran another piece on the James brothers: "CAPTURED.—The notorious James Brothers, of Missouri, on their way from Northfield, Minnesota, passed through Sac County, stopping over night at Mr. Granley's, in the west part of the county. One of them had a sore knee, and spent fifteen minutes in cursing it when he rose in the morning."

The article ended with a misnomer: "This one, Frank James, has just been captured in Missouri by Pinkerton's detectives, and Jesse is in close quarters."[43]

The Pinkertons were on the trail, though, and conducted raids on houses owned by friends of the outlaws, whom they thought could be hiding the fugitives. Allan Pinkerton nearly always knew who he was pursuing.

> Each criminal, [he later told an audience], has his or her marked, personal technique that gives them away every time: On reading a telegraphic newspaper report of a large or small robbery, with the aid of my vast records and great personal experience and familiarity with these matters, I can at once tell the character of the work, and then, knowing the names, history, habits, and quite frequently, the rendezvous of men doing that type of work, am able to determine, with almost unerring certainty, not only the very parties who committed the robberies, but also what disposition they are likely to make of their plunder, and at what points they may be hiding.[44]

Unable to pick up the outlaws' trail, and their own horses played out, the posse at Sac City returned to LeMars. They felt confident, however, that the Jameses were headed for Timber and planned to cross the Northwestern Railroad for Missouri.

The officers said the trail they were following was undoubtedly that of the outlaws. The gray horse one of the robbers was riding was shod with a shoe resembling a mule shoe in shape, and the taller of the two men was so lame, he limped badly. He had to step on the toe of his boot to walk. Stations along the Northwestern and Rock Island roads were alerted.

Upon hearing the officers' report, a local man, C.W. Hepburn, rode up to the river crossing, picked up the robbers' trail, and found they had swum with their horses across the river five miles above Correctionville at Jacob Bunn's farm. A posse was organized quickly and found the trail on the east side of the Little Sioux River, on the road leading up Moon Creek in the direction of Ida Grove. Farmers living along the road told the posse they had seen the two men pass about noon on Thursday, riding at a gallop.

Near the Zupe farm, they discovered the robbers had stopped on the road to talk with one of the farmer's little daughters. They asked her what she was eating, and when she answered raw potatoes, they laughed heartily, telling her they didn't want any, and continued on down the road.

The posse followed the outlaw's trail to within seven miles of Ida Grove, and with night coming on, they stopped at a farm house. Here they learned the sheriff of Plymouth County and a well-armed posse had passed only a couple hours before in the direction of Correctionville. The Sioux City party ate their supper, fed and watered their horses, and took off after the other posse. About midnight, they met the other group and learned the Jameses had been tracked to the Coon River, but, with a two days start on both posses, the lawmen gave up the chase.

Meanwhile, a *Sioux City Daily Journal* reporter visited William McFarland in his jail cell and conducted an interview. The reporter was introduced to the prisoner by Sheriff McDonald and graciously received. "The first information the (prisoner) condescended to impart, after acknowledging the reporter's presence by a stiff nod of the head, was that he had 'a little matter to settle with the editor of that damned paper,' and that he should not 'go for him with a barrel stave either.'" McFarland added his character and reputation had been seriously damaged because of the *Journal*'s branding him a James boy.[45] The interviewer had come to the jail expecting to get a confession out of a cool, calm James brother who would admit to being a James in name and heart, spill how many men he had killed, and identify some of the other gang members. When he found McFarland in a very agitated state, he decided for his own safety to conduct a mild interrogation.

McFarland told the reporter he was not a James brother, and he had never been arrested before in civil life. He admitted to being placed under arrest in the army for drunkeness and other minor violations of which he did not specify. When the interviewer said he was told McFarland lived in Crawford County, the prisoner replied, "I do not. Never was in Crawford County. I have a mother and brothers and sisters living in Davis County. I don't live long at a time anywhere; but stop and work in one place a short time and hen (sic) move on to another place."

When asked if he ever lived in Missouri, McFarland said he had not but had traveled through the state several times. He stated emphatically he had not heard about the attempted bank robbery in Minnesota until he was arrested. McFarland talked of people he had worked for recently, remembering names but not faces, and told the interviewer he carried no extra baggage. He also said he was a veteran of the Civil War with the Second Iowa Regiment and the Eighth Michigan.

The reporter later wrote: "As regards the matter of his arrest, he says that he was pulling onions when the officer rode up unbeknown to him. On straightening up McFarland says he looked into the muzzle of the rifle in the hands of the officer, who ordered him to hold up his hands. Prisoner replied, 'Go to hell!' The officer said, 'Hold up your hands or I will shoot!' 'Shoot and be damned!' said McFarland. But he gave himself up."

The following morning, McFarland was released.

Shortly after the abduction of Dr. Mosher, the trail of the very real Frank and Jesse James grew thin and eventually disappeared altogether. Numerous reports of robber sightings made headlines but the real outlaws left the area with nary a trace. G.W. Hunt, pioneer editor of the *Sioux City Democrat*, claimed to have the answers as to the whereabouts of the Jameses after the Dr. Mosher affair. His account, however, is not taken seriously; no copies of the *Democrat* exist today and almost no material on the *Democrat* can be found. Hunt's alleged story also ran no byline.

Hunt, who held a great admiration for the James brothers, contended that he interviewed Dr. Mosher upon the physician's escape to the city. Taking advantage of Deputy Sheriff Dan McDonald, brother of the sheriff, John, who let him read dispatches concerning the outlaws' whereabouts, Hunt decided to do everything possible to prevent them from being captured. This included his discouraging of a plan by Dan McDonald to patrol four skiffs on the Missouri River.

Hunt, whose undated article (with no byline) was found years later by Dan McDonald's daughter, wrote: "By this time we discovered that Sheriff McDonald and a well-armed party were on the fresh and well-defined scent of the Jameses and must capture them if not thwarted. Hitching up our team, we (Hunt and an unidentified companion) started out after the sheriff's party, soon overtaking them, and by a little strategy succeeded in turning them off in another direction."[46]

Hunt claimed that he and his friend met the James brothers four miles from the village of Woodbury, on the Sioux City and Pacific Railroad. Hunt said as the brothers rode up, he identified himself, even telling them he knew who they were, and offered to strike up a deal. In exchange for their giving him an exclusive interview on the Northfield affair, he would help guide them back to Missouri. Although the brothers laughed, they consented. Leaving their horses behind to graze, the brothers climbed into the wagon, but when riders approached, they asked Hunt to lead them away by the shortest possible route.

According to Hunt, he accompanied the James brothers: "That night we camped at a point adjacent to the Missouri River, nearly opposite the village of Sloan, not desiring to risk the chances of stopping at a house. During the night they proposed and we acceded to an oath or pledge that we would not under certain circumstances reveal what facts they gave us until their safe arrival among friends, of which fact they could acquaint us either by telegraph or letter, and in addition, under certain other circumstances pending on the arrest and trial of the Younger brothers, we would not disclose certain other information given us . . ."

After sleeping in prairie grass that evening, the wagon proceeded down the Missouri Valley in the direction of Council Bluffs. Where the Little Sioux River runs into the Missouri, the strange party discovered a skiff moored to a stake by a small chain. Having procured provisions from Ed Haakinson's store in Sloan, the Jameses left their newfound friends, and floated along the river at night until they reached Nebraska City. From that point on, they felt it safe enough to travel by day and reached St. Joseph, Missouri, within eight days of taking leave of Hunt.

Other accounts relate the Jameses made their way to Fort Dodge, Iowa. Mrs. John Rolow was a seven-year-old girl when the Jameses allegedly came to her parents' door near Fort Dodge. The men arrived at sunset and were armed with knives and revolvers. The family was alarmed when the men said they were going to spend the night.[47]

This same courteous, soft-voiced stranger is supposed to have stopped at the George Armes home in the backwoods near Fort Dodge. Posing as a wealthy land buyer, he said he was seeking lodging while he negotiated for several farms in the area. He paid liberally for his board and helped with chores. The Armeses, however, wondered why he never removed his gun and cartridge belt, but since many men went armed, they gave it little more thought.[48]

Armes showed the stranger around and took him to local farms, several of which the newcomer agreed to purchase. When Armes agreed to take him to Fort Dodge to draw up the necessary papers, the stranger gave his small-caliber pistol in appreciation of his services. At Fort Dodge, the stranger asked Armes to wait at a corner while he met a friend to obtain some money. He never returned.

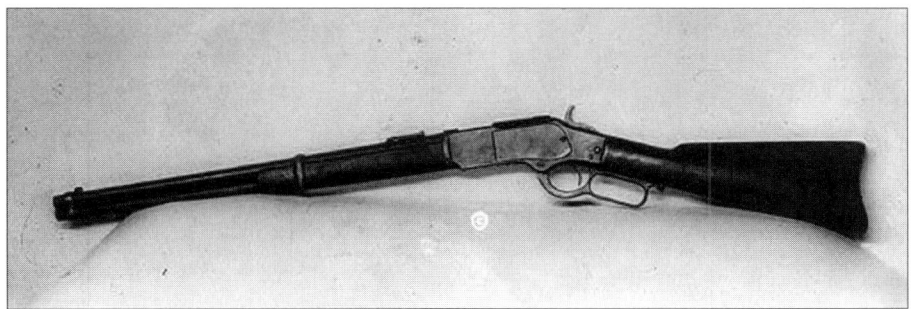

Jesse's Winchester rifle. (Courtesy of the Library of Congress)

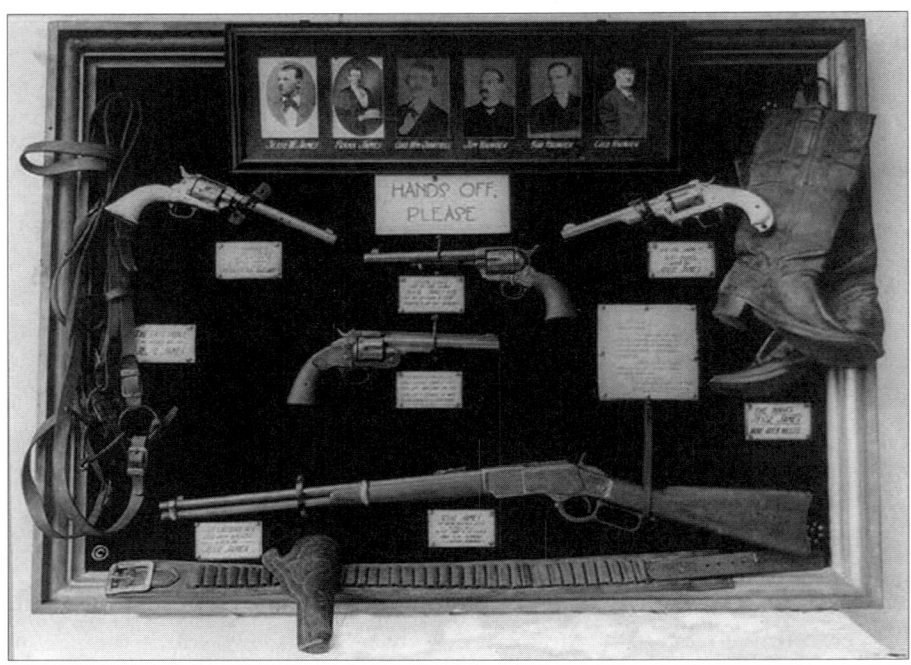

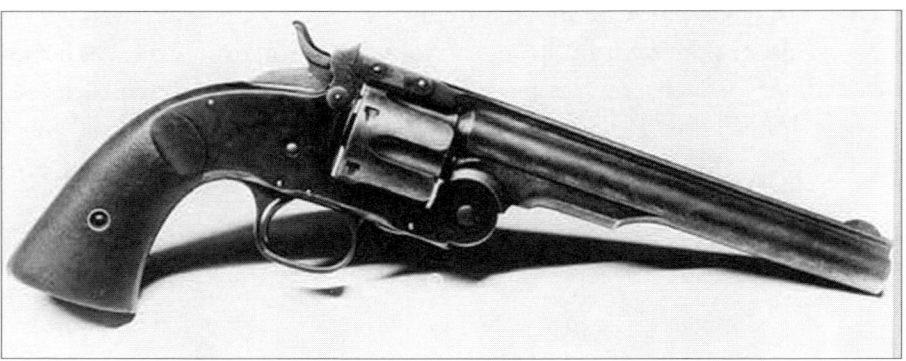

The last gun used by Jesse James, a .45 Schofield. (Courtesy of the Library of Congress)

Soon Armes learned the identity of the stranger. Armes moved his family to Saunders County, Nebraska, in 1881 and several years later relocated in Oregon, where he died in 1897, the pistol still in his possession.

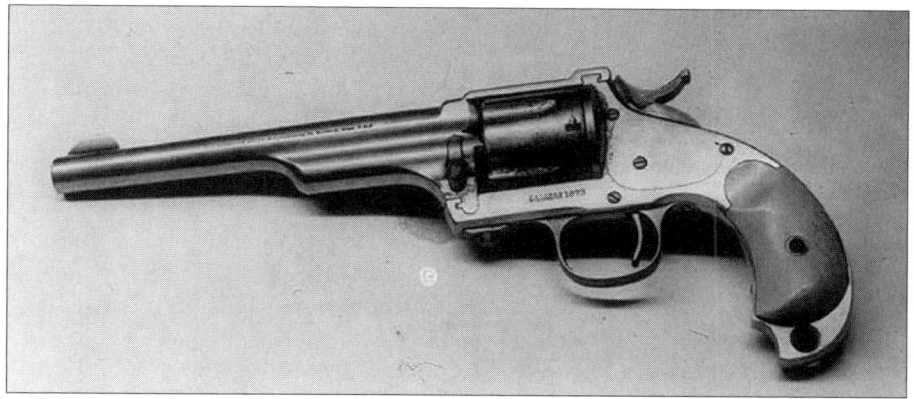

Jesse James's .44 Hopkins & Allen pistol, 1873 model. (Courtesy of the Library of Congress)

It is possible the Jameses left the heavily-guarded Missouri River and turned eastward toward Fort Dodge. They were aware that authorities in Missouri were watching for them. They could catch a train in Fort Dodge for Kentucky, where they had relatives who would hide them, and they may have been waiting for news of the Youngers, whom they could possibly intercept at Fort Dodge. If news of the Youngers' fate did reach them in the vicinity of Fort Dodge, they would most-assuredly catch a train to Kentucky rather than ride into the arms of Missouri officers.[49] The Jameses had lived in Midway, Kentucky, located in the northern section of Woodford County, and the Youngers had relatives there.[50] Frank and Jesse would return no more to Iowa and Frank would quit the outlaw trail for good.

Few persons in Iowa would mourn Jesse's murder in 1882 at the hands of nineteen-year-old Bob Ford. Peace and prosperity had come at last. Iowa farms, which initially produced wheat, later developed into major producers of corn, soybeans, cattle, and hogs. Rural agricultural communities, increasingly connected by rail, enjoyed the prosperity and suffered the recessions of boom-bust national economic cycles. Urban centers became increasingly interconnected with the national and international political economy via developing road, steamboat, and rail transportation networks, social and business ties, and involvement with the arts, religion, communications, education, and government.[51]

Jesse James would take a long, well deserved rest from his outlaw antics. But, like the Confederate guerrillas he had ridden with as a youth, he would one day strike again, and again, and again. . . .

## Notes

[1]*Faribault Democrat*, December 15, 1876, "The James Boys."

[2]T.D. Griffith, "Aces, Eights and Number 10, Wild Bill Hickok's Death," *Historic Traveler Magazine*, November 1996.

[3]*Black Hills Pioneer*, August 5, 1876.

[4]Homer Croy, *Jesse James Was My Neighbor*, New York, Dell Publishing Company, Inc., 1960, p. 93.

[5]Robertus Love, *The Rise and Fall of Jesse James*, New York, Blue Ribbon Books, 1935, p. 190-191.

[6]*Mankato Weekly Review*, October 3, 1876.

[7]Homer Croy, *Jesse James Was My Neighbor*, p. 94.

[8]Tom Ryther letter to author dated October 27, 1982; William A.Settle, Jr., *Jesse James Was His Name*, Lincoln, University of Nebraska Press, 1977, p. 95; George Turner, *Secrets of Jesse James*, Amarillo, Baxter Lane Company, 1975.

[9]Homer Croy, *Jesse James Was My Neighbor*, p. 94.

[10]Frank Triplett, *The Life, Times and Treacherous Death of Jesse James*, New York, Konecky & Konecky, 1970, p. 135.

[11]Homer Croy, *Last of the Great Outlaws*, pp. 82-82/

[12]Robert L. Dyer, *Jesse James and the Civil War in Missouri*, Columbia and London, University of Missouri Press, 1994, p. 66.

[13]Anonymous letter from Woodward, Iowa, to author dated December 14, 2004.

[14]George Huntington, *Robber and Hero: The Story of the Raid on the First National Bank of Northfield*, p. 9-10; Don Coulston, "The Youngers 'Rebels with a Cause,'" *The* (Stillwater) *Prison Mirror*, pp 8; Marilynn Cierzan letter to author dated July 13, 1982.

[15]*The Madelia News*, Thursday, November 25, 1915, "Cole Younger's Story of the Northfield Raid."

[16]Chuck Parsons, "James Glispin—Nineteenth-Century Minnesota Sheriff," *Real West*, March 1981, pp. 10-11.

[17]*St. Louis Globe Democrat*, October 16, 1876

[18]George Huntington, *Robber and Hero*, 59.

[19]*Madelia Times*, Friday, September 22, 1876.

[20]*Rice County Journal Extra*, September 1876.

[21]*Sioux City Daily Journal*, Tuesday, September 19, 1876, "The Robbers."

[22]*Sioux City Daily Journal*, Thursday, September 21, 1876, "The Robbers Shot."

[23]*The Sioux Valley News* (Canton, South Dakota), September 23, 1876, "Northfield Robbers."

[24]Frank R. Holmes, *Minnesota in Three Centuries*, Volume Four, Mankato, The Publishing Society of Minnesota, 1908, p. 125.

[25]Charles and Vesta Knapp, signed affidavits, Plymouth County Historical Society, LeMars, Iowa.

[26]J.A. Derome, "Canton Thrown Into Wild Stage of Excitement When Report Was Given That Bandits Were Near," eighth in a series of articles.

[27]A.T. Andreas, *Illustrated Historical Atlas of the State of Iowa*, 1875—Sioux County History.

[28]Ted P. Yeatman, *Frank and Jesse James*, p. 180.

[29]*Sioux City Daily Journal*, Wednesday, September 20, 1876, "The Hunt."

[30]*Sioux City Daily Journal*, Sunday, September 17, 1876, "The Northfield Brigands."

[31]*Sioux City Daily Journal*, Wednesday, September 20, 1876.

[32]*Sioux City Daily Journal*, Friday, September 22, 1876, "The Robbers."

[33]Gertrude Henderson, "Dr. Mosher Makes a Call," *Tales and Trails of Yesterday*, Date Unknown, Northfield Public Library; "Sioux City Family Treasures Bullet Pierced Trousers Worn by One of James Brothers," Date Unknown, Northfield Public Library.

[34]*Sioux City Daily Journal*, Friday, September 22, 1876, "The Robbers."

[35]*Mankato Record*, September 30, 1876.

[36]*Sioux City Daily Journal*, Saturday, September 23, 1876, "The Outlaws."

[37]*Omaha Bee*, Saturday, September 23, 1876, "The Northfield Bank Robbery."

[38]Mrs. Fred Wingert letter to author dated April 1982; *Kingsley* (Iowa) *News-Times*, 1981, Exact date unknown.

[39]*Sioux City Daily Journal*, Sunday, September 24, 1876, "The Robbers."

[40]Sheriff Russell H. White, Jr., Woodbury County Sheriff's Department, 1981, a two-page biography of sheriffs John and Dan McDonald, Sioux City Public Museum.

[41]*Sioux City Daily Journal*, Monday, September 25, 1876, "The Missouri Bandits."

[42]*Sac Sun*, October 6, 1876.

[43]*Sac Sun*, October 20, 1876.

[44]Library of Congress.

[45]*Sioux City Daily Journal*, Tuesday, September 26, 1876, "Busted."

[46]Scrapbook of clippings belonging to Mrs. H.C. Harper; *Sioux City Journal*, July 25, 1954, "How an Early Day Sioux City Editor Helped James Boys to Escape After Northfield Bank Robbery."

[47]David Parker, executive director, Fort Dodge Historical Foundation, letter to author dated May 11, 1981.

[48]*Omaha Sunday World-Herald*, January 22, 1995, "Café Owner Convinced Gun Was Outlaw's"; *Omaha World-Herald*, Date Unknown, "Nebraskan Refuses All Offers for Gun Jesse James Used in Famed Bank Raid"; Chuck Parsons, "A Jesse James Pistol?" *Quarterly of the National Association for Outlaw and Lawman History*, Inc., Volume XVII, Number 1, January-March 1993, p. 20.

[49]Bob Shelburne undated letter to author, postmarked January 17, 1997.

[50]Louise W. Hampton, Scholl Family Research Association of America, letter to author dated March 7, 1983.

[51]Carl A. Merry, "The Historic Period," 1996, University of Iowa Website.

*Chapter Seven*

# Prelude to Disaster

*"An unsolved murder, the lure of hidden gold, endless digging for treasure on a sequestered farm, a strange trial that unwound the mystery only to wind it up more tangled than before, disappointed lives and sudden deaths—all these weave in and out of the story of buried treasure near the village of Siam in southwestern Iowa. Back in the days of the Civil War and for some years thereafter southwestern Iowa was a sparsely settled region where more or less lawlessness prevailed. The James boys, Jesse and Frank, began their picturesque banditry about 1870, and lesser gangs emulated their example. Murder and robbery were not uncommon."*

—The Palimpsest[1]

MATTIE COLLINS WAS A WOMAN of unsavory character who played a significant role as the flamboyant femme fatale in the events leading to Jesse James' betrayal and assassination. Always a lady of mystery, Mattie was the lover or wife of Dick Liddil, a principal James Gang member in later years. Mattie may have gained her reputation because she consorted with Liddil without the formality of marriage. Some sources refer to her as a brazen harlot who had shot and killed a suitor who had jilted her. It was she who contacted the law at Liddil's direction to negotiate a deal to turn state's evidence and betray Jesse.[2]

167

Bob Ford. (Library of Congress)

Mattie and her friends sheltered Liddil and other members of the James Gang when the law was on their trail. Liddel, however, also spent time at the home of Martha "Widow" Bolton while Dick was on the run. The widow was a sister of gang members Bob and Charlie Ford. Her door was apparently always open to the James boys or any member of the gang who needed a hiding place.

During the final months of Jesse's life, Liddil became involved in a personal dispute with Wood Hite, one of Jesse's favorite cousins, while they were hiding out in Kentucky. Later Liddil testified that the quarrel stemmed from an accusation by Wood that he had stolen $100 from the Blue Cut robbery proceeds before the loot was divided.

In December of 1881, the feud between Hite and Liddil ended with a bang in the dining room of the Widow Bolton's house about a mile northeast of Richmond, Missouri. Hite had been hiding out there a few days when Liddil drifted in one night for the same purpose and went upstairs to bed. The widow and her children had breakfast early the following morning and called her guests down for their meal. With Bob and Charlie Ford present, Hite and Liddil met in the dining room. The two men had words over the affections of the Widow Bolton and/or similar interests by the two men in her fourteen-year-old daughter, Ida Bolton. According to Martha Bolton, Hite offered to shake hands with Liddil, and when the latter refused, the shooting started.

The room was quite small. Liddil and Hite were only a few feet apart from each other as each drew a revolver and fired rapidly. Liddil emptied his revolver at Hite and only managed to inflict a flesh wound in his opponent's arm. Hite got off at least four shots, one of which hit his adversary in the leg. As Liddil went for his second revolver, Bob

Images of Jesse James. (Courtesy Library of Congress)

Ford calmly drew his gun and shot Hite in the head (an eerie portent of the future).

The Fords buried Hite's body in an old spring that same night. To add insult to his demise, they purloined all his personal effects, including the clothes he was wearing. Wood was buried in his shirt, socks, and underwear, wrapped in a filthy horse blanket.

The killing of Wood Hite undoubtedly presented a dilemma to Liddil and the Ford boys. They faced a murder charge to go along with their other crimes. They also faced retribution from Jesse James if he should find out about his cousin's murder. Jesse was apt to question the trio and probably would not believe it was a fair fight. They knew Jesse was impulsive and might shoot anybody.

Liddil selected Mattie Collins to act as a go-between if they were to reap any benefits out of betraying Jesse because he trusted her. Mattie visited Whig Keshlear, deputy marshal of Jackson County and asked him to contact William Wallace and cut a deal for Liddil. Wallace responded with a letter to Liddil stating that as prosecuting attorney for Jackson County, he could not make a deal to pardon him for crimes committed elsewhere, and referred him to Governor Crittenden who had the power to do it.

After Mattie acted as intermediary between Liddil and the law to help him gain a pardon by betraying Jesse and others, she was double-crossed by her lover, who jilted her and took up with the Widow [Martha] Bolton.

The Widow Bolton is often considered the mysterious "veiled lady" who acted in behalf of Liddil and the Fords by visiting law officials rather than Mattie Collins. Mattie Collins had made the first trip and talked with Keshlear, but since Liddil had dumped her and the Ford brothers trusted their sister more than Mattie, Martha Bolton was sent on the second visit, which was the meeting with Governor Crittenden. This confusion apparently results from the fact that the Widow Martha Bolton was sometimes called "Mattie" Bolton.

Jesse intended to give up his life of crime and move to a farm in Nebraska with his wife and two children. But one more robbery, a bank in Platte City, Missouri, had been in the planning stages for April 4, 1882. Robert and Charles Ford, newly recruited youthful members of the band, had been staying with Jesse and his family at their temporary residence on the corner of Thirteenth and Lafayette streets in St. Joseph, Missouri. Charles had helped rob the Chicago and Alton train the past September, but Bob, only twenty years old, had never been involved in a robbery.[3]

Jesse James House, St. Joseph, Missouri. Author's Collection

Unbeknownst to the gang, Bob had been meeting secretly over several weeks with Liberty, Clay County, Sheriff James Timberlake, Kansas City

170

Police Commissioner Henry Craig, and Missouri Governor Thomas Crittenden. The governor had related to Bob Ford that, "I want Jesse James brought in, and I will give you $10,000 for him, dead or alive." Commissioner Craig armed Ford with two revolvers belonging to the state. Ford then sent a dispatch to Timberlake stating, "I have gone after Jesse James, and in ten days I'll have killed him or he'll have killed me."[4]

Bob and Charlie Ford watched Jesse every minute and waited for the right opportunity to kill him. Jesse, however, was always heavily armed and ever watchful. They discarded any plan of taking him alive, considering the attempt suicidal. But following breakfast, on April 3, 1882, thirteen days after Bob Ford said he'd get Jesse, the opportunity presented itself.[5]

Charlie Ford and Jesse had been out in the stable preparing the horses for that evening's intended Platte City robbery. Returning inside the house, Jesse said to Bob, who was seated in the room, "It's an awfully hot day." Jesse pulled off his coat and vest and placed them on his bed. Then he said, "I guess I'll take off my pistols, for fear somebody will see them if I walk in the yard" and unbuckled his gun belt. Placing his two .45s—a Smith & Wesson and a Colt, on the bed, he picked up a brush to dust some pictures on the wall.[6]

When Jesse turned his back to his friends, they stepped between him and his revolvers, and at a motion from Charlie, both drew their pistols. Robert drew quicker than his brother and fired at the back of Jesse's head from a distance of only two to four feet. Jesse heard the slight motion and began to turn his head, but he fell to the floor with no outcry. The fatal bullet had entered the back of the skull.

Jesse's wife had been in the kitchen during the shooting, and hearing the shot, raced into the front room to find her husband lying dead on his back and the Fords, each holding a revolver, making for the fence at the rear of the house. As Robert scaled the fence, Mrs. James shouted, "Robert, you have done this. Come back." Robert answered, "I swear to God, I didn't," and came back. Bending over her husband, Mrs. James tried to wipe the blood from his forehead, but it flowed so fast, wiping was impossible. He died, his head in her hands, as the Ford brothers rushed off to report their deed to the authorities.

Robert Ford described to Governor Thomas Crittenden how he had killed Jesse James:

On the morning of April 3, Jess and I went downtown, as usual, before breakfast, for the papers. We got to the house about eight o'clock and sat down in the front room. Jess was sitting with his back to me, reading the *St. Louis Republican*. I picked up the *Times*, and the first thing I saw in big headlines was the story about Dick Liddil's surrender. Just then Mrs. James came in and said breakfast was ready. Beside me was a chair with a shawl on it, and as quick as a flash I lifted it and shoved the paper under. Jess couldn't have seen me, but he got up, walked over to the chair, picked up the shawl and threw it on the bed, and taking the paper, went out to the kitchen. I felt that the jig was up, but I followed and sat down at the table opposite Jess.

Mrs. James poured out the coffee and then sat down at one end of the table. Jesse spread the paper on the table in front of him and began to look over the headlines. All at once Jess said: "Hello, here. The surrender of Dick Liddil." And he looked across at me with a glare in his eyes.

"Young man, I thought you told me you didn't know that Dick Liddil had surrendered," he said. I told him I didn't know it. "Well," he said, "it's very strange. He surrendered three weeks ago, and you was right there in the neighborhood. It looks fishy."

He continued to glare at me, and I got up and went into the front room. In a minute I heard Jess push his chair back and walk to the door. He came in smiling, and said pleasantly: "Well, Bob, it's all right, anyway."

Instantly his real purpose flashed upon my mind. I knew I had not fooled him. He was too sharp for that. He knew at that moment as well as I did that I was there to betray him. But he was not going to kill me in the presence of his wife and children. He walked over to the bed, and deliberately unbuckled his belt, with four revolvers in it, and threw it on the bed. It was the first time in my life I had seen him without that belt on, and I knew that he threw it off to further quiet any suspicions I might have.

He seemed to want to busy himself with something to make an impression on my mind that he had forgotten the incident at the breakfast table, and said: "That picture is awful dusty." There wasn't a speck of dust that I could see on the picture, but he stood a chair beneath it and then got upon it and began to dust the picture on the wall.

As he stood there, unarmed, with his back to me, it came to me suddenly, "Now or never is your chance. If you don't get him now he'll get you tonight." Without further thought or a moment's delay I pulled my revolver and leveled it as I sat. He heard the hammer click as I cocked it with my thumb and started to turn as I pulled the trigger. The ball struck him just behind the ear and he fell like a log, dead.

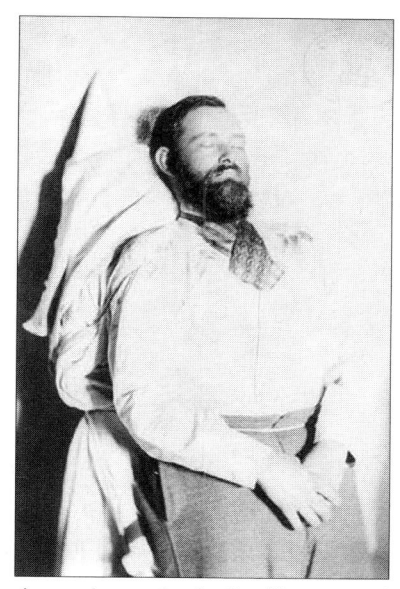

Jesse James in death. (Courtesy of the Library of Congress)

Mattie Collins was on the scene as thousands of curious citizens swarmed the city of St. Joseph, Missouri, following the sudden death of Jesse James, and because Mattie had known the deceased outlaw personally, she was among those who identified the body.[7] In a later newspaper interview she vehemently denied that she had ever contacted Sheriff Timberlake or Governor Crittenden to betray Frank and Jesse, and fingered the Widow Bolton.

Frank James was with his family in Lynchburg, Virginia, when Jesse was killed. Only Frank had been able to stay away from crime, and even though Jesse had informed his family he was going to give up outlawry, Frank believed his brother would have had a difficult time leading a normal life.[8]

After Frank surrendered to the governor and went to trial at the opera house in Gallatin for his alleged participation in the Winston, Missouri, train robbery, Mattie Collins was there. Dick Liddil, under

Jackson County Prosecutor William Wallace's quiet questioning, was the prosecution's star witness, and described how he ridden with Jesse, Frank, Clarence Hite, and Wood Hite to rob the train at Winston.[9] He told the court he had told a friend that he had stayed with—Ben Morrow—a not quite true version of the robbery:

"I told him about the robbery, told him I was in it. I also told him that Frank, Jesse, Wood Hite, and Clarence, and a man by the name of Johnson from Texas was in it. I did not want to tell on Charlie Ford is the reason I gave him this alias."[10]

Despite his testimony, Liddil was unable to convince the judge and jury that Jesse and Frank had shot and killed conductor William Westfall and passenger Frank McMillan as was alleged.[11]

*The Judge*, a satirical magazine in its first year of publication, proposed on April 22 that a monument be erected in Jesse's honor. While focusing on train and stage robberies, the monument would also feature a model of Jesse's home. Guns, daggers, and revolvers would be displayed within the house as well as three plaques bearing the messages: "Bless Our Home," "What is a home without a Revolver," and "What a Friend I Have in Jesus and My Revolver."[12]

Jesse was dead, but thirty-three years later, the strange tale of the Siam murder mystery came to light in July 1915. At that time people of Bedford, the county seat of Taylor County, Iowa, experienced a week of excitement such as had seldom if ever before stirred the feelings of that placid community. Four old men, each well-known in his respective community, had been arrested for the alleged robbery and murder of a wealthy cattleman and his boy companion after a lapse of nearly half a century. Nathaniel Harrison (Hank) Damewood, a lank kindly-faced man, sixty-one years old, was the youngest of the group. His brother John, shorter and with the same pleasant type of face, was sixty-four. Sam Scrivner, a dark, grim man, a splendid farmer and worth, it was said, $50,000, was seventy-four; and Bates Huntsman, tall, lean, with the eyes of a mystic and the beard of a patriarch, was seventy-seven.[13]

According to the story that quickly went the rounds of the town, these four men, together with Dr. C.R. Huntsman, Dr. A.M. Golliday, and Jonathan Dark, had waylaid a wealthy cattle buyer who had been lured to the vicinity of Siam in 1868. The victim, it was said, had traveled with an ox team and wagon to Taylor County from somewhere to the east, bringing a boy with him as a companion, and a truck full of money, $90,000 or thereabouts.

This gang of daring young fellows, so the story ran, had met the two travelers not far from Siam, shot or clubbed (versions differed) the man to death, and dumped his body into an old well. The boy tried to escape during the confusion attending the murder of his older companion, but he had not run far before a member of the gang overtook him and killed him also. His body was buried in a locust grove not far from the well into which the body of the man had been thrown. The gang then buried the swag, carefully making a plat of the farm and marking the location of the trunk.

Everyone in the county had heard the story. It was a tradition. This gang of counterfeiters back in 1868 had operated from ten acres they owned adjoining the property which Sam Anderson purchased a few years later. Sam used to dig for treasure nearly every day on his acreage.[14]

The counterfeiting gang used a nearby cave for their operations and allegedly committed most of the crimes perpetrated throughout the heavily forested area of southwestern Iowa. As time went by, the bandits could not get their nerve up to go back and dig up the treasure. During their procrastination, a fire destroyed the Huntsman cabin where the map was hidden, the map included. When the outlaws finally returned to dig up their treasure, fate dealt them another blow—they could not find it!

In 1881, the year before Jesse James was assassinated, Sam Anderson came into possession of the farm where the Siam Treasure was buried, and he knew it was there. He dug up the place day and night for fifteen years, and when he failed to find it, he moved to Maryville, Missouri. Still, however, he made trips back to Siam and resumed digging before giving up about 1903.

When the newspapers picked up the story during the summer of 1915, however, it was sensational. Two wealthy, well-known, longtime residents of Taylor County were under arrest and being charged as members of the counterfeiting gang which had murdered the cattle buyer and his son forty-seven years earlier. Not only did the law have a long arm, but it had a long memory!

In early coverage, the *Maryville* (Missouri) *Weekly Tribune* reported on the results of an investigation conducted by the Iowa Attorney General's office. Mrs. Henry Porter of Quitman, Missouri, seventy-one years old, was the only living witness to a murder which had occurred in September of 1868. Bates Huntsman, seventy, had been arrested and charged with being a member of the counterfeiting ring which was believed to have committed the murders. Huntsman was a lifetime resident and member of a widely known family living near Bedford, Iowa. Henry Scribner, a wealthy cattleman of New Market, Iowa, was also under arrest and a warrant had been issued for an unidentified third suspect.

According to the attorney general, five counterfeiters had operated in 1868 near Siam on ten acres adjoining and subsequently occupied by Sam Anderson. That particular year the Anderson cabin was occupied by Mrs. Floyd Collins, a widow, and her children. A daughter had married Jonathan Dark, a member of the counterfeiting gang, and the couple lived nearby.

On that bright moonlit night in September 1868, fourteen-year-old Maria Collins (later to become Mrs. Henry Porter of Quitman) heard a noise outside the cabin and stepped outside to investigate. She came face to face with the members of the counterfeiting gang carrying the body of the wealthy cattleman they had murdered, wrapped in a quilt. A young member of the gang held a team of oxen hitched to a wagon containing a large chest of gold.

"As the party with the quilt came nearer, I saw that there was a body of a man in it," recalled Mrs. Porter years later. "I saw his legs and feet dragging on the ground, and then from the conversation of the party, all of whom I knew and recognized, I learned that they had way-laid and murdered 'Old Than,' a cattle buyer who was passing through the district with a trunk full of gold. . . ."[15]

After the cattle buyer was slain, his young son begged for his life. A member of the gang bashed in his head with an axe and buried him in a nearby grove of locust trees. Under the threat of death, the men made Maria Collins swear to not tell what she had seen. They buried the cattle buyer in an abandoned well and buried the chest. Maria was forced to wash the bloody quilt and wash the blood from the men's clothing.[16]

After Maria's experience with the killers, she feared for her life and with a sister moved to Quitman, Missouri. In Quitman, she alleged-ly told Frank James about the Siam Treasure, and he was soon seen in the Iowa town apparently looking for the gold. Local residents also reported that Jesse James and his band had once visited Siam and attempted to locate the treasure but came up empty-handed.

Members of the Siam Gang allegedly learned that Maria was telling others about her experience and the treasure and sent Jonathan Dark to silence her. Before Dark could do so, he was shot and killed by an older Collins sister before he could use his own gun. According to Maria, she had cradled Dark's head as he breathed his last, but she would have felt more sorrow for a dying dog. She said, "Dark was a foul scoundrel who got what he deserved." In his final moments, Dark claimed to have seen an apparition of the boy he had murdered and told the others that he regretted killing the boy more than any other crime he had ever committed.

The arrests of the local residents had come about because Sam Anderson of Lucas, Iowa, had attempted to file a civil suit to force them to give him one-fourth of the $90,000 treasure which had been found on his farm. He claimed that Huntsman, Scribner, and a third man had found the chest twelve years earlier and did not give him his share under an agreement they had made with him.

According to Anderson, after his marriage some thirty-five years earlier he had settled down on his father-in-law's farm adjoining that of the Huntsmans. Soon after he located on the farm he received a visit from his neighbors. They told him that he had better move on, as the farm was poor and the place haunted. Anderson replied that he was not afraid of "haunts," he did not fear dead men, was not much afraid of live ones, and proposed to stay where he was.[17]

Later the Huntsmans visited him again. They told Anderson on this occasion that there was a lot of gold buried on the place—$90,000 in one place, $50,000 in another, and $12,000 in a third. They wanted Anderson to help them dig for it and promised him one-fourth of whatever amount he found. "Doc" Huntsman explained that the money had been obtained from the sale of a large farm in Missouri. Fearing that he might be robbed by outlaws who infested that part of the country, he claimed to have buried the money for safe keeping on the land he was then farming. He had then made a chart of the burial places, but the fire which had consumed the Huntsman cabin a few years earlier had likewise destroyed the chart. Huntsman had forgotten the markings and now sought to recover the treasure by digging for it. Anderson agreed to help, and the three drew up a contract whereby the former agreed to dig whenever the Huntsmans wanted him to do so. This agreement commenced their quarter-century search for the hidden gold.

"One of the Huntsmans was always with me whenever I dug, sometimes both of them, and I know they watched me night and day," Anderson later told reporters. Deep furrows were run here and there about the farm and trenches were dug in locations pointed out by his employers.

Not long after the search began, the ghostly visitation about which Anderson had been warned allegedly made its appearance. One lonely moonlit night, when trees cast eerie shadows and the stillness of the night magnified every unusual sound, Anderson and Bates Huntsman were walking near the former's home. Off a hundred yards or so a shadowy figure made a sudden appearance, striding back and forth in a ghostly vigil.

Anderson ran into the house for his shotgun and returned to battle the apparition. One shot from the old muzzle loader was sufficient to send the ghost scurrying for cover. The specter never reappeared, but for days Huntsman appeared nervous and shaken.

As the years drifted on and the search revealed nothing, the Huntsmans became more impatient and persistent. Anderson never knew just when he would be called away from his farm work to renew the digging. Sometimes he would have to leave his plowing or harvesting in the middle of the forenoon to do the bidding of the brothers.

On one occasion, Bates Huntsman asked Anderson to bring a team with him. He took the team over to the Huntsman place and hitched the horses to a plow-like apparatus for cutting the surface of the ground. Both the Huntsmans and Damewoods were present on this occasion, declared Anderson, and "Doc" Huntsman had an iron rod he would push into the ground here and there. After a time Anderson struck a soft spot with the plow apparatus, and "Doc" Huntsman said they would stop for the day. As Anderson and his brother passed this spot the next day they noticed that it had been dug out. Investigating the freshly turned dirt, they found a bone about eight inches in length, apparently that of a boy. Anderson's brother took the bone and when Bates Huntsman came along, handed it to him. Huntsman said, "I never had anything to do with it," and his jaw fell.

Some time later, while digging in a designated spot, Anderson uncovered three stakes set in a direct line. The tops of the stakes were charred as though by fire, and they appeared to have been in the ground a long time. Doc Huntsman urged him on. Spurred on by the vision of one-fourth of the fortune, which was to be his, Anderson dug away feverishly, while the doctor made no effort to conceal his eager anticipation.

"I first came onto some white sand," he told reporters. "I followed the sand up a hill a distance, and found a box about as long as my arm. There was a rock on the box. The box was zinc or iron."

Believing he could knock the top off the metal box, Anderson hit it a whack with his spade. Despite the fact that the hole was twelve or thirteen feet deep and muddy at the bottom, Doc Huntsman jumped into it forthwith, and ordered Anderson to get out as they would not go any farther that night. Anderson replied that they had found what they were hunting for and that he wanted his share as pay for his work. Just then Charles Huntsman, a son of Doctor Huntsman, came up. He said nothing, but he had a gun in his hand and Anderson crawled out of the hole. Doc Huntsman told Anderson that they could not count the money until later, and then they would pay him. Trusting and credulous as he was, Anderson left the Huntsmans in possession of the box. He never saw it again.

The next spring, Doc Huntsman died suddenly, gripped by a stroke of paralysis. "I have asked for the money once or twice a year since that but have always been put off by Bates saying he wanted to look a little further," Anderson told newspapermen. So the years ebbed on. Weary of long waiting for his share of the treasure which he believed he had uncovered Sam Anderson at last unburdened his woes to Attorney Bulman.

Anderson visited Attorney W.W. Bulman of Chariton, Iowa, and information was collected over several years. Bulman then placed his findings before the attorney general of Iowa and the criminal arrests and investigation soon followed. Bulman claimed that $43,000 of the treasure had been recovered.[18]

A press dispatch from Fresno, California, quoted C.P. Huntsman, son of the deceased Dr. C.R. Huntsman and nephew of the accused Bates Huntsman, to the effect that his father and uncle did bury the bodies and the $90,000 belonging to the cattleman, but they did so at the orders of the James boys. According to his story, on the night in question, his father, who had been visiting at the home of Bates Huntsman, was summoned to attend Mrs. Floyd Collins, who was ill at the cabin of her son-in-law, Jonathan Dark. Bates Huntsman accompanied the physician. Just before reaching the cabin they stumbled upon the James boys and their gang soon after the murder had been committed.[19]

"The two men were backed up against a tree, and then Bates Huntsman was forced, under the threat of death, to bury the two bodies while Dr. Huntsman buried the gold," insisted C.P. Huntsman. "Although members of the family sought to have Dr. Huntsman reveal the hiding place, he died without giving its location, although in his later years he was sorely touched by poverty."

Shortly after this story appeared in newspapers, Cole Younger, the only surviving member of the James gang, uttered a vigorous denial of any participation in the affair by the James boys. "Frank James was in California from 1866 to 1870," he declared, "and the gang was not organized until he returned." Both of the boys were far from Iowa when the murder was committed. "What's more," he added, "it's a joke to think of the James boys having anything like $90,000, the amount they claim the cattleman lost. I frequently loaned them money in those days, and I know they never had more than they could carry in their pockets."

As to the identity of the victims, the stories finally sifted down to two men, Nathaniel Smith, a rich ranchman of northern Missouri, who disappeared in the late sixties, and William Hedrick, a horse trader, also a resident of northern Missouri, who dropped out of sight in Civil War days. Volunteer witnesses, however, came forward to show that Hedrick lost his life in border warfare in the early days of the Civil War, and so the remaining surmise indicated that Smith was the victim of whose murder the four old men were accused.

The preliminary hearing began on July 14, 1915. "With such a background of alleged crime, of fortune and strange quests, the trial began," penned a reporter from the *Kansas City Star*. It was only a preliminary hearing before Justice of the Peace M.A. Sawyer, but the court-room was packed with curious sightseers both from Belford and distant points. A tiptoeing, jostling line extended out into the hallway and every window of the dimly lighted court-room was filled with eager listeners that hot July night when the trial began.[20]

Every eye watched fixedly the front of the room as Maria Collins Porter, a little, brown-faced woman with wisps of gray hair showing beneath her simple bonnet, took the stand. Attorney Bulman put the usual questions for the state. The little woman answered them quietly, but with a vigor that belied her years. She gave her age, told where she lived at various times, and her acquaintance with the defendant, Bates Huntsman, who of the four accused men stood trial first. She told how her sister, Elizabeth, had married Jonathan Dark, and they had come to live near the Collins homestead. She related how she and another little girl playmate had wandered one day into a cave near the cabin and had found there a lot of metal dies, acids, and some quarters and dollars. Afterwards, she said, they had seen the Damewood boys, Sam Scrivner, Jonathan Dark, Doc Huntsman, and Doc Golliday about the cave and wondered what they were doing there.

"I had come to Dark's house to take care of my sister's baby," Maria told the court. "About [eleven] o'clock I heard voices outside and I went to the door and looked out. Some men were approaching the gate. I stepped back in the shadow and watched them. I saw they were carrying a heavy object in a quilt or blanket. Then I recognized Doc Huntsman's voice. He was saying, 'I've felt his pulse and the old stiff won't be able to tell anything now.' I distinctly saw a hand and a leg dangling from the quilt."

The attorney interrupted. "How close were you?" he asked.

"As close as I am to Uncle Bates Huntsman," she replied, pointing slowly to the old man whose fate hung upon her story. He was sitting as one in a dream, his face lit up by the same simple curiosity and interest which showed in the countenances of men in the audience.

"Dark saw me there," she continued. "He swore, 'Damn you, I've a notion to kill you now. If you ever breathe a word of what you have seen I'll wash my hands in your heart's blood.' Bates Huntsman, Doc Huntsman, Sam Scrivner, and Doc Golliday were carrying the body. Hank Damewood was walking along by it. John Damewood was out holding the team. As they went on I heard them say, 'We'll divide the money later, when it is more suitable time.'

"They argued about how to dispose of the body and one suggested throwing it into the well. Another said to put it in a ditch and cover it up. I don't know how they finally settled the matter, but I never saw the body again. The next day Jonathan Dark brought home a quilt. He told me to wash it and again warned me to keep quiet about what I had seen.

"After I moved away from there and went to Quitman, Missouri, Jonathan Dark followed me. He threatened me often. When he would get me alone he would say, 'I'm going to kill you some time because dead people never talk.' One day when he was at our place he declared, 'I've got you now,' and started toward me. My sister, Mattie Collins, shot him. He died in a few minutes. I held his head with one hand and held a bucket to catch the blood with my other hand."[21]

But during the vigorous cross examination, the emphatic assertions of the aged woman began to break down, and her memory appeared rather unreliable. Maria could not remember the exact year the killings took place. She said they occurred the year her father died and she was fifteen at the time, but a witness testified that her father's tombstone bore the year 1876, not 1868. Nonetheless, Maria stood up well against harsh cross-examination and maintained the accuracy of her recollections.[22]

Maria's sister, Mrs. Zella Benson, of Dover, Oklahoma, also testified. Zella admitted she was the former wife of Jonathan Dark and had killed him years ago when he tried to kill Maria, although she denied having any knowledge of the Siam, Iowa, murders.

The case might have proceeded further, but there was no body, no witness to establish definitely that Nathaniel Smith was in the vicinity of Siam at the time of his disappearance, and no one who could give positive evidence that he had been killed on the Klondike farm. The mysterious search for buried treasure, persistent rumors of highway robbery, and the discovery of a miser's hoard of old money could not be definitely connected with the alleged murder.[28]

At the conclusion of the testimony offered by the State, Bruce J. Flick, the young attorney who handled the defense, moved that the case against Huntsman be dismissed. Following the motion and remarks, by

Flick, Attorney General Cossen addressed the court. The testimony offered by the state, he believed, established the fact that there had been considerable digging on the Huntsman place. Mrs. Porter, too, undoubtedly believed that she was telling the truth. Nevertheless, no one in the vicinity had seen the murdered man alive, and his identity had not been established. In view of the age of the defendants and the circumstances surrounding the case, he felt there was not sufficient evidence to bind the defendants over to the grand jury. Therefore, he recommended that the motion of the defense be granted. The court so ordered. Then he asked that the dismissal apply to all defendants in the case, and without comment Justice Sawyer complied with the suggestion.

Thus the strange case came to an end although questions of Siam gold and the "Klondike" farm remain unanswered. Even to this day they puzzle all who try to find the answer to this unsolved mystery.

The Great Siam Treasure Trial turned out to be one where the accusations were exciting but the facts weak. The James boys had been connected with the Siam Treasure before the trial via a tradition that they allegedly searched for it. Such yarns were a common delight at the time, and still very much so even today. A flood of old-timers in Iowa, Minnesota, and Missouri have claimed they had shod Jesse's horse, played pool with him or Frank, or been visited by the gang. People paid little attention to such claims, and apparently no one seemed overly concerned about the James brothers' connection with the Siam Treasure.

More important, on the very day the Siam Treasure Trial was dismissed, the *Democrat-Forum* ran a wrap-up piece which mentioned that Mrs. Zella Collins Benson, of Dover, Oklahoma, had another name—Mattie." A week later, the same newspaper ran a follow-up story focusing on the recollections of Judge G.M. Adams, Sr., of Buckner, Missouri, who had been both a judge and schoolmaster near Siam in 1868.[24]

Judge Adams had known the Collins family connected with the Siam trial quite well. Maria had been a student of his, and, he added, a good student to boot. Lloyd Collins and his family had purchased a farm in Buckner in 1868 following the Siam murders. The next year they moved back to Maryville, Missouri, where Lloyd died about 1870. The widow moved back to Buckner with her children, which included Mattie and Maria. According to Kansas City newspapers, it was Mattie who later married Siam Gang member Jonathan Dark.

Maria moved to Quitman, Missouri, as did a Siam Gang member named George McGraw, who had married Abigail Collins.[25] Mattie and Maria were popular with young men, and laughter, music, and dancing were common evening activities at the house. When Jonathan Dark moved into the house with Mattie, he quickly put a stop to the merriment and ordered the men away.

One of the young men, however, didn't pay much attention to Dark. According to the February 4, 1879, edition of the *Kansas City Journal*, this suitor is referred to as a young man named Bast.[26] The following day, the same newspaper spelled his name "Bass."[27] However, the July 22, 1915, edition of the *Democrat Forum*, Maryville, Missouri, stated the man was none other than Dick Liddil.[28]

The suitor was visiting Mattie one evening when Dark approached brandishing a revolver in each hand. Mattie and her friend barricaded themselves in a room and remained there all night. The suitor told her he would probably never come back if he managed to get out alive. Mattie replied he could come back because Dark would not be there next time.[29]

The Widow Collins was alarmed over the incident and sent her son Dock to see Judge Adams for help. When Dock returned home with the judge, Mattie was wildly stalking about with a revolver in her hand and the family huddled in a corner. Mattie told the judge she would "see Dark's blood before sundown," and insisted she would kill him if he interfered.

The judge and Widow Collins left the house. Hearing a shot, they rushed back to the house when Mattie rushed out crying she had just killed Dark. Judge Adams had to restrain Dock Collins, who was, in turn, threatening to kill her.

During the Siam trial in 1915, no newspaper apparently discovered that the witness, Mattie Collins, had once been intimately connected to the James Gang. Obviously, if it had become known that Mrs. Zella Benson of Dover, Oklahoma, may have actually been the infamous Mattie Collins associated with the James Gang, it might diminish her credulity as a witness. Having allegedly shot and killed Jonathan Dark, was bad enough, as was her being the infamous vixen who had been wife or consort to James Gang member turned traitor, Dick Liddil. And what if it had been known that she had played an active role in the betrayal and death of Jesse James?

Most of Mattie's endeavors over the years turned sour before they even began, such as her debut in a variety act in Kansas City's Coliseum Theatre when her show-business career ended abruptly after she chased the theatre manager three blocks down the street with a revolver after he reprimanded her for being noisy while entertaining friends.

When Mattie was in jail on February 7, 1879, charged with second degree murder for killing Dark, a group of ladies visited the jail looking after the spiritual interests of the female prisoners and providing them with uplifting reading material. The ladies reported that Mattie was bearing herself with the utmost composure, was very courteous to all visitors, and stated that she had no special regret over killing Dark, except for the necessity that compelled her to do so.[30]

A week later, Mattie made $5,000 bond for bail—the principal being Martha E. Collins, the signers George W. McGraw, William Swiney, and Thomas McDevitt. Another warrant was said to be in the hands of the marshal for her arrest in case the bond should be approved.[31]

Granted, Mattie Collins was not exactly a paragon of virtue, but people change. Judge Adams once recalled that he had run into Mattie in 1895, and she proudly reported that she was not only a church member in Springfield, Missouri, but also taught Sunday school. It should also be remembered that during the Siam Treasure Trial, Mattie did not confirm her sister's testimony regarding the Siam murders.

Maybe goodness and light did prevail once her wild days were over and maybe as she aged and the passions of youth subsided, Mattie Collins had repented, become a useful church-going member of the community, led a useful life with no need for a Jesse or Frank James, and lived happily ever after.

Or maybe she just lied to the judge!

## Notes

[1] *The Palimpsest*, July 1927, Volume VIII, Number 7.
[2] Emmett C. Hoctor and Virgil C. Julian, "Who was Mattie Collins, or Jesse James, Mattie Collins and the Treasure of Siam, or the Family, Friends, and Thrilling Adventures of Mattie Collins (also necessarily concerning the life of her sister Maria Collins or What the Heck was an Olio Girl?" *Violent Kin*, Issue 29, January 1996; *Democrat Forum* (Maryville, Missouri), July 15, 1915.
[3] *The* (St. Joseph) *Daily Gazette*, Wednesday, April 5, 1882—EXTRA, "Jesse, By Jehovah"; William A. Settle, Jr., *Jesse James Was His Name*, pp. 117-118.
[4] *Frank Leslie's Illustrated Newspaper*, April 22, 1882, "The Jesse James Tragedy," p. 135.
[5] *The* (St. Joseph) *Daily Gazette*, Wednesday, April 5, 1882—EXTRA.
[6] Ibid.
[7] Emmett C. Hoctor and Virgil C. Julian, "Who was Mattie Collins, or Jesse James, Mattie Collins and the Treasure of Siam, or the Family, Friends, and Thrilling Adventures of Mattie Collins (also necessarily concerning the life of her sister Maria Collins or What the Heck was an Olio Girl?" *Violent Kin*, Issue 29, January 1996.
[8] Stella Frances James, *In the Shadow of Jesse James*, Thousand Oaks, California, The Revolver Press, Dragon Books, 1989, p. 30.
[9] Emmett C. Hoctor and Virgil C. Julian, "Who was Mattie Collins, or Jesse James, Mattie Collins and the Treasure of Siam, or the Family, Friends, and Thrilling Adventures of Mattie Collins (also necessarily concerning the life of her sister Maria Collins or What the Heck was an Olio Girl?" *Violent Kin*, Issue 29, January 1996; *The Trial of Frank James for Murder with Confessions of Dick Liddil and Clarence Hite and History of the James Gang*, New York, Jingle Bob/Crown Publishers, Inc., 1977 facsimile reprint of original 1898 edition, p. 4.

[10]*The Trial of Frank James for Murder with Confessions of Dick Liddil and Clarence Hite and History of the James Gang*, New York, Jingle Bob/Crown Publishers, Inc., 1977 facsimile reprint of original 1898 edition, pp. 202-203.

[11]Emmett C. Hoctor and Virgil C. Julian, "Who was Mattie Collins, or Jesse James, Mattie Collins and the Treasure of Siam, or the Family, Friends, and Thrilling Adventures of Mattie Collins (also necessarily concerning the life of her sister Maria Collins or What the Heck was an Olio Girl?" *Violent Kin*, Issue 29, January 1996; *The Trial of Frank James for Murder with Confessions of Dick Liddil and Clarence Hite and History of the James Gang*, New York, Jingle Bob/Crown Publishers, Inc., 1977 facsimile reprint of original 1898 edition, p. 4.

[12]Roger A. Bruns, *The Bandit Kings From Jesse James to Pretty Boy Floyd*, New York, Crown Publishers, Inc., 1995, p. 24.

[13]*The Palimpsest*, July 1927, Volume VIII, Number 7.

[14]Emmett C. Hoctor and Virgil C. Julian, "Who was Mattie Collins, or Jesse James, Mattie Collins and the Treasure of Siam, or the Family, Friends, and Thrilling Adventures of Mattie Collins (also necessarily concerning the life of her sister Maria Collins or What the Heck was an Olio Girl?" *Violent Kin*, Issue 29, January 1996.

[15]*Democrat Forum* (Maryville, Missouri), July 15, 1915.

[16]Emmett C. Hoctor and Virgil C. Julian, "Who was Mattie Collins, or Jesse James, Mattie Collins and the Treasure of Siam, or the Family, Friends, and Thrilling Adventures of Mattie Collins (also necessarily concerning the life of her sister Maria Collins or What the Heck was an Olio Girl?" *Violent Kin*, Issue 29, January 1996.

[17]*The Palimpsest*, July 1927, Volume VIII, Number 7.

[18]Emmett C. Hoctor and Virgil C. Julian, "Who was Mattie Collins, or Jesse James, Mattie Collins and the Treasure of Siam, or the Family, Friends, and Thrilling Adventures of Mattie Collins (also necessarily concerning the life of her sister Maria Collins or What the Heck was an Olio Girl?" *Violent Kin*, Issue 29, January 1996.

[19]*The Palimpsest*, July 1927, Volume VIII, Number 7.

[20]*Kansas City Star*, July 14, 1915.

[21]*The Palimpsest*, July 1927, Volume VIII, Number 7.

[22]Emmett C. Hoctor and Virgil C. Julian, "Who was Mattie Collins, or Jesse James, Mattie Collins and the Treasure of Siam, or the Family, Friends, and Thrilling Adventures of Mattie Collins (also necessarily concerning the life of her sister Maria Collins or What the Heck was an Olio Girl?" *Violent Kin*, Issue 29, January 1996.

[23]*The Palimpsest*, July 1927, Volume VIII, Number 7.

[24]Emmett C. Hoctor and Virgil C. Julian, "Who was Mattie Collins, or Jesse James, Mattie Collins and the Treasure of Siam, or the Family, Friends, and Thrilling Adventures of Mattie Collins (also necessarily concerning the life of her sister Maria Collins or What the Heck was an Olio Girl?" *Violent Kin*, Issue 29, January 1996.

[25]Emmett C. Hoctor and Virgil C. Julian, "Who was Mattie Collins, or Jesse James, Mattie Collins and the Treasure of Siam, or the Family, Friends, and Thrilling Adventures of Mattie Collins (also necessarily concerning the life of her sister Maria Collins or What the Heck was an Olio Girl?" *Violent Kin*, Issue 33, January 1997.

[26]*Kansas City Journal*, February 4, 1879.

[27]*Kansas City Journal*, February 5, 1879.

[28]*Democrat Forum* (Maryville, Missouri), July 22, 1915.

[29]*Kansas City Journal*, February 4, 1879.

[30]*Kansas City Journal*, February 7, 1879; Emmett C. Hoctor and Virgil C. Julian, "Who was Mattie Collins, or Jesse James, Mattie Collins and the Treasure of Siam, or the Family, Friends, and Thrilling Adventures of Mattie Collins (also necessarily concerning the life of her sister Maria Collins or What the Heck was an Olio Girl?" *Violent Kin*, Issue 32, October 1996.

[31]*Kansas City Journal*, February 14, 1879.

# Bibliography

## Books

*A Little Bit of Paradise*. Aspinwall, Iowa centennial book, 1992

Andreas, A.T., *Andreas Illustrated Historical Atlas of the State of Iowa*, 1875— Sioux County History.

*Annals of Iowa*, Volume VI, Number 7, October 1904, 3D Series, "Pioneer Perils."

*Annals of Iowa*, Vol. XVIII, No. 5, Des Moines, Iowa, July 1932, Third Series, F.L. Herriott, "The Origins of the Indian Massacre Between the Okobojis, March 8, 1857."

*Annals of Iowa for 1870*, William L. Toole article on history of Louisa County, Iowa.

Axelrod, Alan, *The War Between the Spies*, New York, The Atlantic Monthly Press, 1992.

Bartholomew, Ed, *Wyatt Earp: The Untold Story*, Toyahvale, Texas, Frontier Book Company, 1963.

Beights, Ronald H., *Jesse James and the First Missouri Train Robbery*, Gretna, Pelican Publishing Company, 2002.

Boatner III, Mark M., *Civil War Dictionary*, New York, Vintage Books/Random House, Inc., 1991.

Bower, Donald E. Bower, *Ghost Towns & Back Roads*, Stackpole Books, Harrisburg, Pennsylvania, 1971.

Brant, Marley, *The Illustrated History of the James-Younger Gang*, Montgomery, Elliott & Clark Publishing, 1997.

Brant, Marley, *Jesse James: The Man and the Myth*, New York, Berkley Books, 1998.

Brant, Marley, *The Outlaw Youngers: A Confederate Brotherhood*, Lanham, New York, London, Madison Books, 1992.

Breihan, Carl W., *The Complete and Authentic Life of Jesse James*, New York, Frederick Fell, Inc., Publishers.

Breihan, Carl W., *The Day Jesse James Was Killed*, New York, Bonanza Books, No Date Given.

Breihan, Carl W., *Outlaws of the Old West*, New York, Bonanza Books, 1957.

*Brief History of the Founding and Early Growth of Scuyler County, Compiled from Caywood's 1888 History of Adair*, Putnam, Sullivan & Schuyler Counties, *The 1878 Atlas of Schuyler County*, information collected by the Office of Historic Preservation, files of Schuyler County newspapers and personal interviews as reported by Nelle George.

Bruns, Roger A., *The Bandit Kings From Jesse James to Pretty Boy Floyd*, New York, Crown Publishers, Inc., 1995..

Buel, J.W., *The Border Outlaws: An Authentic and Thrilling History of the Most Noted Bandits of Ancient or Modern Times, The Younger Brothers, Jesse and Frank James, and Their Comrades in Crime*, Syracuse, Alvord & Sleight, 1883.

Croy, Homer, *Jesse James Was My Neighbor*, New York, Duell, Sloan & Pearce, 1949.

Croy, Homer, *Cole Younger Last of the Great Outlaws*, Lincoln and London, University of Nebraska Press, 1956.

Dale, Henry, *Adventures and Exploits of the Younger Brothers, Missouri's Most Daring Outlaws, and Companions of the James Boys*, New York, Street & Smith, Publishers, The Secret Service Series—No. 32, 1890.

Dobie, J. Frank, *Legends of Texas*, Austin, Texas Folk-Lore Society Number 3, 1924.

Drago, Harry Sinclair, *Outlaws on Horseback*, Lincoln and London, University of Nebraska Press, 1964.

Dyer, Robert L., *Jesse James and the Civil War in Missouri*, Columbia & London, University of Missouri Press, 1994.

Erwin, Richard E., *The Truth About Wyatt Earp, Carpinteria*, California, The O. K. Press, 1993.

Fitzgerald, Ruth Coder, *Clell and Ed Miller, Members of the James Gang*, 1987.

Folwell, William Watts, *A History of Minnesota*, Volume III, St. Paul, Minnesota Historical Society, 1969.

Gardiner, Abigail, *History of the Spirit Lake Massacre! 8th March 1857, and of Miss Abigail Gardiner's Three Months Captivity Among the Indians*, New Britain, CT., L.P. Lee, Publisher, 1857.

*Good Bye, Jesse James*, Liberty, The Jesse James Bank Museum, 1967, first printed in the *Kansas City Daily Journal* in 1882.

Gue, Benjamin F., *History of Iowa From the Earliest Times to the Beginning of the Twentieth Century*, Four Volumes, New York, Century History Company, 1903.

*The History of Daviess County, Missouri*, Kansas City, Missouri, Birdsall & Dean, 1889.

*The History of Polk County, Iowa*, Union Historical Company, Birdsall, Williams & Company, 1880.

Holmes, Frank R., *Minnesota in Three Centuries*, Volume Four, Mankato, The Publishing Society of Minnesota, 1908.

Horan, James D., *Desperate Men*, New York, Doubleday & Co., 1962.

Huntington, George, *Robber and Hero: The Story of the Raid on the First National Bank of Northfield.*

James, Stella Frances, *In the Shadow of Jesse James*, Thousand Oaks, California, The Revolver Press, Dragon Books, 1989.

Laird, Charlton Grant, *Iowa Legends of Buried Treasure*, Lincoln, Foundation Books, 1990.

Lavine, Sigmund A., *Allan Pinkerton—America's First Private Eye*, New York, Dodd, Mead & Co., 1963.

Love, Robertus, *The Rise and Fall of Jesse James*, Lincoln and London, University of Nebraska Press, 1990.

Macintyre, Ben, *The Napoleon of Crime*, New York, Delta Books, 1997.

Mercer, A.S., *The Banditti of the Plains*, Norman, University of Oklahoma Press, 1954.

Miller, Donna, *A Glimpse of Greene Valley*, 1964.

Nagel, Paul C., *Missouri: A History*, Lawrence, University of Kansas Press, 1977.

Nash, Jay Robert, *Western Lawmen & Outlaws*, New York, Da Capo Press, 1994.

Patterson, Richard, *Train Robbery: The Birth, Flowering, and Decline of a Notorious Western Enterprise*, Boulder, Johnson Books, 1981.

Riley, Glenda, *Frontiers woman: The Iowa Experience*, Ames, Iowa State University Press, 1981.

Romine, Scott and Miller, Steve, *History of Kinross, Iowa*, 1979.

Sabin, Henry, L.L.D. and Sabin, Edwin L., *The Making of Iowa*, Chicago & New York, A. Flanagan Company, 1900.

Schwieder, Dorothy, *Iowa State Register*, History of Iowa.

Settle, Jr., William A., *Jesse James Was His Name*, Lincoln & London, University of Nebraska Press, 1966.

Springer, Arthur, *History of Louisa County, Iowa, from Its Earliest Settlement to 1912*, Volume I, The S.J. Clarke Publishing Company, 1912.

Steele, Phillip W., *Jesse and Frank James: The Family History*, Gretna, Pelican Publishing Company, 1987.

Steele, Phillip W., with Warfel, George, *The Many Faces of Jesse James*, Gretna, Pelican Publishing Company, 1995.

Stuart, Theodore M., *Past and Present of Lucas and Wayne Counties*, Volume I, 1913.

Tefertiller, Casey, *Wyatt Earp: The Life Behind the Legend*, New York, Wiley & Sons, Inc., 1997.

Thompson, George A., *Throw Down The Box!*, Dream Garden Press, Salt Lake City, Utah 1989.

Time-Life Books, editors of *The Wild West*, Alexandria, Virginia: Time-Life Books.

*The Trial of Frank James for Murder with Confessions of Dick Liddil and Clarence Hite and History of the James Gang*, New York, Jingle Bob/Crown Publishers, Inc., 1977, facsimile reprint of original 1898 edition.

Triplett, Frank, *The Life, Times & Treacherous Death of Jesse James*, New York, The Swallow Press, 1970 reprint of the 1882 edition.

Turner, George, *Secrets of Jesse James*, Amarillo, Baxter Lane Company, 1975.

Ulyatt, Kenneth, *Outlaws*, Philadelphia and New York, J.B. Lippincott Company, 1976.

Wall, Joseph Frazier, *Iowa: A History*, New York, W.W. Norton & Company, Inc., 1978.

Waters, Frank, *The Earp Brothers of Tombstone*, Lincoln & London, University of Nebraska Press, 1960.

Wilson, R.L., *Colt: An American Legend*, Artabras, New York, London, Paris, Abbeville Publishing Group, 1985.

Yeatman, Ted P., *Frank and Jesse James: The Story Behind the Legend*, Nashville, Cumberland House, 2000.

Younger, Cole, *The Story of Cole Younger*, St. Paul, Minnesota Historical Society Press, 2000.

## Magazines, Pamphlets, Dissertations

Bell, William, "The Reno Gang's Reign of Terror," *Wild West Magazine*, February 2004.

Boggs, Johnny D., "Following Wyatt Earp," *True West*, November/December 2005.

Boyer, Glenn G., "On the Trail of Big Nosed Kate," *Real West*, March 1951.

Chatterley, L. Matthew, "Explore Iowa's Historic Mormon Trails," Iowa Mormon Trail Association.

Coulston, Don, "The Youngers 'Rebels with a Cause,'" *The* (Stillwater) *Prison Mirror*, date unknown.

Derome, J.A., "Canton Thrown into Wild Stage of Excitement when Report Was Given That Bandits Were Near," eighth in a series of articles Canton newspapers.

E.S. "A Visit to Fort Armstrong." *Rock Island Banner* and *Stephenson Gazette*. Rock Island, 1840.

Fleming, Charles A., Oklahoma State University, Bret Harte, DLB 79.

Gilles, Albert S., "Jesse, Frank and Cole," *Frontier Times*, September 1969.

Gilmore, Donald L., "When the James Gang Ruled the Rails," *Wild West Magazine*, August 2000.

Golemba, Henry L., Wayne State University, Bret Harte, DLB 74, "American Short-Story Writers Before 1880."

Griffith, T.D., "Aces, Eights and Number 10," *Historic Traveler Magazine*, November 1996.

Henderson, Gertrude, "Dr. Mosher Makes a Call, Tales and Trails of Yesterday," Date Unknown, Northfield Public Library.

Henderson, Victoria, "Bret Harte: 1836-1902," Internet.

Hines, James, "Robbery," *Kentucky Living Magazine*, June 2002.

Hoctor, Emmett C. and Julian, Virgil C., "Who was Mattie Collins, or Jesse James, Mattie Collins and the Treasure of Siam, or the Family, Friends, and Thrilling Adventures of Mattie Collins (also necessarily concerning the life of her sister Maria Collins) or What the Heck was an Olio Girl?" *Violent Kin*, Issue 29, January 1996.

Hoctor, Emmett C. and Julian, Virgil C., "Who was Mattie Collins, or Jesse James, Mattie Collins and the Treasure of Siam, or the Family, Friends, and Thrilling Adventures of Mattie Collins (also necessarily concerning the life of her sister Maria Collins) or What the Heck was an Olio Girl?" *Violent Kin*, Issue 32, October 1996.

Hoctor, Emmett C. and Julian, Virgil C., "Who was Mattie Collins, or Jesse James, Mattie Collins and the Treasure of Siam, or the Family, Friends, and Thrilling Adventures of Mattie Collins (also necessarily concerning the life of her sister Maria Collins) or What the Heck was an Olio Girl?" *Violent Kin*, Issue 33, January 1997.

Jackson, Lorena Farris, "James Gang Quietly Invaded Downtown Columbia in 1872," *Columbia Magazine*, September 2002.

Merry, Carl A., "The Historic Period," 1996, University of Iowa Website.

Michelson, Charles, "The Trade of Train Robbery," *Munsey's*, February 1902.

Anthony Monachello, "Struggle for St. Louis." *America's Civil War*, date unknown.

Orbelo, Captain William R., "Colt Model 1851 Navy Revolver," *Western Frontier 1980 Annual*, Summer 1980.

Parsons, Chuck, "James Glispin—19th-Century Minnesota Sheriff," *Real West*, March 1981.

Parsons, Chuck, "A Jesse James Pistol?" *Quarterly of the National Association for Outlaw and Lawman History*, Inc., Volume XVII, Number 1, January-March 1993.

Perry, Michael J., "A Territorial Period Site in Dubuque," Office of the Iowa State Archaeologist Archives.

"Sioux City Family Treasures Bullet Pierced Trousers Worn by One of James Brothers," Date Unknown, Northfield Public Library.

*Treasure Cache Magazine*, January 2002.

Weaver, Dwight, "Missouri's Historic Border Battles," *Missouri Resources Magazine*, Summer 1999.

Webb, Dottie, "Local Color: 19th Century Regional Writing in the United States Bret Harte: Popularity, Poetry, and Performance," 23 August 1998.

## Newspapers

*Adair News*, July 28, 1922; April 22, 1954.

*Adair News Special Addition*, Summer 2003.

*Black Hills Pioneer*, August 5, 1876.

*Chicago Tribune*, undated article by Max Rothstein.

*Columbia, Missouri, Herald*, August 28, 1903.

*Council Bluffs Nonpareil*, July 22, 1873; July 25, 1873; July 29, 1873.

*Daily Iowa State Register*, July 22, 1873; July 23, 1873.

*Davenport Gazette*, July 25, 1873

*Faribault Democrat*, December 15, 1876.

*Frank Leslie's Illustrated Newspaper*, April 22, 1882.

*Gallatin North Missourian*, April 4, 1993.

*Huntington Advertiser*, August 3, 1903; August 10, 1903.

*Kansas City Daily Journal of Commerce*, December 9, 1869.

*Kansas City Journal*, April 4, 1882; February 4, 1879; February 5, 1879; February 7, 1879; February 14, 1879.

*Kansas City Star*, July 21, 1881; July 14, 1915.

*Kansas City Times*, October 15, 1872; September 27, 1873; January 31, 1875; August 18, 1876.

*Kingsley* (Iowa) *News-Times*, 1981, Exact date unknown.

*Lexington Caucasian*, September 5, 1874

*Liberty Tribune*, February 16, 1866; June 21, 1870; July 5, 1870; July 22, 1870; June 16, 1871; January 29, 1875.

*Louisville Courier*, March 24, 1868.

*Louisville Daily Journal*, March 21, 1868.

*Madelia News*, Thursday, November 25, 1915.

*Madelia Times*, Friday, September 22, 1876.

*Mankato Record*, September 30, 1876.

*Mankato Weekly Review*, October 3, 1876.

(Maryville, Missouri) *Democrat Forum*, July 15, 1915; July 22, 1915.

*Missouri Democrat*, September 29, 1864

*Nashville Banner*, March 22, 1868.

*New York Times*, August 4, 1864; October 2, 1864; July 23, 1873; July 25, 1873; July 26, 1873; July 27, 1873; July 29, 1873; July 30, 1873; August 7, 1873; August 21, 1873; September 9, 1873; September 12, 1873; March 23, 1874; September 10, 1874.

*North Missourian*, December 19, 1864.

*Omaha Bee*, September 23, 1876.

*Omaha World-Herald*, January 22, 1995; Date Unknown; June 1, 1998

*Osceola Republican*, June 8, 1871.

*The Palimpsest*, July 1927, Volume VIII, Number 7.

*Palmyra Whig*, December 26, 1839.

*Rice County Journal Extra*, September 1876.

*Rock Island Daily Argus*, July 24, 1873; July 25, 1873; August 7, 1985.

*Sac Sun*, October 6, 1876; October 20, 1876.

*St. Clair County Courier*, May 6, 1976; May 13, 1976; May 27, 1976

*St. Joseph Daily Gazette*, Wednesday, April 5, 1882—EXTRA.

*St. Louis Daily Globe*, July 23, 1873.

*St. Louis Dispatch*, January 1874; June 9, 1874.

*St. Louis Globe Democrat*, October 16, 1876

*St. Louis Weekly Globe*, May 30, 1873.

*Ste. Genevieve Fair Play*, May 29, 1873.

*Sioux City Daily Journal*, September 17, 1876; September 19, 1876; September 20, 1876; September 21, 1876; September 22, 1876; September 23, 1876; September 24, 1876; September 25, 1876; September 26, 1876; July 25, 1954.

*Sioux Valley News* (Canton, South Dakota), September 23, 1876.

*Terrell* (Texas) *Transcript*, April 26, 1907.

*Wellman Advance*, February 14, 1893.

## Letters

Anonymous letter from Woodward, Iowa, to author dated December 14, 2004.

John Caldwell letter to author dated December 9, 2004. Author's Collection.

Marilynn Cierzan letter to author dated July 13, 1982.

Louise W. Hampton, Scholl Family Research Association of America, letter to author dated March 7, 1983.

Mabel Guth Ohde letter to author dated September 22, 2002. Author's Collection.

Mabel Guth Ohde letter to author dated September 24, 2002. Author's Collection.

David Parker, executive director, Fort Dodge Historical Foundation, letter to author dated May 11, 1981.

Excerpt of a letter written by E.A. Rea, Corydon, dated August 15, 1929. Author's Collection.

Claire Ryan letter to author dated September 20, 2002. Author's Collection.

Tom Ryther letter to author dated October 27, 1982.

Bob Shelburne undated letter to author, postmarked January 17, 1997.

Mrs. Fred Wingert letter to author dated April 1982.

Cole Younger letter to J. W. Buel dated October 20, 1880.

## Public and Private Records

"Breakfast with Jesse James," F. Eugene Barber Papers, in collection at Prairie Trails Museum, Corydon, Iowa.

Burton, William Lee, "Adam Ripper, Corydon Resident for 62 Years, Tells of Town's Thrilling History," 1932, in collection at Prairie Trails Museum, Corydon, Iowa.

Draper-McClurg Family Papers, 1838-1981 (C3069), Western Historical Manuscript Collection, Columbia, Missouri.

Dunihue, Daniel, "Journal of Occurrences, August 1832," Indiana Humanities Council, Indianapolis, Indiana.

1850 Federal Census for Marion County, Iowa.

Scrapbook of clippings belonging to Mrs. H. C. Harper.

Emmett C. Hoctor Collection, Plattsmouth, Nebraska.

"Jesse James and the Colt," F. Eugene Barber Papers, in collection at Prairie Trails Museum, Corydon, Iowa.

Charles and Vesta Knapp, signed affidavits, Plymouth County Historical Society, LeMars, Iowa.

Library of Congress.

Missouri State Archives, Soldiers Database, Records Services, Abstract of Wars & Military Engagements.

Stirling, Dave, untitled document in collection at Prairie Trails Museum, Corydon, Iowa.

Wayne and Appanoose counties, Iowa, Biographical & Historical Record, 1886, in collection at Prairie Trails Museum, Corydon, Iowa.

Sheriff Russell H. White, Jr., Woodbury County Sheriff's Department, 1981, a two-page biography of sheriffs John and Dan McDonald, Sioux City Public Museum.

William Hull Family Papers and biography.

## Unpublished Manuscripts

Diess, Ron, "Fort Armstrong at The Rock Island Rapids."

# Index

Acres, Green B., 78, 79.
Adair County, Iowa, 8, 86.
Adair, Iowa, vii, viii, 24, 84, 86, 88, 90, 92, 96, 97, 101, 108, 114, 116.
Adair, John, 86.
*Adair News*, vii, 111, 112.
Adams, Judge G.M. Sr., 184-186.
Alcorn, Miles, 67.
Alcott, Louisa May, 61
Alford, Chauncey, 123.
Allerton, Iowa, vii, 66, 67, 73.
Anderson, "Bloody Bill," 46, 48-50, 61, 104, 115.
Anderson, Charlie, 86.
Anderson, Sam, 175-180.
Anita, Iowa, 92, 96, 100, 101.
Anthony, Susan B., 59, 60.
Appanoose County, Iowa, 31, 44, 45, 82, 83, 197.
Armes, George, 161, 162.
Askew, Dan, 129, 132.
Aspinwall, Iowa, 28-30, 32.
Atlanta, Georgia, 49.

Atlantic City, Iowa, 17.
Austin, Texas, 126.
Avard, Sampson, 6.

Banditti of the Plains, 19, 31, 192.
Bang, Jennie, 108.
Barclay, Hugh, 154, 155.
Bartlett, Iowa, 24.
Baxter, Richard, 9, 10.
Beard, Ed T., 22.
Bedford, Iowa, 174, 176.
Beloit, Iowa, 145-147.
Benson, Mrs. Zella, 183, 184, 186.
Benteen, Frederick, 134, 135.
Berry, F.M., 26, 121.
Bethany, Missouri, 73.
Big Sioux River, 145-147.
Bird, Greenup, 51.
Bishop, Arthur C., 65.
Bishop, Jack, 103.
Black Hawk Purchase, 5.
Black Hawk War, 3.
Bligh, D.T. "Yankee," 56, 78.

183, 185-187.
Collins, Mrs. Floyd, 176, 180.
Columbia, Kentucky, 76, 78.
*Columbia* (Missouri) *Herald*, 23.
Conover, William, 78.
Coon River, 156, 158.
Cooper, Ben, 51.
Corbit, John A., 73, 74.
Cordna, Henry, 12.
Corinth, Mississippi, 128, 129.
Correctionville, Iowa, 156-158.
Corridan, Johnny, 25, 26, 120, 121.
Corydon, Iowa, vii, 8, 15, 19, 25, 59, 65-68, 70-76, 99, 104, 105.
Council Bluffs, Iowa, 8, 24, 25, 90-92, 98, 101, 102, 110, 160.
Council Bluffs Nonpareil, 114.
Cox, Frank, 97.
Cox, S.P., 61.
Craig, Henry, 171.
Craven, Montgomery, 78.
Cravens, Isaac, 78.
Crawford County, Iowa, 28, 154, 159.
Creston, Iowa, 19, 109.
Crittenden, J.J., 135.
Crittenden, Thomas, 170-173.
Crowe, Pat, 28.
Cummins, Jim, 123.
Custer, George Armstrong, 134, 135, 139.

Dalmanutha, Iowa, 90.
Damewood, Nathaniel Harrison, 174, 179, 182.
Damewood, John, 182.
Daniels, Edwin, 125.
Dark, Jonathan, 174, 176, 177, 180-186.
Davenport County, Iowa, 8.
*Davenport Gazette*, 98.
Davenport, George, 8, 9.

Davenport, Iowa, 22, 25.
Daviess County, Missouri, 5, 61, 62, 64, 73, 76, 86, 104, 115.
Davis City, 72.
Davis County, Iowa, 14, 15, 159.
Davis, Sheriff, 154.
Deadwood, Dakota Territory, 109, 138.
Dean, Henry Clay, 15, 16, 68-71.
Decatur County, Iowa, 72.
Deer Lodge, Montana, 114, 116.
Denison, Iowa, 29, 152, 156.
Denver, Colorado, 24, 115.
Des Moines, Iowa, vii, 5, 93, 96, 101, 109, 116.
Des Moines River, 11-13, 36, 93, 147.
Dickinson County, Iowa, 13.
Dodge County, Missouri, 45.
Dodge, A.C., 43.
Doose, David, 39.
Dover, Oklahoma, 63, 183, 184, 186.
Drake, F.M., 65.
Dubuque, Iowa, 43, 97.
Duke, Basil W., 107.
Dunihue, Daniel R., 3, 4.

Eagleville, Missouri, 73.
Earp, Morgan, 20.
Earp, Nicholas, 21.
Earp, Virgil, 21.
Earp, Wyatt Berry Stapp, 19-21.
Eastwood, Maximilian, 39.
Edie, John R., 90.
Edwards, John Newman, 79.
Elder, Katherine "Big Nose Kate," 21.
Emmet, Robert, 80.
Estherville, Iowa, 12.
Ewing, John, 87.

Fairview, Iowa, 24, 27, 121.
Farmington, Iowa, 39, 40.

Sac County, Iowa, 28, 156.
*Sac Sun*, 156.
Salt Lake City, Utah, 21.
Samuel, Dr. Reuben, 2, 48, 65, 130, 136.
San Francisco, California, 110, 119.
Sandusky, Ohio, 9.
Saunders County, Nebraska, 162.
Savannah, Missouri, 52.
Schuyler County, Missouri, 41.
Scioto County, Ohio, 35.
Scott County, Iowa, 9.
Scribner, Henry, 176, 177.
Scrivner, Sam, 174, 182.
Sedalia, Missouri, 97, 98.
Seventh Kansas Volunteer Cavalry, 34, 135.
Seymour, Indiana, 84, 86.
Seymour, Iowa, 66.
Sheets, John W., 61, 62, 64, 75.
Shelby, Jo, 107, 122, 126.
Shelbyville, Kentucky, 77.
Shepard, George, 53, 56, 105, 106.
Shepard, Oliver, 51, 53, 56.
Shepherd, Jack, 80.
Shepherdstown, Virginia, 35.
Sherman, Texas, 110.
Shing, Wong, 93.
Shuelson, Andrew, 145.
Siam Gang, 177, 184-186.
Siam, Iowa, 167, 174-177, 183, 184.
Siam Treasure, 175, 177, 184.
Siam Treasure Trial, 184, 186.
Sidominadotah, 11.
Simmons, Thomas H., 54, 55.
Simms, Benjamin, 2, 136.
*Sioux City Daily News*, 145, 152.
*Sioux City Democrat*, 159.
Sioux City, Iowa, vii, 4, 12, 13, 146-154, 158, 160.
*Sioux City Daily Journal*, 145, 148,

158.
Sioux Falls, 146.
Sioux River, 146.
*Sioux Valley News*, 146.
Sisson, Abner, 91.
Sitting Bull, 134.
Sloan, Iowa, 160, 161.
Small, Eleazer, 14.
Smith, A.E., 135.
Smith, Joseph, 5-7.
Smith, Nathaniel, 181, 183.
Smith, Otto, 22.
Smith, William A., 93, 95, 100, 102.
Smoot, Daniel, 62.
Spirit Lake, Iowa, 11, 12.
Springfield, Dakota Territory, 146.
Springfield, Massachusetts, 93.
Springfield, Minnesota, 11.
Springfield, Missouri, 146, 186.
St. Clair County, Missouri, 97, 110, 124, 125.
St. Joseph, Missouri, 27, 116, 161, 170, 173.
*St. Joseph* (Missouri) *Herald*, 110, 114.
*St. Louis Dispatch*, 114.
St. Louis, Missouri, 22, 49, 63, 107, 108, 120, 123, 124, 143.
*St. Louis Republican*, 172.
*St. Louis Weekly Globe*, 87.
St. Paul, Minnesota, vii, 107, 116, 148, 149.
Stanton, Elizabeth Cady, 59.
*Ste. Genevieve Fair Play*, 88.
Ste. Genevieve, Missouri, 80, 87, 104, 108.
Stevens, S.S., 93.
Stevens, Tom, 72.
Stiles, Bill (*See also* Bill Chadwick), 81, 139, 140, 142.
Stowe, Harriet Beecher, 61.